The International
Television News Agencies

This book is part of the Peter Lang Media and Communication list.
Every volume is peer reviewed and meets
the highest quality standards for content and production.

PETER LANG
New York • Washington, D.C./Baltimore • Bern
Frankfurt • Berlin • Brussels • Vienna • Oxford

CHRIS PATERSON

The International Television News Agencies

THE WORLD FROM LONDON

PETER LANG
New York • Washington, D.C./Baltimore • Bern
Frankfurt • Berlin • Brussels • Vienna • Oxford

Library of Congress Cataloging-in-Publication Data

Paterson, Chris A.
The international television news agencies: the world
from London / Chris Paterson.
p. cm.
Includes bibliographical references and index.
1. Television broadcasting of news. 2. Broadcast journalism.
3. Foreign news. I. Title.
PN4784.T4P38   070.4332—dc22   2011013898
ISBN 978-1-4331-1078-8 (hardcover)
ISBN 978-1-4331-1077-1 (paperback)

Bibliographic information published by **Die Deutsche Nationalbibliothek.**
Die Deutsche Nationalbibliothek lists this publication in the "Deutsche
Nationalbibliografie"; detailed bibliographic data is available
on the Internet at http://dnb.d-nb.de/.

The image of Reuters Television photographer Bassam Masoud is used
with his permission; the photo was taken by Khalil Harmra and is provided
by the European Pressphoto Agency. The image of the Reuters Television
London newsroom is by Henrik Andersen and is provided courtesy of
Thomson-Reuters.

The paper in this book meets the guidelines for permanence and durability
of the Committee on Production Guidelines for Book Longevity
of the Council of Library Resources.

This book is dedicated to all journalists who face peril to illuminate injustice, document history, and give a voice to the voiceless.

Contents

Preface

There are many first-rate books detailing the side of international journalism we do see, but none—at least recently—dealing with the side we don't. One that did thirty years ago was *The International News Agencies*, and in that work Boyd-Barrett (1980) developed the distinction between the "retail"—packaged, glossy, localized—news we consume every day and the "wholesale" news most of us are substantially unaware of, unless we work for a news organization. If you do work for such an organization, you know all too well that without a reliable flow of words and pictures from news agencies (and, unfortunately, increasingly from public relations firms as well) you would have little to offer your audience. (The days when newsrooms emptied during the day as staff "pounded the pavement" for stories are sadly long past.) You depend—perhaps more than you like to admit—on the wholesale side of the news industry.

This is the story of the television side of that wholesale industry sector and more specifically the international (as opposed to domestic[1]) television side: *The International Television News Agencies*. Remarkably, their story has remained substantially untold for fifty years. They either created, or globally distributed, most of the iconic television images of international events anyone with exposure to TV tends to recall, thereby playing a leading role in determining how we understand our world, yet they remain unknown outside the small segment of the global television industry concerned with international news. Despite the intense scrutiny of international news inspired by the New World Information and Communications Order debates of the late 1970s, such essential elements in the production and dissemination of international television news have never been thoroughly examined and revealed. This book is an attempt to rectify that. It is also an attempt to describe a system of news production that has shaped our shared visual history since the 1950s.

Currently the international television news agencies are Associated Press Television News (APTN) and Reuters Television; these are part of global information conglomerates and are also the leading wire services and providers of international news online. There has been little study of them and of what they do, and yet the world we all understand to exist (because we see it on our televisions) is shaped every day by the fairly small number of journalists in these few organizations. As veteran British television correspondent Jonathan Dimbleby put it (in Harrison and Palmer, 1986, 76),

> as we're technically capable of becoming more and more informed and better and better informed, we're at risk of becoming less and less informed by fewer and fewer people.

It is important to acknowledge that the entire project on which this book is based, spanning over twenty years of data gathering, document analysis, video content analysis, news production ethnography, interviewing, and generally being a nuisance to busy news agency journalists, owes everything to the companies that have assisted me and the journalists and news managers who have helpfully revealed to me (most of) their work. I hope this book will serve as a tribute to this small and largely unknown tribe of journalists who bring us international television news pictures, and also as a warning about the harm to public understanding that the system in which they operate may be doing. The thorough reader may note that from chapter to chapter this author's approach and style vary: some chapters privilege the theoretical, others institutional history, and others ethnographic detail. While all scholarship is subjective, some of these chapters strive to present a distanced and dispassionate account, while others don't disguise my opinion. The reader will judge if this variety of approaches succeeds.

Revealing a Hidden Industry

Ironically, given their professional mandate to communicate to the public, media workers tend to be a secretive lot: it is professionally safer, and more pleasant, to be observer than observed. One veteran television news agency journalist shared with me his view that, typically, television news agency managers are "not the most confident specimens of the human race," inclining them toward excessive secrecy. For corporate executives (and the most corporatized journalists) everything boils down to reputational harm or reputational gain, and the impact of those factors on customer confidence and shareholder value. The possibility that exposure, transparency, and critical analysis by people from outside of their industry should have importance beyond those ends does not sit well with such a perspective. A perpetual dilemma in this project, as with many media ethnographies (for instance, Schlesinger, 1978; Gans, 1980; Born, 2004), is that organizations risk criticism when they permit independent analysis of what they do: what makes sense in the context of their business may look irresponsible or arrogant to people outside of that context. It is rarely the intention of researchers to create discomfort for those who have assisted them, but the conclusions drawn from independent analysis—the view standing apart from a narrow instrumental lens of the television news industry—can make for uncomfortable reading.

But for news agency workers there is a tension between yearning for the public (and students of journalism) to know about their unappreciated and unacknowledged role in international news, and a long tradition of quietly working in the background of global media, as the clients who pay the tab—the television networks and big newspapers—get the glory. And corporations in competition with other corporations tend toward secrecy because any unplanned disclosure of information might have commercial consequences; the more a media outlet defines itself in commercial—as opposed to public service—terms, the more this is the case (this is discussed further in Paterson and Zoelner, 2010.) And so, as helpful as they have been, the companies described in this book have been mostly tight-lipped about the finances at the heart of every journalistic decision. I have done my best to overcome that shortfall in data, but it constrains this analysis.

A lack of accessibility to researchers remains common in the media industry and points to the integrity and courage of the leadership at WTN, Reuters, and the Associated Press in permitting access to this researcher, with his often skeptical view of their industry. They have demonstrated that, despite the hidden nature of their sector of the media, they accept their vital social role and accountability to society, and so have made the difficult decision to permit significant transparency. The former WTN made this commitment even before the current industry leaders, AP and Reuters. If some WTN staff appear in a less responsible light than those of the other two agencies, it is because I use examples from their work and quote from their staff more extensively to reduce the potential for embarrassment of the two contemporary companies. I apologize for that necessary bias and point out to the reader that no organization was more forthright about its work, overall, than was WTN.

The information I am working from is inevitably incomplete, and open to multiple interpretations. Where I have had reason to suspect a point of information could be commercially sensitive or portray a company or individual negatively, I have taken extra steps to verify it or have excluded it where that hasn't been possible. Where journalists or managers have disputed my interpretations, I have included their views as fully as possible and sought to correct or remove disputed information. Ultimately, this book presents my interpretation of the research I've done, the things I've seen, and the stories I've heard, and I am responsible for any inaccuracies, for which I apologize in advance, especially to the generous journalists and news agency managers who have assisted me. I hope the value of seeing their fascinating story told offsets any concern.

As noted by Schlesinger (1980) and others, the process of gaining the access to conduct long-term observational research within media organizations can be challenging, and that access, when granted, can be tenuous. APTN and Reuters, previously as WTN (and before that UPITN) and Visnews, respectively, had never permitted extended access to their newsrooms by outsiders (by known accounts, for more than a day), and each had followed a tradition of silence. My main observation in agency newsrooms took place over the course of two to three weeks at each company in the 1990s, but I had had intermittent contact with WTN personnel since 1989, when I was researching a master's thesis about television coverage of Africa. Reuters, with a very private corporate culture, provided less access than did WTN, although since about the year 2000 they have been generous in accommodating every research request, and APTN, under the management of Nigel Baker and Sandy MacIntyre, has hosted me on many occasions and offered unprecedented access to information about agency operations. Both companies have offered me generous access to their archives. At WTN and APTV, and later APTN, I was permitted access to daily and weekly editorial meetings, and some access to meetings was provided at Reuters Television. Since the 1990s I have returned frequently to the newsrooms of APTN and Reuters Television to conduct interviews and occasionally observe production operations again and reflect on the changes taking place. I have most recently done so with both news agencies in 2010 during the final preparation of this book. Only senior news agency managers and broadcasters who have specifically given me permission to do so are named in the quotes I provide; other quotes are anonymized for the protection of the many news workers whom I interviewed.

Acknowledgments

I cannot name everyone who assisted me (though I mention key contributors to this project below), so I offer my thanks to all and especially to those who went beyond the call of duty with numerous interviews, or comments on past writing, or opening doors for me that had previously been closed to researchers. Many managers and executives of television news agencies have given generously of their time and the resources of their organizations to assist my research over the course of nearly twenty years. These include many, but far from all, of the leading figures in shaping the two modern television news agencies. Chief among these (and including broadcast as well as news agency people) are Nigel Baker, Lou Boccardi, Eric Braun, Stephen Claypole, Chris Cramer, Tony Donovan, David Feingold, David Kogan, Lowdnes Lipscomb, Sandy MacIntyre, Reese Schonfeld, Richard Wald, and Lloyd Watson. Many other senior journalists from television news agencies have been extremely helpful, either during their tenure with news agencies or in their retirement or, in some cases, both. These include Andrew Ailes, Mohamad Amin, Eric Bremner, John Connor, John Clarke, Paul Faithful, Terry Gallacher, Toby Goode, Nigel Hancock, Liz Havern, John Jirik, John Mahoney, Ralph Nicolson, Sally Reardon, Stuart Sutton-Jones, and Yann Tessier. Some assisted during brief tenures with television news agencies, while others helped build the agencies from their earliest days; some assisted by correspondence, but most in person. Several dozen additional journalists and other staff from news agencies Visnews, WTN, Reuters, and Associated Press; broadcasters CNN, YLE, BBC, ITN, and others; and from Eurovision, have provided interviews and other assistance; they are too numerous to mention here, but they all have my thanks.

I undertook the research described in this book as a former local television photographer in the United States, interested in the mechanics of television news, and as someone dismayed by the bizarrely negative television portrayal of the African continent. I discovered the fascinating story of the television news agencies, and I hope I do it justice. This long project began as master's research at Boston University and evolved into Ph.D. research at the University of Texas at Austin, so thanks are due to both sets of dedicated and inspirational supervisors, as well as to the journalism and communications faculties at Tampere University (Finland) and the University of Westminster (U.K.), for hosting me during portions of this research, and, of course, to colleagues and the many outstanding student assistants at the institutions I've worked at since. Richard Wild assisted with the design of the industry time-line in chapter 3. Thanks are due to Peter Lang Senior Acquisitions Editor Mary Savigar for her enthusiastic support and considerable patience, and finally I am grateful to my father for his unflagging support and editorial help, my son Oliver for inspiring me, and Simone for her magic.

Note

1. In many countries there is a highly developed domestic wholesale television news sector operating in tandem with the international news agencies, and often redistributing their global product domestically. Local television journalists may indeed only be familiar with the domestic variants, as with ANI in India, or CONUS, CNN, and other domestic television news distributors in the United States.

Moving the World's News

This is a book about how television news provides images of the stories of our times unfolding in faraway places. It is widely assumed that each station, national network, or satellite channel to which we are tuned simply sends a member of its staff with a camera to those places, and *voilà!*—all that matters appears before us in our living rooms. On practical grounds we can see the problem: with thousands of independent or semi-independent television broadcasters around the world (over 3,200 in China alone[1] and more than 200 satellite stations in India[2]), most of what we see presented as international news would have to take place in front of a stadium full of photographers—should each individual broadcaster desire its own, exclusive, image (television news people love to have an exclusive image). And imagine the number of interviews those news elites—Obama and Cameron, Merkel and Madonna—would have to give! The thought of 10,000 television cameras trained on each combatant in every war is surely a joyful one. (Would innocent civilians continue to be the principal victims of war if that were the case?) Some broadcasters—those with both the will and the cash—do cover distant stories on their own, on occasion. Most do not.

The pictures of international news we see, for the most part, come from television news agencies, as they have since television news began, which is anywhere from four to six decades ago, depending on where you live. The wholesalers of TV news visuals, sounds, and textual information operate at a level of the industry traditionally hidden from the television audience (lest broadcasters lose the limelight in which they thrive). These are the visual counterparts to the wire services Associated Press (AP), Thomson-Reuters, and Agence France-Presse (AFP) (and their national counterparts, like the Press Association in the U.K. or DPA in Germany). And since the beginnings of television news (save a few years in the 1950s, mid-1990s, and again in 2000), broadcasters around the world have had *just two* of these television news agencies to choose from for their images of foreign news. In this book I'll describe these few organizations, from their origins to their contemporary incarnations, and I'll argue that it is more consequential than most scholarship suggests that *our world comes from London*. That is to say, the television news-provided image of the world we (and our governments) believe in, and act upon, is manufactured by two small sets of people in two rather similar newsrooms in London, the news capital of the world.[3]

News agencies, as Fenby (1986, 171) puts it, are all about "the impression of omnipresence"—seeming to be *everywhere*, so a news organization's reporters don't have to be. Is it any wonder that the foreign news content on television seems to have very much the same sorts of pictures of the same sorts of stories from the same sorts of places, year after year? I hope to show that it is not quite as simple as that, but we might speculate analogously that should you buy IKEA furniture year after year (I write from experience), your house will look a bit like an IKEA store, and a bit like your neighbor's home as well, since they do the same. But I digress. This is about international television news.

Organizations at the first tier of television news are essentially "wholesalers" of visuals, sounds, and textual information. The foremost international examples are Reuters Television and Associated Press Television News (APTN), along with the cooperative news exchanges. (More on them later.) Organizations at the second tier are "packagers" and distributors of news constructed from the "raw material" of the first tier. In truth, a quite significant part of what the audience sees is barely modified at all from the output of the news agencies. I will demonstrate this later in regard to television news, but have also shown this to be the case in regard to international news at the leading news websites, which are almost entirely barely reworked wire service words (Paterson, 2007). The "retailers" are primarily the television networks of every country and their surrogate newsfeed operations providing news to affiliates, and the ubiquitous international rolling news channels. As in other information industries, they can be seen as simply adding value to existing information and reselling it. CNN effectively overlaps both tiers, and the news agencies occasionally do so as well (in creating finished productions for broadcast, for example).

The process has not been well described because it is a relatively recent phenomenon, the product of broadcaster foreign newsgathering reductions and industry realignments. The academic literature has neglected this crucial internal structure, although its key elements are revealed in a few studies of some of its constituent parts: Hjarvard, 1995a, 1995b; Cohen et al., 1996; Johnston, 1995. Boyd-Barrett

(1980) originally described a wholesale/retail model in the context of print news agencies. Figure 1 presents a model of international television news flow based upon the conception of a two-tiered distribution structure. It shows the major providers and broadcasters of television news, and indicates the flow of television news pictures (and related sound and data) among them.

The growth, both in volume and importance, of wholesale international television news is both a product of, and a contributor to, larger trends in global television:

1. deregulation and privatization of television, which was, in turn, a by-product of the 1980s neoliberal agenda expounded, primarily, by the minions of Reagan and Thatcher. For our purposes this process had two important effects in regard to international television news: (a) it reversed a long trend of expansion and investment in international newsgathering by American television networks and most large commercial and public broadcasters worldwide, and (b) it led to the creation of new commercial channels requiring, at minimal cost, large amounts of content for their news programs.
2. growth of 24-hour news channels, or, more precisely, what Cushion (2010) terms the "third phase" of that growth, its rapid expansion at a mostly regional level during the past decade.

This two-tiered structure of wholesale and retail news became more relevant due to these trends. Television news agency dependence grew with cutbacks by major broadcast networks around the world involving the downsizing of television news divisions: television news companies had to provide the illusion they were still covering the world when they were not. Many commentators lamented these cuts and their implications (Dominick, 1988; Waite, 1992; Katz, 1991; Carter, 1992; Winseck, 1992; Utley, 1997; Cottle, 2009). For example, with substantial cutbacks to its own news operation, in 1993 Britain's ITN began exclusively using the international footage of its shareholder, Reuters. Thus, Reuters was supplying international news to every major British television newscast (BBC, ITN, and Sky), virtually giving the British television viewer a single window on the world.[4]

The U.S. networks, along with many others around the world, faced another set of massive staff and bureau cuts in 2010 as a result of declining audiences and advertising revenues (Harmon, 2010), and dependence on agency video is likely to increase again as a result. At the time of this writing (and in an echo of the U.S. cuts two decades earlier), Australia's public broadcaster is facing condemnation from national legislators as its executives conduct "an assassination tour" of the world, closing bureaus while speaking of greater dependence on APTN for international

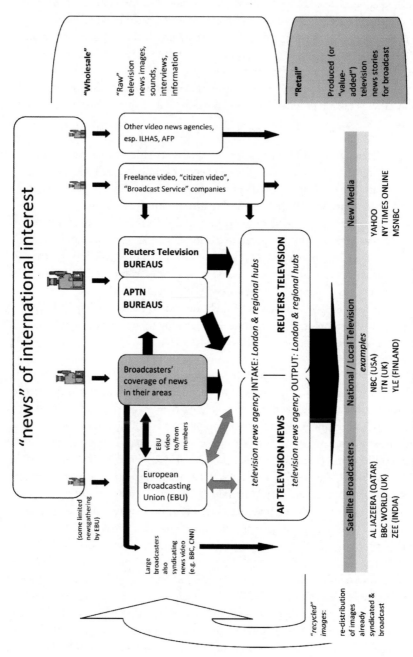

Figure 1. Major providers and broadcasters of television news

coverage (Meade, 2010). Cushion and Lewis (2010) found in their examination of the characteristics of news on the many 24-hour channels that "it was largely routine, predictable, institutionally derived, and often wholesaler sourced" (cited in Bromley, 2010). But it is also worth noting, as many non-American agency staff and broadcasters have pointed out to me, that even before the 1990s the U.S. television networks did little international news coverage relative to their European counterparts, and almost none from developing countries (evidenced by Larson, 1984).

In the United States, the concern about cutbacks to television news divisions twenty years ago led to congressional hearings. Frank (1991, 411) cites a now-classic example of the efforts by corporate owners to swat back at the criticism. He relates how Thornton Bradshaw, chairman of RCA (then the immediate owner of NBC), justified extensive cuts at NBC News by saying, "There's no reason that all three networks need to have people sitting around in Zimbabwe." Frank took the comment as an insult to good television reporters everywhere, but neglects to mention that the comment, originally made to *The Los Angeles Times*, was also disinformation. U.S. broadcast networks had never based anyone in Zimbabwe or any other African country, except South Africa. But Bradshaw either believed network news divisions were paying people to sit around and wait for news to happen in every small country, or he knew otherwise, but wanted Americans to believe it. An unnamed U.S. network executive told *The New York Times* that his network had saved $70,000 a day covering a major foreign story using only agency footage (Carter, 1992).

But these processes also enabled, depended upon, and thrived from the birth of many new commercial broadcasters, mostly in Europe, designed from the outset to draw heavily from the agencies (for analysis of such a broadcaster, see Helland, 1995). Stephen Claypole, television news agency and broadcast veteran and founding director of APTV, observed in 1995 that an increasing number of broadcasters were depending exclusively on news agency video for their images (Claypole, 1995). Euronews was founded on the basis of having a steady stream of mostly news agency-originated video: at the outset, it took video both from the Eurovision news exchange and subscriptions to Reuters and WTN. Even the BBC's highly regarded international news channel, BBC World, was originally designed to do little of its own original journalism. According to Preston (1999, 189), "the channel directly commissioned only a couple of reports a week, with approximately 60 per cent of material coming unchanged from domestic News, and the remainder consisting of re-voiced agency material." The many new broadcasters erupted from the deregulation and privatization of the European broadcasting landscape, which was instigated by the neoliberal and commercial agendas emanating from Washington and London in the 1980s, but which was also affectionately embraced by the European Union and European Commission.[5]

The Television News Agency Business

The television news agencies gather videotaped pictures and sound and story information continuously from a number of major bureaus around the world and scores of minor ones, a far larger number of stringers, and from client television stations worldwide. They also, increasingly, organize live pictures of developing news stories whenever it is technically possible to do so. They take from and contribute stories to the European Broadcasting Union's (EBU) news exchange mechanism and other cooperative exchanges. Most in the industry suggest that Associated Press Television eclipsed Reuters Television during the last decade to become the larger of the two. In a critique of the two, journalist Peter Maass (2001) commented, "Their battle has evolved into television journalism's equivalent of Coke vs. Pepsi." As of this writing, APTN claimed "over 80 bureaus worldwide" (of which 63 are promoted as having the necessary television facilities to serve visiting broadcasters—and so are larger, well equipped, and have a substantial number of staff); they also now claim to supply news video to 88% of the world's broadcasters.[6]

The television news agencies edit together their own story "packages" consisting of video and "natural" sound (that is, no added narration—sometimes called "international sound" in agency parlance), and deliver them by satellite to clients in any of several daily scheduled (and sometimes fast-breaking unscheduled) "feeds" (or via the ongoing television news story exchange conducted by the European Broadcasting Union). But it is worth mentioning that satellites are no longer essential; they are no longer the conduit of globalization. Much of the literature of globalization dating to the 1960s links the processes of cultural globalization to the satellite, but this role as agent of globalization has substantially diminished due to the Internet. Since the bulk of news agency video started being transmitted by file transfer protocol (FTP), via the Internet or the news agencies' own fixed data links, the vastly less costly and more capacious undersea cable has taken on at least as important a role.

Some audio commentary and electronic text (sometimes called "scripts" or, in earlier days, "dope sheets") are provided to television news agency clients, providing information to accompany the visuals, and occasionally finished stories that a broadcaster can put right on the air are offered. Strict copyright rules are observed to ensure that no station broadcasts—and no agency distributes—news video that it hasn't paid for or produced itself. As Waite (1992) succinctly observed, at the heart of the international television news business is *the goal of gaining the greatest possible exclusivity of news images for the lowest possible cost.*

Clients pay the agencies from tens of thousands of dollars to many millions of dollars yearly, depending upon a variety of factors including the size of the station's audience, the number and type of news feeds received, and the volume of news video from its home area that the client provides to the agency.[7] In the 1990s, contracts with major broadcasters typically cost several million U.S. dollars each year, and this continues to be the case, although it is rarer now to see public announcements about news agency contracts and their value, and broadcasters and agency staff who deal with contracts are bound to secrecy by their employers (and the contracts' fine print). So the precise values of news agency deals are all but impossible to pin down. For example, in 1991, U.S. network CBS switched to Visnews (soon to become Reuters Television) from APTN predecessor Worldwide Television News (WTN) for, according to Waite (1992), "much less than the $1 million a year the network had been paying WTN." (A common strategy for television news agencies has been to under-price the competition—at a loss—to steal away key broadcasters.) But a few years later CBS returned to WTN with a contract for three years for about $3 million per year. An inflation of more than 200% in three years for WTN's product is implied, evidencing the boom for the agencies that the newsgathering cutbacks at the American networks provided. Another trade article at that time claimed, "US networks each still spend about $1 million a year" on agency contracts.[8] Baker (2004) writes that television news agency subscriptions usually run for three years.

From the late 1980s to the present, the agencies also benefited from the occasional specialized contracts with larger companies, providing far-ranging services over an extended period. As Rupert Murdoch began to build his Sky News channel in the U.K. in 1988, he first spoke to ITN about providing most of the journalism and news pictures (nearly everything, in fact, done away from the studio). When their price was too high, he agreed with Visnews to do so for £30 million (just over $50 million) for five years (Preston, 1999, 251). By the mid-1990s, for Reuters Television, that had increased to £10 million yearly (ibid., 279). The deal involved international news feeds, the provision of crews and facilities to cover international stories, and the establishment of Sky News bureaus around the U.K.[9] The links with Murdoch's Sky were part of what made Visnews valuable enough to Reuters to buy out the co-owners of Visnews in 1992, but were also significant in progressively souring the Visnews relationship with its founder, the BBC (a story continued in Chapter Four).

Prior to the growth of cable news in the United States (CNN, MSNBC, Fox), the U.S. networks had among the largest (and most commercially valuable) audiences of any television news agency clients, so it is reasonable to suspect that television news agency subscriptions currently range from much less to slightly less than the million-dollar figures mentioned above. But for the voracious global rolling news channels, subscription fees are probably significantly higher. In 2007 CNN had a spat with Reuters over pricing and dropped their wire and video service, leaving them with only their APTN subscription (which dated back to their inception in 1980 when the contract was with APTN predecessor UPITN). Reuters announced that the lost CNN contract was worth $3.5 million each year (Li, 2007). Television news agencies also sell smaller, customized services to broadcasters (and the full gamut of media companies from newspaper websites to mobile phone news providers). These are priced by the agencies according to the size of that company's audience, the cost of producing the service, and, it would seem (according to various agency insiders), a fair measure of what the agency thinks it can get away with asking.[10] A recent example provided to me by one journalist working for a large national network was that their regular feed of show business news from one television news agency costs them just over U.S. $40,000 yearly. That is just for a steady supply of images of the comings and goings of celebrities, not the "hard news."

Recently, an APTN executive wrote that among them, the television news agencies share a "subscription market…worth around US $250 million dollars a year worldwide" (Baker, 2004, 70), with Reuters Television and APTN having the lion's share of that market, but some of it going to the European Broadcasting Union and CNN as well. Contemporary sources suggest that subscription rates have not increased significantly since 2000 (see Venter, 2005; and interviews), but the number of clients has (due mostly to Internet news and to the increase in rolling news channels). Financially, the news agencies do slightly better than break even; sources report off the record that they return a small profit for their owners. This is surprising, since from their inception in the 1950s they have mostly existed as barely tolerated loss makers for their owners—almost always hemorrhaging money, but too important to do away with (hence AP's 1994 entry into the business with enormous investment from the newspaper side of its business). Indeed, there are indications within Reuters and AP that the needs of the video service often now take precedence over text and photos on major stories: video has taken its place at the table in two organizations founded on the written word.

From their inception, television news agencies have been mostly owned by, and have mostly catered to, European and American media. Baker (2004) reported that in 2000, just under 52% of APTN revenue came from European clients, 20% from Asian, and about 16% from North America. But it has, on occasion, only been through the support of a few powerful advocates within U.S. and British broadcasters that the television agencies have survived hard times, and those same few people have had a substantial influence over their development, as I will describe further in Chapters Three and Four. These include BBC and later CNN International news chief Chris Cramer; former ITN chief executive Sir David Nicholas; NBC and later ABC (United States) news head Richard Wald;[11] and CNN founder (with Ted Turner) Reese Schonfeld. And without the massive investment in television news authorized by Associated Press President Lou Boccardi in the 1990s, APTN would not exist, and WTN—then the only competition to

Reuters—might well have been consumed by Reuters, leaving a single global television news agency.[12]

A Gap in the Research Literature

The overall lack of recent research exploring television production, global news production, and the influence of corporate ownership on news production has been cited as a gap in our understanding of news (Cottle, 2007; and others). It could be added that "inter-industry" news production—the work of news agencies—is almost entirely unresearched. This book attempts to address these areas while providing ethnographic insight into a massively influential yet nearly invisible journalistic culture. Who are the small set of journalists who decide for the world's broadcasters what "the" images of the day are to be, and what are their motivations and working routines?

Since broadcasters feel an obligation to provide news from outside their own locality or national borders but are rarely willing to allocate the extensive and costly resources to discover and gather such news, most leave the task to the few, and largely unknown, public and commercial TV news wholesalers described in this book. Malik, in his useful 1992 TV news agenda survey, demonstrated the worldwide congruence in international television news coverage: "What our pages show is that the power of the exchange systems and the TV news agencies is much greater than the public generally feel or know." His data showed the same video, of the same stories, from the same sources, running in roughly the same position in newscasts all over the world on the evening of his survey. While the two leading international examples—and the foci of this book—are Reuters Television and Associated Press Television News (APTN), other important providers of television images exist, and some will be described here. These include, in Europe, the public news exchange mechanism Eurovision, and in the United States the commercial TV news cooperative Conus and competing news distribution systems operated by television networks, chiefly CNN.[13]

The 1995 survey of broadcasters from around the world by this author, as part of the global news flow study that year repeating the famous UNESCO-funded study of 1979 (Sreberny-Mohammadi et al., 1984), found essentially the same thing: the same pictures, used in the same ways, around the world. Industry data and further academic studies, described in the next chapter, tell the same story. The recent trends in European television news suggest further homogenization of international news, despite the increase in news channels. As early as 1980, scholars were noting that "TV News and newsreels are largely based on film material from the United States and Great Britain where the UPI, ITN and VIS News [sic] have virtually established a world-wide monopoly,"[14] and, referencing the research of

Batscha (1975), Larson (1984, 37) observed that "since the vast majority of such reports originate from the major international news agencies, they provide a measure of network dependence on those agencies for coverage of international affairs."

Two major studies of agency news were published in the 1980s, though neither included extensive research on the production process (Boyd-Barrett, 1980; Fenby, 1986). Johnston (1995) provided a mostly interview-based examination of the global news wholesalers. The remaining research consists of master's dissertations (Clare, 1998; Venter, 2005), brief accounts of aspects of agency work by those involved in it (Mahoney, 1975; Claypole, 1995; Baker, 2004 and 2009) and some features in other popular or industry media (Waite, 1992; Busfield, 1995a; Edmonds, 2006). Preston (1999), in one of the most exhaustive reviews available of the U.K. television news industry and its international links, details aspects of the agencies' relationships with broadcasters in the 1980s and 1990s. Two disenchanted Reuters journalists wrote about the financial woes of the company in 2003 (Mooney and Simpson, 2003) but revealed little about the news production process. Official (Associated Press, 2007) or semi-official (Read, 1992) company histories of AP and Reuters, respectively, revealed even less about their role in television news.

The Global Public Sphere, Revisited

Most TV news broadcasters will cover events close to home on their own, but with our television pictures of distant events coming from just two fairly similar organizations, is it conceivable that for each of the five billion of us who have access to a television, our view of the world (literally and metaphorically) is essentially identical?[15] Could we speculate that it is not so much the satellites or the broadcasters or the Hollywood studios that make us into McLuhan's "global village" (1962), but the television news agencies? Jeremy Tunstall, who provided an early influential analysis of global communications flow in *The Media Are American* (1977), speculated as much, writing in 1992 (89) that "most TV foreign news professionals would probably agree that Visnews (taken over by Reuters in 1993) has some claim to being the most widely consumed, if least recognized, world brand." That claim now rightfully belongs to the television news agency duopoly of Reuters and APTN. APTN claims that "video captured by AP Television News can be seen by over half of the world's population on any given day" (APTN.com: "company overview"). By analogy, Coca-Cola is everywhere; and, everywhere they are, everyone knows it because more than five cents of every dollar spent on Coca-Cola goes toward marketing their brand to the public.[16] Reuters and APTN, and their predecessors, market themselves to broadcasters, but almost never to the public at large. They are both omnipresent and (substantially) invisible.

For the largest broadcasters they are a tool—an essential component in news coverage—but the broadcasts would go on without them (in how different a form might be fiercely debated in the industry).[17] But for smaller broadcasters and many large, but lean, new satellite broadcasters, they are the flour in the bread: there simply would be no substance at all—visually—without them. (There would instead be many pundits in studios, debating the events of the day—events we would never see.) Everywhere, journalists see television news agency images on the incoming video source screens of their newsrooms (usually prominently suspended above the desks of key editors). They follow their printed agendas and their diaries; they depend on their pictures to construct their stories and on their resources to report their own stories.[18]

Imagine a television world in which broadcasters "did their own thing"—that is, chose their own news (is what matters to me the same as what matters to you?) and constructed their own reports without input from other media (including the non-local news wholesalers). What would such a world on television look like? Without foreign input, it would surely be more local. As such we might suspect it would be massively more *relevant* to viewers, and it would surely be different from what other media channels around the world are broadcasting. So this new global television news environment would unquestionably be diverse. Straubhaar (2007) has well demonstrated the importance of cultural relevance in the popularity of non-English-language television fiction, causing it to succeed even where global trends said it should fail. Continue to imagine, if you will, that the millions spent by television stations (or their parent networks) on news agency subscriptions were spent on scores of eager young reporters (we journalism educators can supply them by the thousands) to "pound the pavement" and dig out the stories, nationally and internationally, that nobody else is doing. I'm surely describing a nightmare for news agency managers (my apologies to them), but for the rest of us, could this describe the diverse media world we so desperately need? More on that in the conclusion to this book.

But don't we all *need* to see the same picture of bombs over Baghdad, of an Obama speech, of foreign ministers discussing global trade, of hungry masses following a disaster? Isn't it those common moving images, with their power over text and sounds and photographs, that bind us together, that give us a common reference on international affairs, that challenge us to act, that identify the threats and opportunities we and our respective governments should be worrying about? Giddens suggested "the global extension of the institutions of modernity [capitalist economy, nation-state system, world military order, industrial development] would be impossible were it not for the pooling of knowledge which is represented by the 'news'" (1991, 77–78; in Archetti, 2008). And as put by Clausen (2004), "international news increases the awareness and interconnectedness of social and political information and actors across borders." It isn't quite the global public sphere that Volkmer (1999) theorized (following Hannerz, 1996; Dahlgren, 1995; Hallin, 1994; Venturelli, 1993)—tied too closely to Anglo-U.S. satellite broadcasters as it was—but the idea seems to fit. Hjarvard (2001) examined the role of news media in the construction of such a phenomenon, and his review of the many approaches scholars have taken confirms the limited attention paid thus far to the source images of television news. But a scholar who has is Clausen (2004, 27), who posits that "the distribution of news through international news agencies enable[s] the global diffusion of information about events, while enhancing the interpenetration of *universal*…concepts and policies" (italics in original).

Volkmer's important study made influential arguments about the nature of global communication, but having spent as much time as I had with the global television news agencies, I was uneasy about a theory of global communications so substantially based on the workings of one American news network. CNN, which even at the time of Volkmer's study was at the peak of its global reach, had relatively little visibility outside of the United States beyond high-priced hotel rooms, and remained, as it had been from its inception, substantially dependent on television news agencies for its images and wire services for its information. CNN had been a presence on cable and satellite systems in Europe, Asia, and Latin America for some time, but had rarely pulled in large audiences outside of the United States (and by this time it was rapidly losing its U.S. audience to the upstart rolling channels).

Volkmer posits the possibility that the global political communications she sees as being "launched by CNN" (1999, 4) leads to a global public sphere. The concept has been developed further by other scholars (some cited above). But if the images at the core of global broadcasting are indeed important (and few have argued otherwise), shouldn't it be *the source of the images* (and their shared properties) that we credit with construction of a global discourse, as opposed to the larger broadcasters who selectively relay some of those images to their audiences? If I want to know the health effects of banana consumption globally, for example, I would be more inclined to research the properties of the banana than to examine a few of the larger banana distributors. Recent scholarship surveying the global landscape of countless news channels in countless languages and with countless agendas (for example, Rai and Cottle, 2010) has been too quick to dismiss the possibility of a global public sphere—that there are *universal, shared elements* in the diversity of televisual babble—while curiously ignoring that just about every one of those channels is showing the *same pictures* to its audiences. It is as though the visual part of television doesn't matter. But we know it does.

Global video news viewers (whether using television, computer, or mobile telephone) seeing the same limited set of pictures of what are "important," is reminiscent of Habermas's conception of a sphere in which we abandon our private selves to be exposed to a collective set of ideas (if one ever existed [i.e., Sparks, 2004]), and to debate those—just as the corporate-dominated and unidirectional nature of the process reaffirms Habermas's concern for the loss of such a sphere. Giddens explained (1991, 187; in Clausen, 2004), "although everyone lives a local life, phenomenological worlds for the most part are truly global." But if those shared phenomenological worlds are constructed by distant television news agency journalists, is this television news agency-created global public sphere one of debate, or a uni-directional fire hose of images from two London newsrooms, aimed at the world? Television is a device cleverly engineered by the marketers who would come to dominate it as a one-way system. As there shall be no debate about why the washing powder you have just seen for thirty seconds will improve your life, there will be no debate about the news image you have been shown—or why you were shown it, where it came from, or what it might mean. Were those Iraqis pulling down the statue of Saddam jubilant about their "liberation" or just caught up in an event staged by U.S. troops? Sorry, the next image is on the way: TV news doesn't permit such reflection. And so it is our very state of knowledge—our global understanding—that is shaped in this unidirectional way.

The television news agencies' view, despite ample and honest efforts by their journalists to uncover multiple perspectives and hidden stories, is a fairly homogenous one, and certainly an ideological one for what it includes and excludes. The routines of professionalism and objectivity widely practiced in television news, especially in the established Anglo-American news operations, have been recognized not merely as a necessary source of structure for television journalists, as Schlesinger (1987) and others have argued, but as the means by which ideology is conveyed (see also Reese, 1990; Bantz, 1985; Tuchman, 1978; Golding and Elliot, 1979). How is it possible to follow a tradition of objectivity and impartiality while all the while reinforcing the hegemony of the powerful? Hall (1988, 86) writes that the media claim of impartiality is itself ideological,

> not because it is false but because it does not adequately grasp all the conditions which make freedom and impartiality possible...it offers a partial explanation as if it were a comprehensive and adequate one...its legitimacy depends on that part of the truth, which it mistakes for the whole, being real in fact, and not merely a polite fiction.

Hall later concludes: "Unwittingly, unconsciously, the broadcaster has served as support for the reproduction of a dominant ideological discursive field" (1988, 88). The global impact of the television news agencies is dependent upon (though not exclusively due to) the influence upon audiences of the portions of television newscasts to which the agencies contribute, that is, the visual component of international stories. (More on this in the next chapter.)

Television news is identical from place to place, the world over, in one way: through the sharing of video images provided by television news agencies. But there is also a considerable element of a circular flow—effectively, a kind of *global recycling*—of images by way of the television news agencies and exchanges. Putnis (1994) and former television news agency producer-turned-researcher John Jirik (correspondence, 2007) have commented on the role of the news agencies in a perpetual, global system of recycling news images. While television news agencies most value the images that they obtain themselves, a large portion (at times the majority) of what they distribute globally are what they term "up-picks," or video from a television station (typically, one of their own clients). Television stations around the world, after all, collectively have far more photographers chasing stories than the two global news agencies could muster and are normally closer to breaking news. And so those images taken by broadcasters in any given region are moved to London (usually by the closest television news agency bureau) and distributed out to the world, including back to the very same broadcasters who obtained the images. I rather simplistically illustrate this in the earlier figure. The extent of this is roughly measurable from day to day using the story lineups that are occasionally available from the television news agencies at their websites. As I write this, about one-fifth of Reuters Television stories currently circulating are labeled as originating with local broadcasters.

Broadcasters then go on to depend on the flow of images from agencies and continually recycle them in updates to their stories. Putnis detailed the process for Australian television in his 1994 research titled *Displaced, Re-cut and Recycled: Filetape in Television News*. He came to similar conclusions, albeit with a different metaphor for this global flow of images (Putnis, 1996, 21):

> Because of the interdependence of the major English language news organizations "standard Western" ways of seeing emerge out of the process. [A story about Haiti] was presented in much the same way in Britain, the US, and Australia. We not only have the same images, but the same interpretations. International news flow is like a world-encircling merry-go-round with multiple (though, ultimately, very selective) points of "uploading" and "downloading."

Steward Purvis, ITN's Chief Executive, told Harrison and Palmer (1986, 76):

> Since the news agencies are putting out pictures which most countries are using, there is a kind of recycling of all the same pictures. And we have sometimes taken a satellite from another country and seen our own pictures and thought: "My God what's the point of that?" Quite often Israeli television coverage of Arab events comes from WTN's coverage so that you don't get any unique insight from watching their coverage of the Middle East. All you see is our pictures with a different commentary.

Jirik (ibid.) observed that

> the "raw material" gets "shaped" according to the logics of the center in an endless cir-
> culation of a fairly limited set of narratives with a new event injected into the mix every
> now and then. Under this model, Reuters (and) AP become more of a clearing and ide-
> ological shaping house than a production house.

The television news agency journalists' view of the world may very much reflect a shared understanding with their fellow journalists everywhere (they would typically argue it does), but this does not negate how influential it is. The steady flow of tele-vision news agency pictures, in themselves, no more comprise a global public sphere than do the broadcasts of CNN, the BBC, or Al Jazeera. But they are the common ingredient in global television news, no matter what the ideology, spin, proprietor's politics, or cultural stance of the broadcaster. The heavy use of the same television news agency images (and information) is consistent across them all. A dramatic image carried on the BBC (or any of the other big broadcasters) won't, on its own, spark global debate, mobilize armies, or move markets. But one distributed by a tele-vision news agency and aired by all broadcasters will. The exception is when that BBC (or other broadcaster's) image is acquired by a television news agency and sent on to the world. Images convey meaning; the selection and editing of those images convey even more meaning; and sequences of agency images used with agency-pro-vided information or audio (as I show in the next chapter is typical, especially for smaller broadcasters) convey a great deal of meaning about what a news viewer should conclude (or "decode" from the news text, in Hall's terms).

Much has been written about the counter-hegemonic ambitions of many newer broadcasters: the wish to present a distinctly different view of the world appealing to large, but previously underserved audiences (as opposed to established hegemonic flows of news from mostly Anglo-U.S. broadcasters like the BBC and CNN). The idea that Latin Americans no longer need to watch themselves por-trayed consistently as criminals (see Reyes Matta, 1979) or Arabs as terrorists (Ayish, 2010; Semati, 2010), or the developing world majority as dependent on Western largess (Dahlgren and Chakrapani, 1982; Fair, 1992), is compelling; new global and regional channels have surely brought a more relevant and sympathetic world view to audiences who previously might have had to experience comprehen-sive international television news coverage through the narrow and tainted lens of an Anglo-American commercial network or a propagandistic state channel.

But, in light of what we have observed concerning the ubiquity of television news agency images, there is reason to ask if the contra-flow of television news which many have described (Boyd-Barrett and Thussu, 1992; Sonwalkar, 2001) is somewhat illusory. Television news agencies act as global public sphere "visual flow regulators" that both regulate and mitigate counter-hegemonic TV news flows.

Many new broadcasters—especially rolling news channels—could not exist without the image flow from the television news agencies. This fosters ideological conformity. Examples might be the perception of Iran as a threat (because its nuclear program gets extensive news agency coverage), or the perception of most nations as insignificant (because most nations get little or no news agency coverage). They regulate in the sense that important, influential images of international events rarely exist independently of them: for those images to become meaningful beyond the home territory of the broadcaster (or individual videographer) who captured them, they need to enter the regional and global distribution systems of the news agencies. That is not a matter of "news value." It is a matter of choice—the choices of the few television news agency editors and managers on duty in London, and (to a lesser extent) other regional agency headquarters, at any given moment.

Imperialism, Revisited

This book's call to look more closely at the global role of some very old institutions—the television news agencies—complements a call to look again at some aging theoretical explanations of mass communications. Two that are vital to these arguments are media imperialism, long dismissed as reductionist, U.S.-centric, imprecise, and dated (see Golding and Harris, 1997; Sreberny-Mohammadi, 1996), and gatekeeping (see White, 1950; Donohue et al., 1972; Becker and Whitney, 1982; Berkowitz, 1990; Reese et al., 1993). With few individuals determining what, if any, stories about the world (the 99% of the world most media don't have easy access to) will be among the dozen or so non-American, non-Western European stories fed to television news agency clients each day, their gatekeeping role becomes clear, leading us to ask how their gatekeeping decisions are made. Gatekeeping studies have stressed various influences affecting gatekeepers' decisions, including the degree to which a gatekeeper identifies with the story source, the degree and nature of consideration of audience, various economic, institutional, and technological considerations, and, potentially, ethnocentric and nationalistic influences.

It must be emphasized that the gatekeeping influences of interest here consist not only of the values and priorities of the London news agency journalists, but also of their perceptions of the news values of their clients, i.e., the executive producers, managing editors, and, indeed, owners of client broadcasters. Determining what the London news agency editors deem newsworthy is not enough; through long-term observation of the television news agencies some estimation is possible of what they believe their most important clients will "buy." When I started my research in the early 1990s (and even prior to that), the names of those "most important" clients were clear: BBC, ITN (U.K.); ABC, CBS, NBC, CNN (United

States); NHK (Japan); ZDF (Germany); the Australian networks, and perhaps only a few others. Van Ginneken (1998, 44) suggested that news agencies have consistently prioritized three categories of clients while ignoring others. Those three are the business world, the media of developed countries, and governments of developed countries (also see Schiff, 1996).

But the television landscape, and television news agency priorities, have changed. It is now the many large regional and international rolling news channels, broadcasting constant "live news" (whether much is either live or news is subject to debate), that command the most respect—and fast action—from the television news agencies. Their ravenous desire for pictures, preferably live (in combination with other factors, like lower video transmission costs and new Internet and mobile clients), gives a new lease on life to organizations that, after fifty years, should be showing signs of wear. Surprisingly, though, the TV news agencies soldier on despite a slew of recent threats: the coming of the Internet, which threatened to make redundant their proficiency at global news acquisition and delivery; the dot-com bust, which devastated a fast-growing online news industry; the press for profit from owners (the Canadian conglomerate Thomson-Reuters, for Reuters Television, and the collective of struggling U.S. newspapers that owns AP, for APTN), when their business is massively costly and historically unprofitable; and, of course, the threat to jail or kill their photographers in the zones of conflict that are their home turf.

This process of so many images being provided to so many people, but being processed and selected by so few, is at odds with widespread predictions since the 1990s of increased and more equitable news flow caused by new news providers and the application of new newsgathering and distribution technologies. Indeed, the central rationale for so much deregulation of broadcasting, and the journalism it entails, has been that these processes facilitate a diverse and vibrant journalism. Like most promises of neoliberal economics, this was wrong (well evidenced by Winseck, 1997; Thussu, 2007). Deregulation spread further the images originating with two companies.

The globalization of television news, while unquestionably a crucial aspect of the processes customarily lumped together as "globalization," seems paradoxically to be the least well-examined, yet most alluded-to, aspect of the globalization phenomenon. Rarely are the specific processes concerning the internationalization of television news detailed and contextualized. Instead, they are all too often used as anecdotal examples of a much broader conception of the globalization of communications, a conception that many scholars tend to relate much more to the spread and cultural impact of entertainment products such as television serials, films, and music. Television news agencies are a "missing link" in the globalization puzzle—a neglected but crucial agent of globalization. The role of mass communications in globalization has been endlessly theorized, and different approaches have gone in and out of fashion; thus it is beyond the scope of this chapter to recount the full history of globalization theory. (For more comprehensive summaries than I could offer here, see, for example, Kavoori, 2009; Griffin, 2002.)

But, crucially, as innovative new ways to think about globalization were being introduced, a perfectly sound approach that retained considerable explanatory value was being marginalized: that of "media imperialism." The concept was concisely described in 1977 by Boyd-Barrett as occurring when "media in any one country are...subject to substantial pressure from the media interests of any other...countries without proportionate reciprocation of influence...." Journalism and international communication scholars were well positioned in the 1980s and 1990s to develop this concept by researching and cataloguing those asymmetrical external influences on the media systems of countries. Some studies did, such as the 1979 "Foreign news in the media" news flow project (Sreberny-Mohammadi et al., 1984), reprised in 1995 with input from this author (and described in Wu, 2003).

Sonwalkar (2001) has argued convincingly that any concept of cultural imperialism must be updated to include regional media powers such as India or Brazil, as much as it focuses on the United States, but Thussu (2007) offers convincing evidence that the bulk of media flow in the world continues to be largely unidirectional: from the "north to the south," "west to the rest," or—most commonly—from the United States to the rest, suggesting that imbalance in global media production evidenced over the last four decades or more (Nordenstreng and Varis, 1974; Tunstall, 1977; De Bens et al., 1992), has not been entirely dismantled by new regional or global contra-flows of media (Boyd-Barrett and Thussu, 1992; Sonwalkar, 2001), including television journalism.

Many scholars in these fields moved with the fashion of discarding media imperialism (and related approaches) before its processes were well understood, and it is my contention that one of the most vital of those is the global flow of television news video (and the "scripts," story diaries, and other information that accompanies it) from the two (and briefly three) television news agencies in London to (nearly) every television broadcaster everywhere on the planet. No advertising campaign, no entertainment product or Hollywood (or Bollywood) celebrity, no piece of music, is as ubiquitous. The images we all share, and which substantially shape our political, economic, and cultural lives, come almost entirely (never completely) from two similar newsrooms in London. That is a process of globalization, and a process of media imperialism. And it is, oddly, all but absent from the last three decades of discussion of globalization.

The Chapters Ahead

In the next chapter this book addresses some general characteristics of the often-seen, but little-understood, product of the television news agencies: the images they feed daily to the broadcasters of the world. We then move, in two stages, through the history of the television news agencies, addressing first, in Chapter Three, their birth (as early as 1947) and development into essentially the form they take today; and then, in Chapter Four, the violent and chaotic 1990s, which saw dramatic shifts in ownership and changes to the agencies' longstanding business model, the death of two agencies and birth of two others, and the transition to the relatively stable, semi-converged, operations of today.

In the following chapters we will examine the television news agency news production process, drawing largely from this author's ethnographic research with these organizations. Chapters Five and Six examine some of the prominent characteristics of television news agency "news manufacturing" and how these have changed over the past decade or so. Chapter Seven presents a case study of a typical international story in order to demonstrate the extensive, and remarkably comprehensive, planning process that enables television news agencies to do what they do. Chapter Eight focuses on coverage of conflict, the most difficult but most sought-after form of news agency journalism. Some conclusions, and recommendations for news agencies, policy makers, and the public at large, are offered in Chapter Nine.

Notes

1. 1997 data via CIA World Factbook, accessed September 27, 2010. https://www.cia.gov /library/publications/the-world-factbook/fields/2015.html.
2. Cushion and Lewis, 2010, 24.
3. See Clarke, 1995, and Tunstall, 1992, for elaboration of the case for London as the world's "news capital."
4. Noted in *Broadcast*, May 28, 1993. ITN and the BBC, of course, covered a great deal of foreign news on their own at this time. Westcott (1995a, 22) confirms that "Reuters now supplies news to all of the major UK broadcasters."
5. As with the 1989 European "Television without Frontiers" directive.
6. APTN website. That doesn't mean that Reuters Television supplies only the other 12%. Many of the largest and wealthiest media companies typically subscribe to both agencies, and Reuter's Television will have a similar number of subscribers. The term "broadcaster" is slippery when used in television news agency promotional material, and indeed is defined widely and variously within academia and the industry. CNN is probably on APTN's list, though it is technically not a broadcaster, while numerous small television

broadcast stations affiliated with larger national networks, which are technically broadcasters, are probably not. In the mid-1990s, Reuters Television's own internal client list showed 214 companies (some non-broadcasters were included) in 83 countries. It noted that affiliates of some of the networks on the list were not shown, since these do not subscribe directly, but may receive Reuters Television pictures through their network.

7. Interviews, trade press reports, and Baker (2004).

8. Interviews; WTN signs $10 million deal with CBS, *Broadcasting and Cable*, September 19, 1994, 42; Production News (1994); *Film and Video*, October 10, 1994; Busfield (1995a).

9. The deal not only relieved the financial pressure on Visnews, which had only earned just enough to survive through the 1980s, but gave it—with the Sky UK bureaus—a source of U.K. news as its relationship with the BBC soured. It also financed an expansion in international newsgathering to service Sky, but which Visnews could sell outside the U.K.

10. An executive who negotiates such contracts for a major broadcaster, and who had previously worked for a television news agency, confirmed to me "there is no formula": the agencies ask for as much as they can get.

11. In my interview with Wald he mentioned once being credited by former ITN boss Stewart Purvis as "creating more jobs in the UK than anybody . . ." for his investments, at the helm of two U.S. networks, in Visnews, UPITN, and WTN.

12. It is not widely known that Reuters attempted to purchase WTN from the Disney Corporation in 1997, shortly before it was sold to the Associated Press (detailed in Chapter Four).

13. For CONUS, see Mater (1989). CNN and the U.S. broadcast networks also operate news exchanges for their affiliated stations.

14. Bruck (1980, 66), quoted in McPhail (1997), 20.

15. And those who watch it with others away from home (as is common in poorer countries). International Telecommunication Union, 2010.

16. Various sources. Coke earned $31 billion in 2009 and spent as much as $2 billion of it on marketing annually in the 2000s.

17. The BBC's Director of Global News Richard Sambrook, for example, explained, "When we take a Reuters feed by and large we want to add our own value to it, take it and put our own judgment on it or put it with something different" (*Broadcast* 2006). Some years earlier, long time BBC Head of Newsgathering Chris Cramer told the trade press, "The BBC and major broadcasters buy agency pictures as fire insurance," compared to "a lot of broadcasters which actually buy in as their entire news supply [sic]," in Busfield (1994a).

18. For instance, at the time of this writing one of the television news agencies has been so overwhelmed by requests from broadcasters to help them produce "localized" reports (i.e., with a broadcaster's own reporter doing a "stand-upper" from the scene) of the rescue of the 33 Chilean miners who had been trapped underground for ten weeks that they have had to limit how many they can serve. As the rescue commenced, some 1,300 journalists from around the world descended on the scene, far more than covered the earthquake that had devastated the country some months earlier (Barrett, 2010).

2

The Nature of
Television Agency News

This chapter draws both from production research and content research to describe how television news agency journalism is constructed and what, in general, it tends to look like. The problem is the dearth of research: news agencies (like most media) neither encourage forensic examination of their procedures nor (often) give away their product to researchers. If the AP is correct in its claim that its video "can be seen by over half of the world's population on any given day" (and Reuters could make a similar if slightly less ambitious claim), we should *all* be expert on the characteristics of television news agency pictures. We are not, and that is because the broadcasters who bring us the news don't want us to be. They have always been content for us to assume that all pictures are *their pictures* (as their newspaper and online counterparts have been happy for us to believe that they—not the news agencies—fill their pages). Indeed, the only people who typically know what television news agencies produce are the small fraction of television news agency employees who see the bulk of the output, and the editors and producers in client companies the world over who use it.

There are two interconnected reasons why it is important to consider television news agency content. The first is whether what the agencies do *actually matters*. Both the agencies, and their clients, frequently suggest it does not. It is just "raw material": the peas and carrots that go into the soup. The broadcasters are the chefs; they tell the stories in an infinite number of ways, as their professional skills dictate. Perhaps examination of content will suggest who tells the story or, to use Hall's (1992; originally 1973) terminology, who *encodes* the meaning. The second reason to examine content is to understand—if the interpretations of the world generated by television news agencies matter (see reason one)—what *the nature of those interpretations* are. Do they favor or disfavor certain parts of the world, certain viewpoints, or certain explanations of international events?

Newsroom observations, in combination with content research over many years, suggest a noticeable dichotomy between claims for the prospects of newsgathering technologies—for example, the "we are able now to cover anything, anywhere, anytime, for all media" outlook expressed by APTN chief Nigel Baker (2004), with the actual diversity of stories the news agencies distribute. The types of stories, the variety of perspectives, and the range of topics covered by these organizations have declined over the past two decades, and content research by this author and others has shown news agencies' range of coverage was already narrow, leading to a very limited "menu" of story possibilities for broadcasters everywhere. If that last sentence sounds like the description of a restaurant, the analogy is apt: the daily list of news stories circulating globally can be seen as a menu, and the menu choices are largely determined by the international text and video news agencies according to the tastes of the customers, who are the retail news media of the world. You will be able to confirm this easily. Check the websites of Reuters, AP, and AFP against the international story choices of big media near you; deviations from the agencies' menus are rare. Reese Schonfeld (2001, 43), who would go on to build CNN, used a similar metaphor to explain his effort in the 1970s to create an exchange of television news pictures in the United States that would be different from the news offerings of the (then) three big U.S. television networks:

> For thirty years, Americans had been taking whatever the networks offered in the way of news....they saw things through the same set of eyes. It was as if you were running the same raw material through the same strainer and expecting different results. No matter how many times you ran it through, the product was always pretty much the same.

What should have been obvious to this author from the outset has become apparent: commercial news agencies have very little interest in being even-handed, pluralistic, eager to challenge stereotypes, or provocative in their coverage of the world. In a sense, this confirms the larger argument well made already by Corner et al. (1997), Jameson (2000), and others, cited in Griffin (2002),[1] "that media systems, as commercially driven enterprises, have no social goals and will never be reliable forces for integrating new communities of citizenship or public culture." The occasional news agency journalist—especially if she or he comes from a typically stereotyped culture (and many do)—may occasionally express such desires, but they'll promote such an agenda at their peril. At the very least, they will be guided back toward established representational frames and story ideas by colleagues.[2] They often say they do not want to "educate" their clients. The two leading television news agencies are, first and foremost, commercial services, with a clientele who possess a clear idea of what international television news pictures they want. News agency staff have internalized that concept of the news and rarely set out to challenge it.

Is it a contradiction that news agencies want to be first with every story, but do not want to educate their clients about those stories? At the very least, it is a conception of news agency work that minimizes the *story selection* role. If a news agency covers a story that other media don't know about—thereby broadening the diversity of news—they are, in effect, educating their clients by teaching them that there are things happening that matter, but which were off their radar. But news agency journalists have come to accept this as the exception, rather than the rule. They see their role instead as specializing in "developments," that is, those trickles of new information about the big stories that most media have already agreed are stories that matter. Most of the time that serves them well. But might it also engender a philosophy among journalists in the field, and editors and managers in the newsroom, that they should not spend the time and money driving across the border to that un-reported country to see if there is a story *there*, because clients are expecting the story from *here*?

Some news agency managers freely admit that there is much they would like to cover, but the economics of their business dictates that they don't. The APTN's Nigel Baker, referring to the industry as a whole, wrote: "The prospect of providing sustained coverage from costly and logistically difficult locations, coupled with the cost of supplying more content on a wider number of platforms, meant broadcasters had to review the way they covered international news....The content of TV news bulletins in most countries of the world is a trade-off between stories which are deemed important and those which are visually interesting" (Baker, 2004, 64–65).

The Ideological Boundaries of Agency Output

Golding and Elliott (1979, 210–211) argued that through what they term its "invariable neglect" of the power relationships between people, nations, and cultures, television news provides a distinctive kind of world view. In so doing television news will "reinforce skepticism about...divergent, dissident or deviant beliefs." Thussu noted influential critiques of international journalism suggesting that "because news is a commodity, there is a built-in discrimination against news events that cannot be 'sold,' resulting in a distorted presentation of events 'to make them more marketable'" (2004, citing Somavia, 1976; Masmoudi, 1979). But the idea that just two organizations continuously reinforce that world view at a global level, maintaining its boundaries and never allowing them to expand, has never been widely acknowledged.

I have argued previously that because they must continuously strive to please all of their clients, television news agencies have to work harder than the retail media to create a chimera of neutrality and objectivity in their story selection and in the nature of their reports. That leads to homogeneity in their reporting and a limiting perspective. The culture of journalistic objectivity—the "meaning-free product"—is deeply rooted in the television news agencies. From the company's inception, the motto of Visnews photographers reportedly was "We don't take sides, we just take pictures" (Read, 1992). Hypothetically, a story about Palestinian families suffering under Israeli occupation would be easy to do—the many Palestinian employees of the news agencies could feature their own families or others they know well—but such stories would be difficult to distribute to clients, because the exaggerated image of neutrality is so commercially vital. But there are no corresponding images of similar suffering in prosperous, developed Israel, and so the simplistic ideal of journalistic balance cannot be achieved, leaving only the option of avoiding such stories (echoing BBC correspondent Martin Bell's famous call [1998] to television journalists to re-assess rigid objectivity in the face of one-sided conflict).

The multitude of strategies used by news agencies to maintain the all-important image of objectivity for their clients is well examined by Stenvall (2003, 2008) in her remarkable study of over four million words of agency news reporting. But that is the textual grammar of news agency reporting; there remains minimal analysis of the visual grammar of news agency reporting. The impact of the television news agencies, if there is an impact, is specifically dependent upon the influence on audiences of the portions of television newscasts to which the agencies contribute— the visual component of international stories. There is little consensus as to whether the messages encoded in television news lie mostly in the sound or the picture (Kozol, 1989; Graber, 1990; Grimes, 1990; Grabe, 1994). Kozol and Grabe describe the use of the visual component of television news to reinforce cultural myths about race and power in South Africa. Tuchman (1978, 107) observes that much of the literature of television news analysis "naively suppose[s] that news film captures reality without imposing its own rules." There are persuasive indications that the pictorial element of television news is most likely to be remembered over the long term by viewers (Grimes, 1990; Gunter, 1987), and that television news can create commonly held beliefs about the social world, despite any amount of evidence that such scripts are wrong or antisocial (Gilliam and Iyengar, 2000).

The images broadcasters use to present the world to their audience are important, and they are most important when the viewer at home lives far from the place being shown on the screen, when he or she will probably never experience that place in person. People who don't routinely travel internationally, especially in the developing world—and this certainly includes most television news viewers—have no opportunity to challenge the conceptions of the "reality" of those faraway countries: conceptions provided by mass media generally and television news in particular.

Many surveys demonstrate this. For example, when asked to "associate freely ideas that sprang to mind in connection with the word 'Africa,' 85% of young people in Denmark (in 1988) said 'hunger' and 'famine,' 75% said 'poverty' and 'underdevelopment,' and large numbers said 'apartheid,' 'war,' and 'dictatorship'" (Image of Africa, 1988). People will be convinced that the image in their heads is real, even though the fleeting news images that mostly show destruction and conflict bear little in common with the material reality for most people in those poorly understood countries, regions, or continents (see, for example, Larson, 1984; Behr and Iyengar, 1985; Ogundimu, 1992; Semati, 2010).

The gradual transition in the last decade to the delivery of (most) television news agency stories by compressed digital file (as opposed to an analog video transmission where a one-minute story takes a full minute of valuable satellite time) has theoretically made it possible for television news agency journalists to, in effect, throw everything they have at their clients (thus allowing, potentially, for richer, deeper, and more varied television stories to be made from their images). Of course, their clients do not want this and have been complaining since the early 1990s of "picture flood": too many stories, too many images to make sense of.

In the days of analog satellite transmission, which put the traditions in place that are followed now, every second of costly satellite time had to be accounted for, so words and images were chosen with great care. Now cost is of less concern, but overwhelming clients remains a danger, so agency "output" journalists still make choices. Content analysis of their product, then, can examine those choices and the choices made by the journalists in the field (reminding us of the classic rejoinder to the tired concept of journalistic "objectivity": that even the choice of where to put the camera and when to turn it on is a subjective one).

However, for many television news agency journalists and managers, the reasons that agency news is the way it is are far simpler than academics and critics (such as this author) suppose them to be. APTN's Nigel Baker's explanation for television news agency story selection (2004, 66) boiled it down to the following:

- The demands of the day
- The anticipated demands of customers in all world markets
- The televisual impact of a story
- The budgetary resources of the agency
- The skills of individual journalists

But as is the wont of academics, I'll strive in this book to challenge, complicate, and problematize those explanations.

Characteristics of Television News Agency Output

During the decade following my initial ethnographic research with news agencies in the mid-1990s, I conducted several content research projects using stacks of videotapes generously provided by the agencies of their major news feeds over periods of a day or two.[3] The quantitative and qualitative analysis of television news agency feeds shows clear patterns in television news agency output and suggests some consistencies between what is provided by agencies to broadcasters and what is provided by broadcasters to audiences. A relatively small set of narratives, themes, frames, or—as put by Dahlgren and Chakrapani (1982)—"ways of seeing," can be easily identified.

The research tends to complicate the conventional wisdom that infinite interpretations of the "raw" images of television news are possible (or likely). The research to date is minimal and might well be contradicted by new and more exhaustive investigation, but what we know now suggests there is little variation among broadcasters in how television news agency visual and textual information is employed to create international news stories. And, more crucially, it appears common for the highly subjective and most ideological aspects of news agency output to be faithfully reproduced in the journalistic narratives of broadcasters the world over.

One of the most consistent aspects of television news agency narratives is a focus on the United States and the U.K. Sreberny-Mohammadi et al. (1984) and other studies demonstrate a tendency in international news reporting toward news concerning countries with political, cultural, and economic ties to the United States (also Galtung and Ruge, 1965; Schiff, 1996). So in the case of the agencies, it is not surprising to find an orientation toward covering Britain and the United States and other wealthy countries—the countries in which the international television news agencies are incorporated and locate most of their staff and editorial control.

Some general characteristics of the output of the video agencies were revealed through content analysis in 1995. Agency stories[4] averaged just over two minutes in length, ranging from 38 seconds to 5 minutes, 45 seconds. The main topic of the majority of stories (n=42 of 256, 16%) was coded as "international military, or defense, or conflict." The second most common topic (n=38, 15%) was "international politics," and the third (n=33, 13%) was "civil war or domestic conflict." These themes are explained by the traditional news agency and Eurovision (Hjarvard, 1995a) focus on conflict. At this point in time, most agency stories were about the

United States and Bosnia, each accounting for 12% of stories. The dominant type of main actor in the coded news agency stories was a state official or "nation" (n=97, 38%). At this point the Associated Press operated a television news agency (APTV) alongside Worldwide Television News (which it would take over two years later) and Reuters Television. This study found almost no difference between what each chose as the stories of the day and the time allotted to those stories.

This congruence (at a time of intense competition between the agencies when they each claimed to be seeking to differentiate themselves from each other) might be explained by several factors described in other parts of this book:

- the similarity of extra-media factors influencing news production
- the similarity of news production routines within the three agencies
- competitive pressure to duplicate coverage by other agencies
- a universal focus on standard frames of news coverage deemed acceptable to clients

In a study of the output of APTN in the same period, Clare (1998) found 73% hard news stories, as opposed to "contextualizing" stories or "soft" news; Europe comprised 28% and the United States 23% of stories. International relations stories were the most common type, at 29%. He observed that the world of the television news agency looks something like this:

> Elite nations are portrayed as having strong leaders constantly flying around the globe trying to broker peace deals…their citizens, meanwhile, appear to be able to choose from a number of cultural pursuits, supported by stable business…while being allowed to make peaceful protests.…[N]on elite nations, in contrast, appear to be constantly embroiled in, or on the point of, violent conflict…while at risk from natural disasters. They have crisis-hit governments, untrustworthy leaders, volatile populations and when they do have elections, they do not meet the democratic standards of the West. (Clare, 1988, 62–63; quoted in Boyd-Barrett, 2000, 314)

I repeated my analysis of television news agency output in 2000, but in that case only with access to a few days of satellite feeds from APTN. Here are some points of comparison between the 1995 and 2000 data. The amount of coverage of developing countries (by population, by far the global majority) had stayed roughly consistent:

- 1995 (all agencies)
  44% (83/188) "West, North, or First World" or "Europe"
  22% (42/188) "South, Third World, or Developing"

- 2000 (APTN)
  64% (63/99) "West, North, or First World"
  28% (28/99) "South, Third World, or Developing"

But a focus on the United States had seemingly increased:

- 1995 (all agencies)
  33% split between the United States and Bosnia

- 2000 (APTN)
  37% U.S. (as direct or indirect subject) and no equivalent other
  country

Topically, international politics was the leading story category, comprising about one-sixth of all coverage during both periods, but conflict stories were more common in 1995 (the height of the Yugoslav wars). In both periods, television news agency news was decidedly the news of men, with the "main actor" in stories totaling just 13% female in 1995 (and the study period was during the United Nations Fourth World Conference on Women) and just 12% female in 2000.

The most notable change in this period was the massive increase in the amount of sport and entertainment comprising APTN news feeds, suggesting some tabloidization of global television news agency output. From less than 1% of the total in 1995, these categories comprised 25% of the total in 2000 (consisting of 14 of 99 stories on entertainment or celebrities and 10 of 99 stories on sports). Various commentators have observed the significant role of 24-hour news in bringing about a "tabloidization" of television journalism generally (Lewis, 2010; Bromley, 2010; Thussu, 2007; MacGregor, 1997).

As observed in the previous chapter and detailed further in Chapter Five, the television news agencies have enabled the rapid growth of those 24-hour channels by providing most, or all, of the live and taped visuals they depend upon. But this tiny snapshot of agency content suggests they were doing more than that. As the news agencies emerged as the key source for the burgeoning 24-hour news genre, they were aggressively shifting their output toward lighter, entertainment-oriented, tabloid news. They have, perhaps, fuelled the tabloidization process in global television. In the late 1990s the then-managing editor of APTN told me of the pressure to move the news agency in that direction, showing me research conducted by external consultants for the agency that demonstrated with lavish graphs and charts that agency clients wanted limits on the amount of news they were being sent, and much more entertainment: celebrities, fashion shows, gossip, and sports (also see Lipscomb, 2002).

Research tells us that Reuters and the Associated Press base news coverage largely on the economic priorities of the major Western powers and the assumed interests of major Western media, and that they focus on a limited menu of news stories and news frames from a small group of elite nations. Indeed, the managers of these companies have become increasingly forthright over the past few decades in declaring as much. The worry is that this instrumental approach sits uneasily with the reality that these organizations significantly determine the nature of international public affairs discourse, because they are trusted by journalists and the public alike, and because they dominate channels of news distribution. They are the main intra-industry agenda setters. This isn't just because their news selection choices are trusted by TV newsrooms everywhere, but because restricted budgets force dependence on these companies for television footage to illustrate stories. A variety of television newsroom production studies have shown that television journalists are less likely to cover a story for which they don't have visual footage (Cohen et al., 1996; Helland, 1995; Rodriguez, 1996; Molina, 1990; Schlesinger, 1987; Golding and Elliott, 1979). Molina notes that at Televisa,

> Television stories whose visual element is available through any of the news exchanges stand a better chance of being included in the program's agenda than those where only text is available.

As stated by Cohen et al.,

> in many instances a [European broadcast] service decides to present a story only because it has footage available.

The author worked with a student in 2007 to produce a new analysis of television news agency output dating from a few years prior. Scripts and videotapes of agency output had been provided to the author by APTN in 2004 for a research project that was later abandoned, and so this was the first time they had been systematically analyzed and is one of the few analyses I know of that considers television news agency content in the past decade (another is described below).[5]

Of 60 stories coded from a 24-hour period of television news agency output, 6 were about developing countries (at 10%, a good deal less than seen above). Developed world stories contained stories from the foreign relations and human interest categories; developing world stories did not. These studies seemed to confirm longstanding critiques of international television (and the press), suggesting that developing nations are only newsworthy at times of crisis. Foreign relations among developed nations lagged only behind national politics as the most common kind of news event. The primary topic of the stories (or, specifically, the nature of the primary event in each story) was most commonly some aspect of national politics (at 33%). Another 25% focused on domestic (internal) conflict and 17% on international conflict, suggesting an increased focus on conflict from a decade earlier. (This was during the ongoing Iraq War.) Countries receiving coverage in this brief snapshot of APTN output were the United States with 23%, Iraq with 10%, the U.K. with 7%, Colombia, France, Mexico, and Israel each with 5%, and 19 other countries sharing the remainder. Foy (2007) noted that the world's two most populous countries, China and India, received 3% and 0%, respectively, of APTN's attention during this period.[6]

Only one of the four stories about developing countries delivered by the news agency in this period contained an element of historical context (a story about a human rights conference in Pakistan); there was historical context in one-quarter of the developing country stories, while historical context was present in three-quarters of the developed country stories. This might be taken as validation of the critique that journalism fails to provide the necessary context to allow understanding of stories from developing countries (see Philo, 2004), but in the television news agency context where *update stories* and *background stories* are often provided separately (with the burden on broadcasters to contextualize the stories as they see fit), it is neither surprising nor sinister. Foy noted one APTN story on Iraq that seemed to be deliberately challenging stereotypes—a cadre of American politicians and military officials visiting Iraq and singing its praises—and noted extended non-news features which APTN was providing to clients during this period, but which were not coded. These provided fairly extensive background analysis of conflict in Uganda and in Haiti.

Finally, it is interesting to examine recent findings from the research of a Brazilian television journalist undertaking doctoral research on the television news agencies (the only such project I am aware of since my 1996 Ph.D.). Cleidejane Esperidião (2010, personal communication) conducted a content analysis of 377 newsfeeds from Reuters Television and APTN, with a focus on their coverage of the devastating Haiti earthquake in January 2010, and a study of 84 feeds from both agencies from a single day in November 2009. Her findings in that one-day study are not dissimilar to the 2004, 2000, and 1995 research findings reported above, suggesting considerable consistency in the nature of television news agency output over at least the past fifteen years. Her results showed the following geographic focus:

1. United States: 30% (25 of 84)
2. Europe: 27%
3. Asia: 25%
4. South America: 10%

The consistency of the United States as *the* television news agency focus between one-quarter and one-third of the time—over fifteen years—is especially notable, and the virtual absence of Africa is also remarkable (discussed below). There is also a considerable thematic consistency with the studies reported above:

1. Diplomacy/international politics: 15%
2. War/conflicts/nuclear weapons: 13%
3. Economy: 11%
4. Global warming or "disasters":   11%

Cleidejane Esperidião also provided some statistical description of the kinds of news distributed by the television news agencies. Six percent of stories were exclusive to the news agency; 17% could be classified as breaking; and 40% as running, or continuing, stories; 21% concerned pre-scheduled events. The source of the pictures being delivered by the agencies was the agency itself in just 37% of cases; the remainder consisted of images from pool arrangements with other companies (or distributed by organizations) or images bought or otherwise acquired from other companies.

The Haiti earthquake was a story the news agencies invested heavily in because it was inaccessible and difficult to cover for broadcasters, because global concern was significant, and because they already had considerable experience in covering Haiti (usually from their Washington and Miami bureaus). Cleidejane Esperidião's detailed study will be published in her doctoral work, but a striking finding was that, of the stories about Haiti during her study period that also mentioned another country, the vast majority—more than double any other part of the world—concerned the United States. This suggests that the U.S. military takeover of Haiti's international airport after the earthquake was also an effective takeover of international news coverage.

Globalization v. Domestication

A good bit of the discourse about globalization over the past decade or two has sought to challenge the notion of an ever-more-homogenous global culture—whether imperialized, Americanized,[7] Westernized, or simply a diluted mix of the most powerfully marketed global brands, ideas, and icons drowning out all that is local and authentic. The challenger is the concept of *localization*. This was based initially on evidence that the most successful globalizing corporations were not those that applied the same formula everywhere, but those that adapted their product to local tastes and customized it with local talent. The case of MTV in India was a common example (Ang, 1996; Volkmer, 1999; Juluri, 2003).

So, to the extent that television news plays a vital role in shaping understanding of the world, an obvious question was whether the representations of news from global providers are universally reproduced by broadcasters, or whether these form just a minor element in storytelling strategies that vary considerably from place to place, based on local interest in a story, local journalistic custom, and the integration of a broad range of visual and informational sources in the construction of international news. While perhaps an obvious question, few have researched it. One who has is Clausen (2004), whose exhaustive ethnographic research with Danish and Japanese broadcasters revealed a great deal about how foreign news is localized, or *domesticated*—that is, made relevant for each national television network's audience.

Clausen broadly concludes that international news is made particular to each country through a series of routine processes of domestication that take place in the newsroom, thus confirming the statement made to her (2004, 28) by an NHK (Japanese public television) editor that "Global news in Japan is not like global news anywhere." She suggests this process is determined by the desire to maximize the appeal of stories to audiences, rather than through any overt effort to impose a local identity on stories. Through their comprehensive analysis of popular and powerful new broadcasters in previously poorly served nations and regions, other scholars have supported the claim that the adaptation of Western conventions of reporting and news presentation alone do not lead to a distinctly Western or specifically Anglo/U.S. form of journalism. Sonwalkar (2004, 123), for example, concluded that "globalization ensures that western technologies and professional values are reinvented, localized and customized in non-Western settings."

Clausen's demonstration of specific local cultural traits in the international news storytelling of the broadcasters she examined seemed to confirm the earlier conclusions of Gurevitch et al. (1991) in their examination of the flow of news from the Eurovision News Exchange to public broadcasters throughout Europe:

> Media maintain both global and culturally specific orientations—such as by casting far-away events in frameworks that render these events comprehensible, appealing and relevant to domestic audiences; and second, by constructing the meanings of these events in ways that are compatible with the culture and the dominant ideology of societies they serve. (206)

What both Clausen's (2004) data and my data (Paterson, 2001) strongly concur on is that larger and wealthier broadcasters have a far greater ability to domesticate international news than do smaller ones. In the study described below, which examined one story in detail—anti-colonial rioting in Tahiti in 1995—I found that NHK, the world's wealthiest public network, took 54% of its visual coverage of the story from the television news agencies on the first day of rioting, and that CNN took just 22%. These broadcasters could use news agency footage to supplement coverage that they could obtain from freelancers, from their own staff photographers, or from other broadcasters with whom they had a news-sharing agreement. Smaller broadcasters could not draw from a similarly diverse range of sources. We found that 80% or more of non-local news coverage came from the television news agencies for smaller broadcasters (and it is likely that as much as the remaining 20% may also have come from the television news agencies as well, but we just failed to identify it).

With the help of Clausen and many other scholars around the world, and under the auspices of the "Cooperative Study of Foreign News and International News Flow in the 1990s,"[8] the research team analyzed television news broadcasts from 16 broadcasters from 10 countries, and 10 hours of television news agency feeds of the (then) 3 news agencies (which also included most European News Exchange television stories) over a two-day period in 1995.[9] Of 185 non-local stories in those newscasts, there were 87 (47%) that coders could establish contained images provided by television news agencies. But it is the way in which those agency images were used that matters: the results of this study decidedly contradict the "domestication" thesis of Gurevitch et al., and Clausen.

We sought a number of indicators of whether or not the editorial choices being made by news agency journalists in the field or in their London newsrooms carried through into the stories told by broadcasters to their audiences. The most important of these was the extent to which broadcasters used the editing of images provided by the news agencies, or re-edited those images themselves (thereby re-telling the visual story in their own way). Was the visual narrative global, or local? Strikingly, 61%, or 53 of 87 news stories that could be clearly identified as containing television news agency footage, contained a substantial series of images *edited by the television news agency that took the pictures*, not by the broadcasters.[10] These were stories produced by small broadcasters (Estonian and Lebanese TV are examples) and by major broadcasters with large international news operations of their own, including CNN and Britain's Channel 4.

The minimal re-editing of news agency-provided images is a rational and efficient practice by broadcasters who have paid dearly for the news agency's services, but it makes apparent a very considerable reliance on the editorial decisions of the news agencies. This seems contrary to the notion of domestication. The stories being delivered to audiences in this small study (which corresponded exactly in date to Clausen's research) were told by one or more (of just three) global entities, and not significantly by the local broadcasters. One example I cited in an earlier description of this research (Paterson, 2001, 342) was that

the Finnish public broadcaster, YLE, on September 7, 1995, had as their first international story the aforementioned rioting in Tahiti. Most of this 146-second story contained footage from Reuters Television. In the YLE story, large portions, including all the pictures in the first 30 seconds, were the edited visual text provided by Reuters in the story they fed to broadcasters. The images chosen, and the manner in which they are connected, tells a story of an angry mob invading an airport tarmac, viciously engaging lightly armed police in battle, and then looting the airport.

The example demonstrated that YLE (a large broadcaster with a large editorial staff) chose not to significantly re-edit the television news agency-provided images, nor to add images from other sources—two of the three ways in which it might have changed the tone, or framing, of the global story (thereby "domesticating" it). The third way would be if its audio narration differed significantly from the version of events provided by the news agency (something we could not test). This broadcaster, and the majority of the others we examined, allowed their international television news stories to be told by the global news agencies feeding them: there was little evidence of domestication.

This was clearly a distinct framing of this complex story, a framing that left the viewer in sympathy with the local police and colonial forces of law and order, and disgusted by the protest underway. That was probably not an intention of either the news agency photographers or the London journalists editing and distributing their pictures, but it was distinctly just one side of a complex story about colonial injustice—a story that could have been told from a more neutral point of view or a point of view decidedly sympathetic to the protests. That was not the news agency frame of the day, though (whether deliberately, or because the pictures its photographers could obtain simply would not have allowed otherwise, we cannot know). Therefore, broadcasters did not have visual support for an alternative framing of the story. The framing they chose on this, and most of the other stories we examined, was largely that provided by the available television news agency images.

This visual research was complemented by analysis of the "running order" or "line-up" of stories provided by the television news agencies to their clients. This is the list of stories on each satellite news feed, in the sequence in which they will be transmitted. As with the temporal order of stories in any television news broadcast, journalists assume stories are ranked by importance, with the most important coming first. Where stories go on a newsfeed, and on which feed (that is, to which region of the world) they go on, can be a matter of intensive negotiation in television news agency newsrooms. Preliminary feed rundowns come to television newsrooms around the world in advance of the pictures themselves, to allow local journalists to plan their broadcasts largely on the promise of incoming agency visuals. Helland (1995, 165–166) observed of the Norwegian commercial broadcaster International News:

Because of the central position of the feeds in the news production apparatus, their con-tent was obviously a determining factor in what news stories were selected to be car-ried in the news programs. The perceived quality of the feed sequences was also important for the running order of the news. Furthermore, the selection of the head-line stories was made with reference to the perceived news-worthiness of the available news pictures. . . .

In this 2001 research there was clearly congruence between the prominence given stories by the agencies, and by the broadcasters around the world (though local sto-ries almost always come first, anywhere in the world). Putnis had come to similar conclusions well before my research on the use of news agency content (also see Park, 1994, for a similar analysis). In his groundbreaking 1994 research into how news on Australian television is constructed, Putnis (1996, 20; also 1994) found:

> Except for stories directly affecting Australia or Australians the overseas news agenda for commercial television bulletins is set by overseas news feeds. The rundowns of over-seas bulletins and feeds, quite liberally, form the overseas news agendas considered at news [editorial meetings]. These are dominated by U.S. and British news. News direc-tors select from this predetermined list.
>
> Australia…receives the majority of its overseas material from international news wholesalers.…[T]here is little incentive for small players, such as Australian commercial net-works, to go out and get their own footage.

The claim that there is no global story—only local ones—is questionable at best. As I sought to illustrate as well in regard to international news on the Internet (Paterson, 2007), there are a small number of global stories, and the media most peo-ple turn to are very contented to allow two news agencies to tell them.

Apart from pleading for copies of (wholesale) newsfeeds from the agencies and comparing them, frame by frame, with (retail) television newscasts, as described above, there is one other place to go for evidence of the dominance of television news agency pictures in the bulletins of the world's broadcasters. One can ask the agen-cies themselves. Until quite recently, this wasn't possible: they didn't know. They made educated guesses: anecdotal reports from bureau chiefs and sales representa-tives seeing their footage being used, or a few limited systematic studies by consul-tants seeking to measure use of the product, but no routine and reliable indicator of if, and when, their product was being used. As long as subscription fees came in, that didn't matter (although those sales representatives yearned for evidence of their agency's importance to quote to prospective clients). But during the last decade, and especially as a result of maximizing the exclusivity and protecting the copyright of agency images, various methods have been tried to document the existence of each agency's pictures in the news output of selected broadcasters. In 2000, Reuters

Television threatened to sue one of the major Australian television networks for repeatedly airing their images, which they had allegedly obtained without a Reuters Television subscription (Broadcast, 2000).

Both Reuters Television and APTN use the services of a Dutch company called Teletrax,which inserts an electronic "watermark" in the video of its clients and then searches, with its widely scattered monitoring gear, for that invisible electronic tag in news programming all over the world. An APTN editor demonstrated for me how Teletrax showed her their client broadcasters' use of a particular APTN story about strikes in France on March 28, 2006. In this case, 52 broadcasters used 442 segments from this small set of APTN stories in these 24 hours.

The exact point in their bulletins where the APTN video aired, the exact point of APTN's feeds that were used, and the duration of the APTN material were all provided. An obvious danger is that television news agency journalists start to tailor their global news coverage according to what seems to be popular with their clients, rather than through any journalistic criteria (not to mention the more noble motivations suggested in this chapter). This may already be happening: former Reuters Television Managing Director Tony Donovan is featured in Teletrax publicity as stating that the service "has dramatically changed the way we gather news and distribute [it] to our clients."[11]

A brief example shows what news agencies learn from such data. Teletrax reported to APTN that on March 28, 2006, at 11:19:07 London time, one of China's channels used 38 seconds of footage from the agency's story titled FRA STRIKE 2; and that this was a three-minute-and-ten-second story transmitted by APTN two and a half hours earlier. We can see that Arab satellite broadcaster Al Arabiyah, for example, used APTN video about the French unrest 11 times in 24 hours, while Fox News in the United States used pieces of the story 22 times; Sky (U.K.) 51 times; NTV (Germany) 42 times; and the BBC (across its various channels) 77 times. The same details show for every client. And the system, of course, signals when a news agency's video appears in the broadcasts of a non-subscribing station.

The Teletrax data demonstrates the massive global use of news agency material, but since it does not indicate the proportion of news agency material to non-news agency material in the news programs of broadcasters, it neither directly supports, nor negates, the earlier findings about the broad nature of agency news and the extent of its influence on news broadcasts. But if used in conjunction with knowledge of the duration of news broadcasts, and with a complete set of data for all news agency output on a given day, it would probably do so very effectively. Whether such a study would demonstrate global dependence on these two agencies and an overall lack of domestication of these global news products remains to be seen.

Television News Agencies and Developing Countries

Studies of print news agency journalism have shown a focus on certain parts of the world at the expense of others, parts generally corresponding closely with the strategic and business interests of the United States and U.K. (Boyd-Barrett, 1980; Fenby, 1986; Musa, 1990; Schiff, 1996). We saw above that much of the coverage is of the United States: it is the main "elite" news nation (Galtung and Ruge, 1965). Predating even the influential but media-despised Glasgow Media Group studies demonstrating the power of ideology in British broadcasting, Dahlgren and Chakrapani (1982, 62) concluded that television news (not even considering the agencies that feed it),

> tends to be hegemonic…the ways of seeing which it offers to the public are decidedly in keeping with the needs and interests of the social classes and groups who command economic and political power.

The locations of key news agency bureaus (discussed further in Chapter Five) also map these priorities. Some parts of the world are unmistakably more worthy of news coverage than others, and if all news were regarded more or less equally (a war here is as important as a war there), we might expect a fairly even distribution of stories across the globe, over time. The television news agencies and their parent companies market themselves as global services with no political ties to any one place—to sell their services everywhere, they must do so.[12] But the mix of stories they produce betrays the claim. And the countries where broadcasters are the most likely to be fully dependent on the television news agencies—the smallest and poorest countries least able to produce quantities of their own international coverage—are, sadly, the most likely to be ignored in television news agency coverage (except in the occasional case of extreme disaster or conflict).

The developing world is generally portrayed by television news as savage, primitive, chaotic, and dependent. In television news most of the nations of the planet, and most of the individual societies on the planet, are frequently missing. To borrow a phrase from Tuchman (1978), it is as though television news consists of just a few wealthy nations and cultures talking among themselves. Insofar as television news shapes our reality, this mythical developing world is what we know as real. Smith (1980, 93) recalled that:

> In the 1970s the proponents of a New World Information and Communications Order (NWICO) focused upon the distortions inherent in Western print coverage of the developing world. Western news coverage, in particular that of the international wire services, was deemed to possess a structural bias against the developing world, an inherent ethnocentrism independent of the intentions of journalists.

One of the world's most famous television news photographers was the late Mohamed Amin. Alongside the BBC's Michael Buerk, he revealed to the world the massive 1984 famine in Ethiopia that inspired a massive charity campaign (his son now carries on his journalism business in Nairobi, Kenya).[13] Amin (interview, 1995) once described for me his experience of trying to convince his London Visnews (later Reuters) editors to use his African stories over a few decades, describing the representational frames traditionally sought by those editors:

> I have a lot of grievances with the decision makers, not necessarily with Reuters Television, but all of them. Because I think they live in a different world. They live in a completely different environment. They don't understand Africa. All they want out of Africa is death, blood, famine, corruption, and all that. We've got plenty of that in Africa—there's no shortage of that. But we've also got a hell of a lot of other stuff in Africa which is much more important to the continent than just the various wars that go on. I'm not suggesting for a second that these wars should not be covered—they have to be covered. They're quite crucial in terms of the news coverage, but we should look at other stories as well.

My time in agency newsrooms in the 1990s suggested that a lack of familiarity with non-Western cultures is a factor negatively influencing coverage of developing countries. Of course, quantification of such influence is impossible, but examples emerged during my research. Once in the Reuters Television newsroom a story about the peace process in Angola arrived via satellite from Reuters's Africa Bureau in Nairobi. Much of the tape contained footage of a traditional celebration. The Output Editor commented despondently, "That's an entertainment story, isn't it? Six minutes, a bit of music, a bit of drums. . . ." He deemed it to be improper illustration for a political story (according to preferred news frames), and ordered old file footage of Angolan rebel leader Jonas Savimbi attending meetings from the company archives to illustrate the story in place of the current footage.

The tendency to focus upon the same kinds of stories from developing countries may lead journalists to attach less value to the lives of people from such areas, as expressed by one television news agency journalist:

> When you think of, for example, a bus crash in Turkey or a bus crash in India, you know that the last twenty stories you've had from that part of the world, of India say, four or five of them would have been bus crashes with at least fifty killed or something like this and you say "oh no, not another one. . . ." Third World stories tend to be massacres in Africa or bus crashes in India.

This journalist acknowledges that "what we need is a broader range of stories." He claims there is not a "broader range of stories" because the major clients are not interested in stories from the Third World, so the agency cannot devote more resources to cover Third World stories. But this broader research suggests that the assumption of a lack of interest is often unfounded, since the only substantial communication to agencies from clients is from the wealthiest few.

Africa is particularly overlooked by global news, including by the news agencies, even though it is often the news agencies that are providing the only television pictures of African stories when those stories do get on the global agenda. Africa's only United Nations Secretary General, Kofi Anan, took the issue to the heart of the international television news industry in 2000. Addressing their annual "Newsworld" conference, Anan complained that he was "disturbed by the way the world media is disengaging with Africa, or reporting it only sporadically" (Hodgson, 2000). The head of the new E-TV news channel in South Africa told the conference, "What you show of Africa could lead to more violence and death."

But APTN's Nigel Baker responded with the economic argument "that there was low demand for African stories from western broadcasters" and stated "that Africa accounted for as little as 1% of the income of news agencies" (Hodgson, 2000). He would reiterate a few years on that "There is currently no revenue base there for the agencies, but coverage is provided of African stories of major world interest or of interest to the main agency markets" (2004, 73). He stated than in 2000, 8% of APTN's news coverage budget was spent in Africa, despite almost no revenue coming from there, but he went on to note that his agency's expenditure there was halved the following year as resources shifted to the 9/11 story. A former WTN editor explained that despite wishing to cover a broader range of stories, television news agency decisions are based on value for money decisions, and "you don't waste money and time bribing your way to a story, solving the multitude of logistical nightmares involved in television newsgathering and then either failing or getting the story very late."

Veteran American television executive Eric Braun was the Managing Director of Associated Press Television for much of the current decade, until a few years before the writing of this book. He elaborated on, but broadly confirmed, Baker's perspective from a few years earlier, albeit in the context of more soul-searching:

> We cover Africa some but probably not enough, but then when we look at the uptake among our clients, all broadcasters are not very interested in Africa. Never mind America—[in] the other highly developed, highly evolved media cultures there is little interest...we do what the clients want us to do....I think we do a pretty good job of doing the big stories in Africa, but the truth of the matter is we don't take the time to do the human interest and cultural stories; we do the breaking news, we do the changes of regime....[pauses] I suppose I can beat myself up and say we can do a lot more, but with the resources we have we try to manage them in a way that has yield

for the client; and there is no client base in Africa either…we have very few African subscribers. (interview, 2008)

In the course of my interviews in the 1990s, television news agency managers occasionally expressed strong opinions about troublesome African coverage. Here, a WTN manager described the manner in which clients react slowly, and then over-react, to African tragedies, neglecting the next story to come along:

It was like "do we commit ourselves to this story"? Does anyone apart from the BBC World Service really care about Rwanda? Does America care about Rwanda? America's where a lot of our clients are. You know, do we send a crew in? Do we risk a crew just for a picture of another African bleeding-heart story, you know? And then we said "OK, let's do it," and about two weeks later it was like, Rwanda, you know, everybody knew about Rwanda and then after that, kind of, the area had become embedded into the consciousness of the world. Then it becomes a sort of, you know, this puppet show, this modern puppet show where the Rwanda puppet makes an appearance every now and then.

And it's funny how you…set the kind of agenda and then it's quite hard to sometimes change the agenda. You know, [clients are] just sort of saying well what's happening in Rwanda, and you're saying forget about Rwanda—there's five million dead in Sudan and they said no, no, no, we heard there was another massacre in Rwanda, and it turns out that three people had been chopped up, which, you know, in African terms is nothing. See what I mean? It's kind of funny.

Getting clients to take an interest in the next story the agency has deemed news-worthy is crucial, for the costs of that new coverage must be justified.[14]

It is reasonable to suggest that an ethnocentric and stereotype-laden ideology, characteristic of modern racism[15] (Entman, 1992, 1994; Campbell, 1993), is per-petually produced and reproduced through the continuous delivery to broadcast-ers of ideological representations (news images) by international television news agencies. The production of ideology occurs over time and a "Third World Reality" is shaped over time. Individual news stories cannot be considered in isolation; what matters is the television news agency "super-text" (Browne, 1984), the entire range of visual, auditory, and data communications from agencies to broadcasters around the world, over time.[16] It is a super-text that excludes and stereotypes an entire con-tinent and, more crucially, causes those processes to be replicated in television news everywhere.

As of this writing, the story selections for each day of both television news agen-cies are freely available online. And so it is relatively easy to check from day to day what the "menu" of global news is, as determined by the television news agencies, to determine the extent to which broadcasters lead and follow that agenda, and to determine to what extent the critiques generated by the earlier research referred to in this chapter remain valid. What remains more difficult is to assess individual news stories in detail, for they remain a valued product carefully delivered only to paying subscribers. But to their great credit, both news agencies have cooperated with and facilitated much of the research described here, and I hope they will continue to aid such research well into the future, even when it puts them in a potentially unflattering light.

Notes

1. And to no small extent also powerfully argued by Schiller (1989).
2. Informants at a television news agency in the mid-1990s told of a case of an agency duty editor falling out with management for pursuing what was deemed an inappropriate ideological agenda: in this case, seeking Palestinian perspectives the individual felt were absent. The individual was allegedly dismissed on the basis of performance, resulting in a labor tribunal case that was eventually settled, but details were not possible to obtain and efforts to interview the individual were unsuccessful. The implications for ideological control in the agency newsroom are profound. In the more extensive ethnographic description within my 1996 Ph.D. thesis, I recount an incident I witnessed in a high-level news agency editorial meeting, where a female editor proposed a story in conjunction with a United Nations report on the plight of poor women around the world, and was laughed into an embarrassed silence by her male colleagues. The news agency concerned has disputed my conclusions that, in 1995, there was evidence of sexist behavior in their organization. If their claim is correct, they would have been unusual in the context of British newsrooms at this time, as Delano and Henningham (1995) demonstrate. In my (less extensive) ethnographic visits to both Reuters and AP in the past decade, I have seen no indication that similar sexism persists.
3. One of these studies additionally involved the comparison of television newscasts from around the world with the stories distributed by the television news agencies. Then, as now, there is no technological innovation to make this possible: the process involved student assistants carefully comparing, frame by frame, news agency pictures with broadcaster pictures.
4. An edited assemblage of the latest pictures, sounds, and interviews related to a single issue on the day's news agenda. A typical agency story is designed to be picked apart by broadcasters to use just the pieces they want; but also, should a broadcaster so chose, to be put right out for broadcast with little or no re-editing, with the local news reader narrating.
5. The study (Foy, 2007) examined 24 hours of continuous APTN output from February 10, 2004, a date originally determined at the agency's convenience. News stories, excluding sports or entertainment, were coded across a wide range of categories, and 20% of stories coded were re-coded by a second coder providing a respectable intercoder reliability coefficient of 82%. Coding details are available from this author. It should be noted that these studies are simply the best independent analysis of television news agency output I know

of, but they should be treated with caution. They are small samples and are not drawn from throughout a long period (i.e., a year) of news agency journalism, but focus instead on one or two selected days. And they each represent the bulk of television news agency production in the studied periods, but not all of it.

6. Importantly, this does not mean that APTN was not covering news in either country at the time nor that they were not feeding stories into, or within, either country at the time. It does mean that no stories from these countries were deemed suitable for the global news feed being analyzed.

7. Or even the Dallasification of Culture (De Bens et al., 1992).

8. This was a replication of the landmark UNESCO-funded study of global news flow conducted in 1978, and was organized by two of the original four authors of that study: Sreberny-Mohammadi et al., 1984. The 1995 project, involving researchers gathering and analyzing news from 41 countries, was managed by the late Professor Robert Stevenson of the University of North Carolina and Professor Annabelle Sreberny, then of Leicester University. Details can still be found at http://sunsite.unc.edu/newsflow/ (as of October 2010), and Wu (2003) summarizes many key findings.

9. Videotapes of the main global satellite news feeds for September 7 and 8, 1995, were generously provided to the author by Reuters Television, Worldwide Television News, and Associated Press Television.

10. The conclusion was based both on the use of extended sequences of pictures provided by one news agency or, in some cases, a broadcaster stringing together two or more extended sequences from different news agency feeds and/or different news agencies.

11. Company information from http://www.teletrax.tv/site/Teletrax%20-%20NEWS.pdf.

12. Reuters took this position very publicly and at some commercial risk when it refused to be bullied into accepting a U.S. definition of "terrorism" in post-9/11 news coverage, in stark contrast to most U.S.-based media. Reuters explains its policy in a letter to U.S. newspaper editors, which sparked a firestorm of protest among conservative U.S. publications and blogs. The letter is posted here: http://homepage.mac.com/bkerstetter/writersblock/reuters explanation.html, copied from a now-inactive Reuters webpage. Palmer (2011) explores the history of news agencies' struggle for neutral language in context of "terrorism," and Stenvall (2003) and Bielsa and Bassnett (2009) provide exhaustive investigations of news agency language. Interestingly, Reuters Television's predecessor, Visnews, had taken exactly the Reuters line on neutral language in the 1980s. Visnews editor Tim Arlott told Harrison and Palmer (1986, 75), "We have to be straight down the middle. Of course what they do with it when they get it is a different matter, but we use no pejorative terms about anybody. There are no 'terrorists' in the Visnews world."

13. A senior WTN journalist who contributed extensively to this project observed to me that "there was…only one Mo Amin—not just in the vast continent of Africa, but in the whole world. He was an exceptional, perhaps unique, cameraman and operator." Part of Amin's biography is recounted in Tetley (1988).

14. The overt ethnocentrism expressed in this quotation was not uncommon during my 1990s research, especially among several younger, male, news agency workers.

15. My doctoral thesis argued that television's textual representations of non-white races are framed through a lens of "modern racism." That is to say, modern racism is not only an effect

of reception, but an ingredient of production. This is because through a failure to contextualize and individualize news about non-whites in the same way as is done for news about whites, the three social effects of modern racism are perpetuated: a general hostility toward non-whites; a rejection of non-white political aspirations; and the denial that racism and discrimination continue to be problems.

16. In future research, critical examination of the agency super-text should occur. No researchers have yet attempted this, beyond the limited analysis of agency product described in this chapter and Hjarvard's (1995a) consideration of the news agency component of the Eurovision news super-text. It is a task complicated by the difficulty of gaining access to agency output, legally and technically.

3

The First Four Decades
of Covering the World

The international television news agencies can be well understood only within two broad contexts: the political economy of international television news and the historical development of the global television news distribution system in which they participate. Here I'll describe the early years of the television news agencies from their birth in the days of newsreels to the formation of the organizations closely resembling the modern APTN and Reuters Television. Little has been published that describes this history—a remarkable gap in media scholarship. Such research becomes more critical every year since, as ownerships and internal structures of these companies change and companies relocate, what few document collections exist may be lost or scattered. When the Associated Press bought Worldwide Television News from Disney in 1997, over thirty years of news film and video produced by WTN and its processor, UPITN, were put into storage in a London basement with no long-term plan for its preservation (not to mention commercial exploitation). Many of the records of these companies remain lost or hidden, but in 2008 the AP began a project to catalogue and digitally preserve the "lost" UPITN and WTN footage.[1]

In the 1990s the television news agencies and their corporate parents appeared neither to maintain a systematic archive of company documents nor to employ anyone to oversee their historical records.[2] To their great credit, both Thomson-Reuters (in London) and the Associated Press (in New York) have now established well-organized company archives and are routinely assisting researchers on historical projects. I hope to provide a useful synthesis of the published historical accounts in this overview (in combination with some archival research and interviewing), but my research has not been primarily historical, so this is still far from a comprehensive account. I hope that future researchers will seek to write such an account before the primary documentation of this history is lost, and before the remaining protagonists from early agency days depart for the newsroom in the sky.[3] An important contribution was made in 2009 with research conducted on early television news agency history by Zuzana Zabkova (2009), an Associated Press film archivist.[4] Reflecting on the challenge of uncovering anything of historical value, even as a TV news agency employee, Zabkova wrote that

> vital documentation, such as contracts, business strategies and financial reports seem to be irretrievably lost. Often, the only document of the early television news agencies is the actual product: the 16mm film archives.

The Newsreels

The TV agencies were born not only from the death of the newsreels, but from the birth—or more precisely, the childhood—of television news.[5] Most television stations around the world, but particularly in Britain and the United States, began creating their own newscasts the day they went on the air in the 1950s or 1960s. Early local television newscasts were short and non-visual, for videotape technology, debuting in 1956, was too cumbersome to leave the studio, and live news remotes were all but impossible for their complexity and cost. Thus most television news operations purchased news film from newsreel companies. However, 16 millimeter film, while an excellent newsgathering medium in the field, was costly and required at least three and a half hours to be processed, edited, and set up for the complex process of playing it back into a live newscast (Musburger, 1991).

The international television news agencies are descended from the newsreel companies that had been recording moving pictures of news events since before 1900. Well-archived newsreel collections owned by the international television news agencies today stretch back as far as 1910. Reuters owns some film from as early as 1896.[6] By the early 1950s, demand for theatrical newsreels was waning, and classic newsreel series like "March of Time" came to an end (Barnouw, 1983). Pronay (1972) and other newsreel historians have suggested how the newsreels evolved into news agencies, rather than died away. But Zabkova (2009, 6) takes issue with that hypothesis, pointing out that of a dozen or more newsreel companies active until the 1950s, only two "were directly involved in setting up a television news agency." These were the American companies Fox Movietone and Telenews. And of news agencies existing in the 1950s, only the United Press (UP) and International News Service (INS)—a Hearst company—chose to get involved with television. But the American CBS television network must also be credited with establishing one of the first television news agencies.

It remains a curiosity that more of the newsreel companies failed to invest in TV news by the mid-1950s, when television started to grow at a staggering pace in the United States. Zabkova, following McKernan (2002), points out that newsreels evolved as a product of entertainment, not journalism, and what sustained them was their ability to entertain audiences over many weeks as they went from cinema to cinema. The slow pace of processing and distribution also limited the value of newsreels in providing visual coverage of developing international political stories—although, of course, they eventually established themselves as *the* source of visual news coverage during World War II.

The newsreels were unabashedly patriotic and conservative, not unlike the modern Fox News in the United States, but very much in contrast to a modern news agency striving for global acceptance. One of the first great newsreel cameramen, Paul Wyand, who spent most of his career with Movietone News, said of his filming for Pathé in the 1930s and 1940s:

> As representatives of an American firm we laid particular emphasis on stories with an American angle, and there was keen rivalry between ourselves and cameramen for the other American-controlled newsreels: Paramount, International News, and Fox. Expense was literally no object when it came to getting an important roll of film to New York ahead of our competitors. (Wyand, 1959, 27)

Wyand's description of newsgathering, with technological and logistical details updated, would apply as aptly to the modern television news agencies. The product was competitive and time sensitive (though we might speculate if Wyland could have even imagined modern disinterest in stories that cannot be shown *live*).

Before expanding on the efforts of United Press and the INS agency, an even earlier effort by the Associated Press must be acknowledged. In 1948, U.S. trade magazines reported the flurry of activity by newsreel companies anticipating the television news boom. But there were also reports that the Hollywood owners of the newsreels were unconvinced by proposals to embrace television, delaying the start of such ventures by two years or more. In a 1947 letter explaining the Associated Press's attempt to enter the television news business, AP corporate secretary Lloyd Stratton told *New York Times* publisher Arthur Sulzberger that while researching AP's opportunities in television he was told by "the two leading newsreel companies" that theatrical newsreels were a "dead duck" and had been for months, and that "as far as two years back" they had recommended "retooling" to produce news for television, requests that were "rejected at the top."[7] At around the same time, *Variety* stated that advocates for television services within the newsreel companies were complaining that theatrical newsreels had "been operating in the red since the advent of sound." Sound, along with more services, brought added costs when theaters were not willing to pay more (Anon., 1947).

And so the Associated Press briefly established a television news service for about three weeks in late 1947, but it appears to have produced little more than a single newsreel of Princess Elizabeth's wedding, which it provided to three northeast U.S. television stations (Chase, 1947). Trade magazine accounts reported that the costs of regular news film production for television were higher than the AP anticipated (Anon., 1949; cited in Zabkova, 2009). Intriguingly, Associated Press Executive Director Kent Cooper—credited with much of the AP's modernization during that period—thanked the staff responsible, predicting (in 1947) that "we can and will do better."[8] His prediction was right, though he might not have guessed it would be 45 years before it happened. The AP underestimated not only the cost but also the complexities of running a global motion picture newsgathering operation and wrongly believed that simply providing its reporters with camera equipment would do the job.[9]

The first daily syndicated news film service for television was that of the Telenews newsreel company, which had started producing, distributing, and screening its theatrical newsreels in 1939. They had perceived the changes being wrought by television and established an alliance with the International News Service (INS) newsreel owned by William Randolph Hearst, whose company had been producing newsreels since 1913 (later under the famous brand name "News of the Day"). By the start of 1948, they established a film distribution system where news negatives were flown to New York for processing, and film prints were distributed by air to cities around the United States (Zabkova, 2009, 16).

The United Press news agency entered discussions with newsreel producer Universal in 1948, seeking to establish a daily television news service, but that effort soon faltered (Sultan, 1948; cited in Zabkova, 2009). In October 1951 it began an alliance with Fox Movietone (Zabkova, 2009, 15), adapting the name United Press Movietone (UPMT) (Payette, 1952; Waite, 1992). United Press Movietone would later evolve into UPITN, and then WTN, and eventually into the contemporary APTN. The arrangement called for Movietone to continue shooting news film as it had been, but to work with United Press bureaus to build a network for the rapid distribution of the film to broadcasters (Mahoney, 1975; Waite, 1992). UPMT's manager of television operations claimed in September 1952 that half of U.S. television stations at that time were airing UPMT news film and receiving 100 minutes of new film weekly (Payette, 1952)[10] but as early as 1956, according to Schonfeld (2001, 23), UPMT was in "deep trouble," since broadcasters were increasingly using transcontinental cables to move their news images from city to city, and so had little need for UPMT's air-freighted film. Apart from that problem, by the mid-1950s, all the U.S. television networks were producing more news on their own, leaving INS-Telenews and United Press Movietone to compete for contracts with the remaining non-network stations, many of which were starting to find news too expensive to continue with.

The logical market for growth, then, was in global news. In September 1955 UPMT offered its service without charge to the BBC for a month, as the BBC was attempting to polish its television news offerings in anticipation of competition from the fledgling ITN (the news provider for the new commercial television channel). The BBC was impressed and signed a seven-year contract with the agency. United Press Movietone established a full-time London office to present itself as an international service and attract other non-U.S. broadcasters, and by the end of 1955 it had signed twelve European broadcasters, including some of the largest (Zabkova, 2009, 24).

So the original founders of the modern television news agency industry (if a field with two players can be called an industry) are the following:

Wires	Newsreels	Broadcasters
United Press	Fox Movietone	CBS (U.S.)
INS	Paramount	BBC (U.K.)
Associated Press	Telenews	ITN (U.K.)

The timeline below charts the life of each major company acting as an international television news agency since the 1940s. CBS is the only broadcaster on the chart because it operated as a television news agency from the start of the business, but now many broadcasters syndicate their news video in competition with the major news agencies.

The pioneering U.S. television network CBS, responsible for much early innovation in television news, used the daily INS-Telenews films from 1948, even as it was developing its own news film distribution system. Zabkova details numerous ways in which INS-Telenews effectively invented the modern television news

Timeline of Television News Agencies, 1947–2010

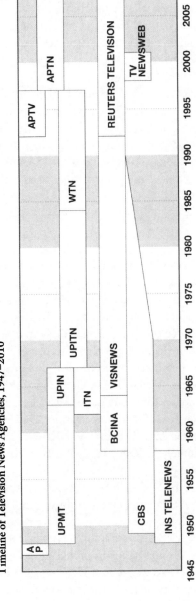

agency service (and UPMT was similarly innovative). Hearst bought out INS-Telenews in 1954, shortly after CBS left the service to pursue its own news distribution system. With international collaborations in newsgathering including the BBC and the French state broadcaster Office de Radiodiffusion Télévision Française (ORTF), and international clients beyond its own U.S. stations (with Mexico's Televisa leading the way), CBS Newsfilm created the structure of a modern international television news agency (Mickelson, 1998, 116), though, with its BBC contract, UPMT "became the first television news agency to operate on a truly international level" (Zabkova, 2009).

United Press purchased the International News Service in May 1958, forming the United Press International (UPI) news agency which continues—albeit in a vastly diminished state—to this day.[11] United Press Movietone originally remained independent of the new agency, but it would later become a UPI subsidiary. In 1963 United Press International broke away from Movietone and established UPI Newsfilm, and Movietone—after a few further years of struggle—went out of the news business altogether.

Visnews

The BBC continued to subscribe to UPI Newsfilm, despite an increasingly heavy reliance upon its own agency, BCINA (Boyd-Barrett, 1980), which is the next part of the story. But since BCINA would become Visnews and eventually the modern Reuters Television, some introduction to the Reuters news agency is in order. Thomas-Reuters resulted from the purchase of Reuters by the Canadian Thomson publishing conglomerate in 2007. Reuters, in turn, had operated Reuters Television since 1992, when it purchased full control of a company that had operated as Visnews since 1964, and as the British Commonwealth International Newsfilm Agency (BCINA) before that. But as described below, Reuters had significant influence over the direction of that company since 1960, when it first acquired stock in the television news agency. The history of Reuters is thoroughly detailed elsewhere (most substantially in Read, 1992; also Boyd-Barrett, 1980; Fenby, 1986; Taylor, 1991).

By 1872 Reuters had cable links to America, Australia, India, China, and Japan. Besides delivering news, Reuters profited immensely from sending private and company messages over its telegraph lines. Its news operations, like its contemporary television news service, typically lost money, and were paid for by these ancillary businesses. Thus an important early precedent was set for funding a prestigious and influential general news service from profit-generating services aimed at transnational business, a strategy characteristic of the modern Thomson-Reuters. During the Boer War of 1899–1902, Reuters placed correspondents on the Boer side, as well as the British side, cementing a reputation for impartiality.

Reuters, Charles Havas of France (the precursor of Agence France-Presse), and Bernard Wolff of Germany dominated international news delivery through the 1930s. In 1916, the company became Reuters Limited, and Roderick Jones, the company's former South Africa manager, became the head of the company until 1941. Jones also served as the head of the Department of Propaganda for the British government during World War I, while Reuters continued to defend its impartiality to its clients around the world. Jones received a knighthood for service to Britain, although he insisted that Reuters should work with the British government and provide information to government agencies, just not permit itself to be directed by government. Reuters claimed it avoided any direct government subsidy, despite intense competition from Associated Press and United Press (Read, 1992, reveals otherwise).

The British Press Association (PA), a domestic news agency owned (mostly) by British newspapers, became a majority shareholder in Reuters in 1925 and in 1930 acquired all but 1,000 shares owned by Jones. Jones was forced out by the PA in 1941, apparently due to his close connections to the British government. Ownership of the company was then divided between the PA and the British Newspaper Proprietors' Association (NPA) and later the Australian and New Zealand domestic news agencies. At this time, the "Reuters Trust" was implemented to ensure that "no single interest comes to dominate its ownership" (Reuters Company Report, 1994). The major activity of the company was providing an inexpensive financial and general news service to the world, until Gerald Long took over as managing editor in 1963. Long persuaded the Reuters board to expand and to embrace new information technologies.

By 1964 Reuters began marketing a desktop computer system that would constantly update stock prices for financial traders, and its systems would later become the main channel for global financial trading. This would turn Reuters into a multi-billion-dollar business and become its primary *raison d'être*. Bartram (2003) reported that "by the mid-1990s an estimated one-half of the world's daily foreign exchange trades worth $1.2 trillion took place on and through Reuters screens." The company's foresight should not be underestimated: in a few decades it built up the business reporting side of the company to become a key source of information driving global economic trading, while profiting immensely from that trading. But it also expanded in the realm of more classical journalism. Apart from the useful loss of competition, Reuters benefited from the collapse of long-time rival United Press International in 1985 by purchasing its news picture business, thus launching itself into news photos and photo archives.[12]

The corporation grew even more rapidly under the direction of Glen Renfrew, who took over as managing director in 1981. Reuters went public in 1984, becoming Reuters Holdings, Plc (providing an unexpected and welcome windfall for the British newspapers that owned shares in the Press Association; see Moncrieff, 2001). At that time, Reuters Founders Share Company was formed to maintain the principles of the Reuters Trust. There was close interaction at the time between media mogul Rupert Murdoch and Reuters's directors, and the possibility of a Murdoch takeover of Reuters was considered credible. Through the Founders Share Company, the trustees and their chairman retain a single share with the power to outvote all other shares to prevent a takeover from a single powerful entity. While the "trust principles" are said to remain intact, the ultimate takeover of Reuters by an international media conglomerate in 2007 demonstrated these were never strong enough to prevent the news agency's acquisition.[13]

So we wind back the clock once more to 1957, when the BBC and other investors created what they believed was a necessary British alternative to the American companies UPMT and CBS Newsfilm. The project was the initiative of Sir Ian Jacob, the BBC director-general from 1952 to 1960 (Curran, 1979). As put by agency and ITN veteran journalist John Mahoney, the British Commonwealth International Newsfilm Agency (BCINA) was created "in a conscious effort to counter the early American monopoly" (Mahoney, 1975; cited in Boyd-Barrett, 1980, 238). U.S.-based news agencies—especially the increasingly successful UPMT—had little incentive to provide serious coverage of countries with colonial ties to Britain, despite the ongoing interest in such places from British television. This meant that there was little flow of TV news images out of the Indian subcontinent or much of Africa, for example, at a time when news from such places provided a vital chronicle of the gradual dissolution of the British Empire.

The BBC joined with the Australian Broadcasting Corporation, the J. Arthur Rank Organization (then a major British film production firm), and the Canadian Broadcasting Corporation (CBC) to create BCINA (Bowden, 1987, 59). New Zealand Broadcasting (BCNZ) joined later as an investor (Curran, 1979). BCINA used the name Visnews from the outset for some aspects of its business, and would go on to fully adopt that name in 1964.[14] The name was the cable address[15] for BCINA (interview, A. Ailes, 2010). While the modern Thomas-Reuters puts great emphasis upon the profitability of its enterprises, the managing director of Visnews in 1979, Sir Charles Curran (1979), wrote, in contrast, that it was

> part of the original constituting agreement that the purpose of Visnews is not primarily to make a commercial profit...that the application of such trading profits as have to be made, in order to fund developments, is directed always toward the improvement of the service....[T]here is no distribution of profits whatever to shareholders.

BCINA began by distributing film footage shot by the BBC, Australia public broadcaster ABC, and CBC staff photographers around the world, but gradually built its own network of staff and stringer camera operators (Curran, 1979). BCINA was headquartered at School Road in west London at an old Rank Film laboratory before moving to a purpose-built facility on Cumberland Avenue in Park Royal in 1975.[16] Both facilities are in an industrial district of west London, and both are near the BBC's White City complex. The Cumberland Avenue site was inconvenient to central London but was chosen deliberately. The location was primarily for ease of access to Heathrow Airport, the transit point for most international news film, meaning an incoming film might be edited and distributed an hour faster than a trip into central London might allow. And only this location, amid heavy industry, had the necessary sewage facilities to dispose of the massive amounts of chemicals used in film processing.[17] The modern Reuters Television continued to use the Cumberland Avenue facility, adjacent to London's Guinness Brewery, for its commercial satellite department, its video and film archives, and its satellite "dish farm."

In 1960, Reuters purchased its first shares in BCINA. After the Reuters partial ownership of Visnews began, a "trust document" (similar to that of Reuters) was established at Visnews (Fenby, 1986, 106). At the time, this partnership between the BBC and Reuters made sense. The BBC already depended heavily upon Reuters for international information gathering (in 1960, the BBC was Reuters's largest subscriber, the only client paying Reuters over £100,000—nearly $300,000[18]—per year [Read, 1992, 277]) and considered Reuters a partner in international newsgathering, so would likely have been glad to share the cost of running BCINA with it. According to Read (1992), "Both the BBC and Reuters accepted that they stood in a special relationship."

Reuters purchased 11% of the television newsreel company's shares,[19] the amount it owned when BCINA officially changed its name to Visnews in 1964 (Johnston, 1995, 22). In 1968, Reuters increased its share in Visnews to 33% in order to equal the number of shares held by the BBC (ibid., 340). Reuters increasing stake in Visnews was precipitated by the decision of the Rank Organization to invest elsewhere—in this case, in British commercial broadcaster Southern Television. Fearing a rejection of its Southern Television investment by the British Independent Broadcasting Authority (IBA), Rank sold its Visnews shares to Reuters.[20] The remaining shareholdings continued to be divided among the public broadcasters from Australia, New Zealand, and Canada.

Visnews made clear its intention of being the British television news agency through its purchase of every major British newsreel collection. These were the British Paramount Newsreel Library in 1959 and the Gaumont, Empire News, and Universal News collections in 1963. It became the leading film and photo archive for Britain and the Commonwealth from 1910 on (the beginning of the Gaumont Graphic archive).[21] Visnews's bureaus and coverage strengths—such as English-speaking Africa[22] and the Middle East—also consistently demonstrated significant colonial ties and an avoidance of U.S. stories, or, at least, an attempt to provide an alternative to U.S. coverage.

A significant example was Visnews coverage of the Vietnam War. An enormous amount of news footage was available daily from the U.S. networks, particularly CBS, but Visnews kept several photographers covering the war nonetheless. One of these was among the dozen or so photographers considered legendary by the industry, Neil Davis. Davis, based in Singapore, covered most of the Vietnam War for Visnews, despite a lucrative 1965 offer to join CBS, and several even better offers later in the war. Davis felt a responsibility to cover non-U.S. angles to the war, and to focus on South Vietnamese troops and those of other nations, such as South Korea and Australia. Despite pressure from U.S. clients to provide more coverage of U.S. troops, Visnews supported Davis' efforts (Bowden, 1987).

Visnews began producing documentary films, mostly for governments and private industry, and by the late 1970s, it had built this business into a significant revenue source subsidizing its newsgathering. It was also profiting from hiring out its international crews and equipment and providing commercial film processing and printing services in London. Visnews staffers were retained by a great many national broadcasting companies, mainly in developing countries, as consultants (and some current Reuters Television staff continue this tradition). Boyd-Barrett (1980, 241) suggests the company may have hoped to increase the prospects of receiving high-quality news film from these new broadcasters by building their TV news departments. Certainly the consultancy business was also an easy way to derive secondary benefit from their international reputation. A flow of reliable news pictures from developing nations' broadcasters to Visnews never ensued in significant measure, perhaps contributing to the culture of mistrust of news from "Third World" broadcasters I saw continuing into the 1990s at the agencies.

In the early 1970s both Visnews and rival agency UPITN were eager to establish reliable and inexpensive alliances in order to provide the extensive coverage of the United States that their major clients worldwide appeared to desire; broadcasters around the world did not want to have to make separate and potentially costly links to U.S. broadcasters in addition to their agency subscription. NBC had worked closely with Visnews since the early 1960s as a subscriber and provider of news footage, but Visnews determined in 1973 that NBC wasn't offering it enough coverage of the United States to support client demand.

Through the early 1970s, Visnews competitor UPITN had been trying to establish a U.S. television news exchange mechanism. But UPITN co-owner

Paramount sold the operation to Television News Inc. (TVN), a television news distribution company targeting local U.S. stations during this period of rapid growth and healthy profits for local television news in the United States. This effectively brought an end to the U.S. operations (but not the London-based global operations) of UPITN. TVN was principally funded by the Adolph Coors Company, which intended to use it to distribute conservative political views to balance the perceived "liberal" bias of the U.S. networks (Boyd-Barrett, 1980). In acquiring the American arm of UPITN, the Coors family retained long-time UPITN news manager Reese Schonfeld, who, five years later, would go on to co-found CNN.[23] In 1973 Visnews, through its co-owner Reuters, invested in a portion of TVN, with the understanding that it would supply international news to the company, and TVN would provide Visnews with a flow of domestic U.S. stories for international distribution. But the Visnews-TVN alliance ended in 1975, leaving Visnews again dependent upon NBC and its own small U.S. presence (principally small New York and Washington bureaus).

Visnews, as with rival UPITN, grew and changed extensively in the 1980s as film was entirely displaced by video, and satellite technology became increasingly integrated into its operations. Occasional satellite use for television newsgathering dates back to the assassination of President John F. Kennedy in 1963, when TV pictures were transmitted to England and distributed globally by Visnews. Until Ku-band satellite transponders became available in the mid-1980s, satellite delivery of news to London was an expensive and less desirable option, and heavy use of airline delivery of film or videotape continued. In 1989, with the fall of the Berlin Wall, Visnews began extensive use of portable satellite uplinks for the delivery of breaking news. Visnews editor Stephen Claypole told Preston (1999, 99–100) that the Tiananmen Square story in China in 1989 was a key moment for Visnews, when the provision of satellite uplink time and support at the scene of a major story became a vital business for the news agency.

> We resolved to make sure that no bureau was ever overwhelmed again at the time of a big event, [by providing] not only news coverage but also facilities. We got heavily into the use of portable ground stations...which had previously only been available to the richest networks in the world....We suddenly liberated a huge group of broadcasters who were able to use our satellite news gathering facilities to do things that were similar to the production values and techniques of the American networks....They would perhaps send a reporter and sometimes send one crew, but what we provided was an enormous picture pool of everything that was going on in the story, and we provided the facility for correspondents to do live crosstalk back to their studios and it became a huge business.

Regular satellite transmissions to clients started in 1975 with the inauguration of a satellite newsfeed for Australian clients, and new satellite feeds to clients were added almost yearly after that.[24] Hjarvard (1994, 2) notes that prior to the growth of agency satellite delivery networks in the 1980s, the Eurovision exchange was the only way the agencies could distribute visual footage electronically (thus, instantly) to their clients: the alternative was putting film or videotape on scheduled airline flights. The editorial priorities of the European Broadcasting Union, therefore, had an extremely strong influence upon the operations of the agencies, certainly more so than today. Visnews began its own subsidiary satellite services company, Brightstar, in 1983, in order to acquire long-term satellite transponder leases for use in news acquisition and delivery, but also for rental to other companies for live news transmission, video press conferences, or other purposes. Brightstar continued to operate after the Reuters takeover in 1992; one of their new television division's profitable enterprises which subsidized television news operations.[25] By the early 1980s, Visnews had a staff of over 300 at Cumberland Avenue (Read, 1992, 340) and was claiming to have "over 400 cameramen around the world,"[26] although just 50 overseas journalists were on staff (Read, 1992, 340).

In 1984, Visnews developed a satellite news service called World News Network, to be marketed directly to cable television operators in Europe. In these early days of rampant privatization of state channels and new cable stations, a growing appetite for a steady stream of international news footage was clear. The service would show the latest news pictures and financial and weather graphics and contained various soundtracks of narration (Fenby, 1986). It was, in essence, much like the plan successfully implemented by Euronews a decade later (further detail may be found in Preston, 1999, 88). The project was eventually abandoned, but it was the predecessor of the full-time satellite news distribution services eventually established by Reuters Television, WTN, and the Associated Press. In the early 1980s, Visnews briefly operated a news feed service specifically for Africa, but terminated it suddenly, apparently because it was "uneconomical" (Tetley, 1988, 237). This feed was coordinated through its Johannesburg bureau and designed primarily for the South African Broadcasting Corporation (to whom Reuters Television continued to provide a special daily feed). No agency made a similar attempt to serve African broadcasters until Reuters Television re-established a daily African service in 2006.[27]

The close connection with Reuters had important logistical benefits for Visnews, enabling it to cover news more efficiently and economically than WTN or major broadcasters. Perhaps most important was its access to Reuters's dedicated cable network around the world for intra-company communications. Some cost sharing and information sharing also occurred on international stories between

Visnews producers or camera crews and Reuters correspondents, although this did not happen extensively until the 1993 Reuters takeover of Visnews, and to this day print-television interaction is not considerable (interviews and observation, 1995–2010).

The connection between Reuters and Visnews through the 1980s was manifest mainly in the boardroom. Reuters Managing Director (until 1981) Gerald Long was the Visnews chairman between 1968 and 1979. In the mid-1980s, Reuters deputy managing director, finance director, and another executive were also Visnews directors (Fenby, 1986, 107). But the relationship between the companies, already soured when Long had wanted to discard Visnews altogether, deteriorated further after 1984 (Read, 1992, 340). That year Reuters attempted to take a controlling stake in the television news agency and was opposed by the BBC and other Visnews shareholders (all of them broadcasters). The fact that Visnews staff, as with any of the television news agencies, came primarily from work with broadcasters and saw their loyalties as lying with broadcasters (with whom they interacted each day), did little to garner sympathy for Reuters.

Due in part to unease with a print and financial service company owning so much of its broadcast-oriented business, Visnews sought to increase the percentage of shares held by broadcasters and was eager for an owner more prepared than Reuters to re-invest the company's meager profits in the technology of television coverage. But Reuters Managing Director Glen Renfrew and Deputy Managing Director Michael Nelson persisted in their fight for a stronger holding in Visnews and succeeded in 1985, when Reuters increased its share to 55%, and the remaining shares were divided equally among the BBC, ABC (Australia), CBC (Canada), and BCNZ (New Zealand) (Read, 1992). In 1987, Visnews approached U.S. network CBS to purchase part of the company, but CBS, itself in the process of major cutbacks, was not interested (Goldman, 1988). In any case, CBS Newsfilm continued to operate as competition to Visnews and WTN, albeit minimally.[28] Soon after, Reuters convinced the other broadcasters to surrender their ownership of the agency and increased their holding to 88.75%, bringing the BBC's share to 11.25%. Visnews lost money in 1987 and 1988, and made a small profit each subsequent year until the Reuters takeover (Waite, 1992).

In 1988, in the United States, NBC was still operating a costly ten foreign bureaus. NBC President Robert Wright was laboring to reduce his network's overseas expenses and felt he could do so in part by acquiring a major stake, and thus editorial influence over (by the admission of NBC executives), Visnews. NBC had subscribed to Visnews since it was BCINA in 1962, and now it saw a chance to close foreign bureaus and use the news agency to generate a large portion of its foreign coverage—a result of across-the-board cost-cutting imposed by NBC's new corporate parent, General Electric (Diamond, 1988). NBC purchased 37.75% of Visnews shares from Reuters, leaving Reuters with 51% and the BBC with the 11.25% it had had since the earlier sale. NBC soon established cost-sharing arrangements with Visnews, including the sharing of bureaus in Paris and Rome (Goldman, 1988). It is probably not insignificant that Visnews had been substantially supported by its heavy subscription payments from NBC through the 1970s, largely at the discretion of NBC News President Richard Wald, who believed in the value of maintaining the independence of the international television news agencies. When Wald fell out with Wright and took over control of news at rival network ABC in the late 1970s, he invested ABC's strong profits in Visnews rival UPITN (later WTN). By buying into Visnews, Wright was hitting back. In the next chapter, we continue the story of Visnews as Reuters finally accomplished its goal of fully acquiring the television news agency.

UPIN/UPITN/WTN

We left the story of the United Press with the departure of Movietone in 1963, and the creation of UPI Newsfilm (UPIN). Burt Reinhardt (who would later work with Reese Schonfeld and Ted Turner's money to build CNN) left Movietone to be its first general manager. The new UPIN had to get up to speed quickly, with the beginnings of major conflict in Vietnam, the space race, racial conflict in the United States, and the November 1963 assassination of John F. Kennedy. But its legacy served it well: Schonfeld (2001, 35) describes how UPIN "salesmen sat working the phones, drinking booze from the bottle, and selling the two Kennedy documentaries" he had made while at UPMT, giving television stations around the world footage of Kennedy's life while they scrambled to produce coverage of their own.[29]

In 1967 UPI Newsfilm was merged with the semi-autonomous international news film syndication service of Britain's Independent Television News (ITN) to form UPITN—United Press International Television News—in which each company had an equal ownership stake.[30] The companies which owned ITN considered the venture an unnecessary risk and were reluctant to provide the funding UPITN needed to compete with Visnews (Cox, 1997). ITN paid UPITN as a subscriber, and UPITN reimbursed UPI for "communications and other facilities" provided by the wire service (Boyd-Barrett, 1980). Boyd-Barrett observed:

> The extent of UPI's operational involvement in UPITN (but not in terms of ownership) seems proportionally greater than Reuters' involvement in Visnews, in that it provides not only the news service and communications but also administers and manages UPITN's overseas bureaux.

Upon the merger with ITN, the television news agency stopped supplying news film to ITN's rival, the BBC. This action ensured total dependence by the BBC upon Visnews, and therefore a secure future for UPITN's only competition. This was perhaps the first in a series of missteps that plagued the UPITN (later WTN) organization until its acquisition in the 1990s by the Associated Press, and helped to keep it (for most of this period) a distant second to Visnews, and later Reuters Television (despite its far earlier start in the television news agency business). UPMT, UPIN, and then UPITN—like Visnews—gradually built ancillary businesses that proved more profitable than the provision of news to broadcasters (always a costly and unpredictable enterprise). One example was Roving Report, a weekly recap of world news distributed by airmail to broadcasters around the world, which WTN took over from ITN.[31] The program continued to be a success for WTN until that agency's demise (Johnston, 1995).

WTN would also win a contract with the British government's Foreign and Commonwealth Office to produce British Satellite News (BSN). Like the U.S. government's Worldnet and other national propaganda services, BSN is delivered free to broadcasters around the world to provide a British perspective on current events and promote British interests. For example, in the 1990s, the Arabsat news exchange distributed the service to broadcasters through the Middle East.[32] WTN executives claimed there was no interaction between BSN and the news division, but WTN staff routinely moved between each division in London and in the field, and I witnessed indications that coverage costs and produced stories were, at least occasionally, shared, effectively amounting to a British government subsidy of WTN's news operations.[33] BSN came back to haunt APTN when it took over the contract from WTN. London staff were angered when the Associated Press in New York decided at the last minute, in 2000, to no longer bid to produce the service, given the perception of collusion with the British government (Conlan, 2000). BSN was taken over by a public relations company and finally lost its government funding a few years ago.

In 1971 UPITN was still facing a struggle to find the funds to expand from ITN's shareholders and so the United Press and ITN took the decision to each sell half of their shares to a U.S. film company, Paramount Pictures, to rapidly build a strong U.S. presence. They each retained 25% of UPITN (Fenby, 1986). UPITN feared that Visnews had an edge in the distribution of U.S. television news, having no strong partnership of its own with a U.S. broadcaster (as Visnews had long had with NBC). Cox (1997) writes that Paramount was "flush with cash after the success of The Godfather…They hoped to base a new fourth television network in the United States on a nationwide UPITN nightly news show." Ironically, Paramount had been—decades earlier—a rival to the newsreel predecessor of UPITN, Fox Movietone.

Visnews saw the increased U.S. activity of its competitor and formed its 1973 Visnews alliance with Adolph Coors's U.S. news video distributor, TVN, described earlier. But a UPITN-Paramount news exchange system in the United States based on the use of AT&T cables[34] was never fully developed, and was sold within a year to rival TVN. In late 1974,[35] Paramount had had enough of television news (having seen little return on its investment) and sold its 50% of UPITN for $1.35 million to a U.S. newspaper, the *Sacramento Union* (owned by one John McGoff, described below). Burt Reinhardt had been responsible for trying to establish the U.S. news distribution system for UPITN-Paramount, and he remained with Paramount to develop its home video business. The collapse of UPITN's effort at a routine exchange of news among U.S. stations left UPITN in a weak, money-losing position in the United States. Hence it was eager for another chance to participate in a national news exchange project when Schonfeld, who had fallen out with the Coors brothers at TVN, decided to invent his own exchange and alliance of stations in 1975 in the form of the Independent Television News Association (ITNA).

UPITN's Washington bureau would supply the main political coverage, UPITN London would provide international stories, and member stations who bought in would provide news from their various cities and regions around the country. But ITNA soon started taking international news from the Eurovision News Exchange and built up its own Washington staff, so it had less need for UPITN. Schonfeld grew increasingly alarmed at the biases and motives of UPITN's new U.S. owner, Michigan publisher John P. McGoff (in no small part after hearing McGoff complain vociferously about "niggers" while sharing a table with him at a White House press dinner) (interview, 2010). He dropped the UPITN contract in 1977 and allied ITNA to Visnews. An ITNA staffer was even based at Visnews to voice-over Visnews reports each day in an American accent with the tagline "from London" to appease ITNA's U.S. affiliates, and ITNA helped Visnews build a stronger Washington presence (Schonfeld, 2001, 49).

The *Sacramento Union* newspaper (UPITN's new half-owner) had just been purchased by the Star Newspaper Company (owned by McGoff,[36] the owner of Panax Corporation), which at the time held 8 daily U.S. newspapers, 28 weeklies, and various printing interests. Panax later became Global Communications Corporation. Through this convoluted chain, U.S. businessman McGoff owned half of one of the two international television news agencies, and it would be many years before the world found out why. McGoff was a close friend of then-President Gerald Ford and had close ties to the Republican Party (Engleberg, 1986). Although McGoff owned 50% of UPITN, his arrangement with the news agency split editorial control of the company three ways among Panax and original owners ITN and UPI (Boyd-Barrett, 1980). McGoff became a joint chairman of UPITN, and Dusty Rhodes, a director of his corporation, was installed as UPITN's president in London (Fenby, 1986; and interviews). UPITN editors began to notice that Rhodes had a particular interest in one story: South Africa. The reason why became clear when, in 1979, the South African government appointed the Erasmus Commission to investigate the "Muldergate" scandal, involving the apparently unauthorized spending of millions of Rands on domestic and foreign propaganda and international influence. The scandal would later result in the downfall of South African president John Vorster.

A witness to the commission claimed that McGoff "sought financial backing of over \$11 million" from the South African government to purchase the *Washington Star* and, later, UPITN (Boyd-Barrett, 1980). The money went to the Star Newspaper Company, disguised as a non-interest-bearing loan.[37] McGoff failed to obtain the *Washington Star* but used the money to purchase the *Sacramento Union* and, through it, half of UPITN (Engleberg, 1986). Regarding UPITN, a South African official told the Erasmus Commission that McGoff told him, "My understanding is that I represent you in that company" (Fenby, 1986). In 1986, after 18 months of unsuccessful plea bargaining, McGoff was charged in Federal District Court in Washington for having acted as "an unregistered foreign agent" for South Africa since 1974. The U.S. prosecutors contended that McGoff had received \$11.35 million from the South African government (by the admission of that government). According to the charge, he had been

> engaging in political activities, disseminating political propaganda, by serving as a publicity agent and a political consultant and by disbursing money or other things of value within the United States for or in the interest of South Africa. (Fenby, 1986)

The charges were eventually dismissed by a federal judge (Shaw, 1987). McGoff also settled, at minimal expense, a civil suit by the Securities and Exchange Commission in 1983 charging him with working for South Africa and concealing his holdings. McGoff promised not to do it again (Lewis, 1986).

The scheme must have seemed a brilliant one to South African propagandists Eschel Rhoodie, then Information Secretary, (whose conviction in South Africa was later overturned), and Cornelius Mulder (who was forced to resign as Information Minister), who together had spent close to \$72 million in their domestic and foreign propaganda efforts.[38] Throughout the 1970s and most of the 1980s, the South African government had been embarrassed by the international distribution of television pictures of the various manifestations of apartheid oppression. By controlling approximately half of the international television coverage of South Africa, it seemed that negative coverage could be reduced and positive coverage increased. Rhoodie was convinced that they succeeded. He told a British reporter in 1984:[39]

> What we did there was we purchased fifty percent of the shares in UPI-ITV [sic]. As you know it was a very useful program: 100 companies around the world with about 130 different clients....[W]e gave the money...to a Mr John McGoff, a newspaper publisher from Michigan in the United States. He bought 50 percent of the shares on our behalf. He was just our [man] in this operation and he put...a Mr Rhodes into London as the Chairman [keeping in] contact with me. And then Rhodes himself came out to South Africa to do an interview with Mr Vorster and that interview was then used and heard all over the world .....I wrote most of the questions for Mr Vorster [asked by UPITN President Rhodes] and most of the replies [from Vorster]. And this was one way that we used United Press International Television, getting across to the public things that would normally be absolutely impossible....[I]t went all over the world and it was a very successful project if I may say so myself.

The literature reveals no analysis of whether or not the South African government objectives were achieved. Scholars (for instance, Fenby, 1986) have generally been quick to side with former UPITN managers (and McGoff himself, whose denial is noted in Boyd-Barrett, 1980), who insist that there was no pro-South African editorial slant, while others ignore the question (for example, Johnston, 1995). Fenby writes:

> Whatever the South Africans may have expected, they were disappointed. The news-film agency's editorial operations were insulated from the board by an editorial committee on which UPI and ITN controlled two-thirds of the seats. It was, however, an embarrassing episode for UPITN. . . .

It is probably premature to dismiss the one-third of editorially influential seats held by McGoff, as well as the influence of his appointee as president of the company. Historically, major UPITN and WTN operational decisions, such as major resource deployments and politically difficult editorial decisions, have been referred to the president of the company.[40] John Connor of Reuters Television, at the time a senior journalist with UPITN, told me that McGoff's company "sent instructions on what to put on," but that UPITN staff refused. In a clear indication of how the transnational operations of a multinational communications conglomerate may avoid regulation and oversight (see Schiller, 1989), the U.S. government never investigated McGoff's influence at UPITN. It did, however, charge that at the shareholding company, the Sacramento Union, McGoff created an editorial policy "designed to promote a positive and favorable image of South Africa and to support and promote closer cooperation between the United States and South Africa" (Engleberg, 1986).

In a forthcoming publication, this author hopes to address South African control of international television news from 1975 to 1979 through examination of archived documentation and videotapes of UPITN feeds from the period. Preliminary analysis suggests that any influence, if there was one at all, was minimal. In 1979, ITN purchased all of McGoff's shares in UPITN for $1.4 million, increasing its stake to 75%.[41] Thus ITN's influence in the international news agency business had become far larger than that of the BBC, which then held just 33% of Visnews (Boyd-Barrett, 1980). In 1981, UPITN remained eager to find a U.S. partner to provide U.S. news footage and increase its U.S. distribution. ABC, then starting to cut back on the costs of its own international newsgathering, acquired 30% of UPITN shares from ITN "under an agreement aimed at modernizing and expanding the agency's operations" (Fenby, 1986). ABC had subscribed and had close links to UPITN prior to this. Australia's Channel Nine network purchased the remaining shares in UPITN.

In the early 1980s the UPI news agency found itself in continuing financial trouble and finally, in August 1984, sold its one-third share in UPITN for $1.3 million to ITN and ABC (Jones, 1984). UPI filed for bankruptcy on April 28, 1985 (Johnston, 1995). With UPI gone and the UPITN name tainted by the McGoff affair (company managers may have been aware that McGoff was plea bargaining in Washington, and that the U.S. case against him could go public at any time), UPITN changed its name in early 1986, becoming Worldwide Television News (WTN). The early and mid-1980s had been a difficult time for UPITN/WTN, with McGoff, the bankruptcy of UPI, and the highly publicized 1986 abduction of WTN Beirut Bureau Chief John McCarthy.[42]

But UPITN fared reasonably well as a television news agency throughout this period, offering wealthy broadcasters more news footage—or a greater variety of news footage—than a Visnews subscription alone would provide and building a loyal clientele of its own. It had moved out of the ITN building in London in 1983 to further develop its own production facilities (Preston, 1999). The most crucial, and influential, of that loyal clientele in the 1980s were part-owner ITN and new and fast-growing U.S. client CNN. The Cable News Network started in 1980 and immediately subscribed to UPITN for its international coverage. It remained exclusively a WTN client until 1992, when it added Visnews (as it was becoming Reuters Television) to meet its enormous appetite for news (Johnston, 1995), and CNN would also subscribe to APTV soon after that service began.[43]

CNN's loyalty to UPITN/WTN, despite its lack of a financial interest in the company (as ITN had), was curious, given that Visnews was a more stable company during the 1980s and might have better provided for CNN's enormous appetite for international news images. That loyalty was crucial to WTN's survival through the

1980s and can be explained by personal ties as much as other factors. Schonfeld and Reinhardt, mentioned earlier, had been with UPITN through the early 1970s and had worked there with new UPITN boss Kenneth Coyte, who had started his long television news agency career in the first London office of UPMT. In 1979, Ted Turner called on Schonfeld to start CNN, and Schonfeld hired his old boss, Reinhardt, to assist him. Their loyalty to former colleagues at UPITN seems natural in light of their years building that agency and—perhaps—in view of years of accumulated hostility toward Visnews. UPITN offered CNN a bargain price of $50,000 in its first year,[44] and Preston (1999) reports how ITN managers were incensed that UPITN (later WTN) would provide ITN's finished news packages to CNN, where they were often aired at knock-down prices, while ITN was contractually unable to sell its own material to wealthy UPITN/WTN clients such as CNN. Reinhardt's continued presence at CNN (later becoming vice-chairman), continued to benefit WTN. A former WTN executive told me that at one point in the late 1980s CNN considered buying WTN, a deal facilitated by Kenneth Coyte's son, who worked for CNN at the time.

All the while, Visnews grew steadily with support from the BBC, NBC, and Reuters, and few public embarrassments. Visnews also thrived on the publicity surrounding its 1984 story on famine in Ethiopia, which set off an enormous worldwide fund-raising drive culminating in the Live Aid events featuring "Do They Know It's Christmas?" and "We Are the World." After losing money each year of the past twenty,[45] WTN had begun to make a small yearly profit by 1990 (Waite, 1992) and, it seemed, put its difficult past behind it.[46] In the next chapter, I will examine the turbulent 1990s, which saw the end of Visnews and WTN and the start of Reuters Television and Associated Press Television, as well as the dawning of the digital revolution in television news.

Notes

1. AP promoted the idea that it was revealing to the world a "lost archive" in 2009, although of course the UPITN/WTN footage was never lost, just made unavailable due to the disinclination, for a decade, to archive it.
2. According to managers within Reuters Television and the Associated Press. In the case of Reuters Television, this was confirmed by Reuters's corporate historian, Donald Read, in correspondence with the author.
3. The limited historical record of the television news agencies exists as brief accounts within books addressing broader aspects of international news distribution (Hjarvard,

1995b; Boyd-Barrett, 1980, 1992; Fenby, 1986), the contemporary television news industry (Johnston, 1995; Friedland, 1992), Reuters's history (Read, 1992), or the biographies of news cameramen (Tetley, 1988; Bowden, 1987; Wyand, 1959). Boyd-Barrett's is especially detailed, despite his focus on the print services of the agencies.

4. Zabkova's (2009) useful account of early television news agency history is complemented by Althaus's (2010) review of the waning days of the newsreels; also see Fielding (2006).

5. Partially adapted from Paterson (2004).

6. Reuters Television promotional material. Reuters and AP, of course, maintain vast archives of their still photographs and wire text as well.

7. AP internal document, December 16, 1947, courtesy AP archive.

8. Associated Press internal document, letter from Kent Cooper, November 17, 1947, via AP archive.

9. This is perhaps a historical point worth noting for contemporary news agency managers, who often argue that technology now allows individual reporters to simultaneously report for multiple types of media, with no consequent impact on journalistic quality.

10. For detail of day-to-day UPMT operations in the 1950s, see Schonfeld (2001).

11. For more on United Press, see Boyd-Barrett (1980); Boyd-Barrett and Rantanen (2004).

12. *Reuters World* (internal magazine), Ten Years of News Pictures: A Tumultuous Decade, 20–24, Issue 104, June 1995.

13. Journalists' unions protested the takeover on these grounds; see Press Gazette, 2007.

14. Visnews chronology in an advertisement from *EBU Review*, 1978.

15. All larger companies had a cable address in this period; this was the teletype system used widely by international businesses at the time, based on the original telegraph cables lines—and long since displaced by fax, and then the Internet.

16. John Mahoney, WTN, interview (1995).

17. Andrew Ailes, Reuters Television, interview (1995).

18. http://www.measuringworth.com/exchangepound/.

19. Read (1992, 340). Taylor (1991) claims Reuters was a co-owner of Visnews from 1959 on, but Read and other sources dispute this.

20. Rank's ownership of Visnews and Southern would contravene two IBA objectives: preventing regional broadcasters from providing non-local news coverage themselves, and reducing ownership of regional stations by large conglomerates with other media interests. See, for example, Tunstall (1992).

21. Visnews chronology in an advertisement from *EBU Review*, 1978. Apparently Visnews was unable to negotiate the rights to the original newsfilm from most of its collection between 1944 and 1950. This film resides, instead, with Britain's National Film Archives. (Hodgson, J. and Ailes, A., *A Visnews Newsroom Operating Handbook*,

1979). Perhaps the oldest and largest single British newsreel collection remains in the hands of its original creators, at least in name. That is the British Pathé collection, dating to 1896 (British Pathe Plc., promotional material).

22. Visnews has historically been the primary supplier of television news from the developing world, and particularly from Africa. See, for example, Melnik (1981, 125). Mohamed Amin of Reuters Television claimed that inter-agency competition was rarely an issue in Africa, since Reuters, and Visnews before it, so dominated coverage. Only on the largest stories of the 1980s and early 1990s did he see WTN providing coverage, and he claimed shortly before his death in 1996 that AP television had, up to that point, little African presence (though examples provided in Colart and Venter [2004] suggest otherwise).

23. Schonfeld was told by the Coors family that the objective for TVN was to act "like a tugboat, pushing ships that were veering to the [political] left back to the right, just a little bit, day by day" (Schonfeld, 2001, 39).

24. Ailes (1994); and interview with Ailes (2010).

25. Ibid.; these operations are described further in the next chapter.

26. Visnews advertisement appearing in the *EBU Review*.

27. According to Mohamed Amin, who was uncertain of the exact date of the service. Ailes writes that a daily South Africa satellite feed began in May 1980. This is probably the feed Amin refers to (Ailes, 1994).

28. In a 1979 internal guidebook to its operations, Visnews stated to its staff, "we have two major competitors: UPITN…and the Columbia Broadcasting System (CBS)" (Visnews, 1979).

29. Reinhardt bid for the famous Zapruder film of the assassination, but Zapruder chose to sell it to *Time* despite Reinhardt's higher offer. UPIN would later buy film from a Dallas postman, the film widely reported to show a second gunman, but Schonfeld (2001, 36) insists, "I spent ten years of my life working that film over and over, and I know there's nothing there."

30. Boyd-Barrett (1980) and interviews.

31. However, WTN promotional material claimed that "United Press Movietone created Roving Report in 1957 'on a budget of 800 pds. a week,'" so its origins remain hazy.

32. Apparently in an arrangement established by WTN on behalf of the British government (WTN promotional material).

33. BSN video, when useful, would find its way into regular WTN news stories, according to a senior editor. But when APTV asked to use any story containing taxpayer-funded BSN video, WTN news staff were pressured to stop the practice. Ironically, at the time of my research with WTN, it was aggressively biting the hand that fed it, in this case, the British government. WTN was suing the government for $220,000 it claimed it was owed when the Meteorological Office abruptly canceled a contract to use a WTN studio (*Broadcast*, June 30, 1995, 7).

34. *Broadcasting* (U.S.), January 26, 1987, 79.
35. Sources differ on whether the sale occurred in late 1974 or early 1975.
36. *The Wall Street Journal*, May 5, 1975, 20, via Lexis/Nexis.
37. Lewis (1986). McGoff's goal of creating an influential Washington newspaper to push a conservative and pro-South African agenda was finally realized in 1982 when *The Washington Times* began publishing with financing from the Unification Church. McGoff served on the advisory board of the newspaper, even as he was facing charges for the *Star* scandal. David Shaw, in a 1987 article for *The Los Angeles Times*, demonstrates the pro-South African slant at *The Washington Times*, along with its consistent anti-Soviet and anti-Nicaraguan themes, its strong influence at the Reagan White House, and its murky connections to the South Korean CIA (Shaw, 1987). Shaw does not disclose that the pro-South African slant was built into the editorial structure of the paper from the outset. The newspaper's foreign editor was Holger Jensen, who, as a *Newsweek* correspondent in 1983, had been denied entry into Zimbabwe for a series of articles critical of that country's new, anti-apartheid government (Paterson, 1990).
38. Much of the money went toward a pro-apartheid, English-language newspaper in South Africa, and some was reportedly used to try to influence African and Western politicians, including U.S. Presidents Ford and Carter, who received campaign financing from the fund (Murphy, 1980).
39. "The British Desk: South Africa's Intelligence Operations in Britain," ITV, May 8, 1984, courtesy Bodleian Library, Oxford University.
40. I base this assertion upon interviews with current and former WTN managers and the historical record of the influence of WTN presidents Kenneth Coyte and Robert Burke through the 1980s. See, for instance, McCarthy and Morrell (1994).
41. *The Wall Street Journal*, June 15, 1979, 22, c1, via Lexis/Nexis.
42. McCarthy tells his story in McCarthy and Morrell (1994).
43. One report intriguingly recounts that at a dinner in Atlanta in 1992 as Ted Turner celebrated CNN's new relationship with Visnews/Reuters Television, he asked the Reuters executives present if they were planning their own 24 hour network. After a moment's hesitation they said no, and Turner replied if they had answered yes he would have probably shut down CNN, given the fear of Reuters' move into television (Stone, 2007).
44. CNN founder Schonfeld's deal with his ex-colleague from UPITN Kenneth Coyte— the new chief executive of UPITN—was "if he could help us [CNN] over the first two years, we would help him [UPITN/WTN] over the long haul. We agreed on a contract price: $50,000 for the first year and $75,000 for the second" (Schoneld, 2001, 64; and interview, 2010). At that time, these were far below the going rate for an international television news agency subscription for a U.S. network. Schonfeld later found out that Visnews owner NBC had forbidden it from supplying CNN, fearing the com-

petition. Schonfeld observes that Coyte could then have asked any price for the UPITN subscription but honored his verbal deal with Schonfeld, saying Coyte "contributed more to the success of CNN than many of those who worked there" (ibid). Reinhart's biography is briefly presented in *Broadcasting* (U.S.), January 26, 1987, 112, 79, via Lexis/Nexis.

45. By the admission of Coyte in Busfield (1994b).

46. Discussed further in the next chapter. This degree of financial loss was disputed by WTN Managing Editor Lowndes Lipscomb in 1995, who insisted to me (without providing figures) that the company had made a profit consistently since 1986, and that profit "has been put back into the product."

4

The Turbulent 1990s
to the Present

As television news agencies Visnews and WTN bade farewell to the 1980s, they began what most staff sensed would be a rough ride into a future of challenging journalism, fast-paced technological change, and ever-encroaching pressure from their paymasters. They were in a stable but still hazardous financial position, with their respective long-time (mostly broadcaster) owners losing interest in subsidizing their costly business. But the future looked bright nonetheless. The quantity of potential clients was increasing along with the value of their raw news video product, as broadcast networks everywhere cut back on foreign reporting under pressure from new owners with little interest in journalism, and deregulation worldwide gave rise to new, news agency-dependent, channels.

The world of potential television news agency stories was heating up. The cold war seemed to be ending at remarkable speed, but new wars would soon be on the horizon in the Middle East, the Balkans, and Chechnya. These became the main business of the television news agencies through most of the 1990s, at the expense of a steady flow of television news from parts of the world not embroiled in all-out conflict. Nelson Mandela walked to freedom in South Africa, bringing an end to twenty years of news agency coverage of turmoil in that country (and the start of a new and hopeful story). Newsroom computers had done much to change the processing of news, and satellite news coverage was getting cheaper and easier, but the digital transmission and storage of news video at almost no cost wasn't yet dreamt of.

This chapter describes a decade that ultimately left two surviving global multimedia news agencies dominating the selection and provision of international news across all media. In 1990, as now, most of the global flow of "raw" television news images was managed through two small newsrooms in London: WTN in Camden, north London, and Visnews, in a nondescript industrial park in west London, near Heathrow airport. At that time each of them had few more than fifty core staff and a dozen key editorial staff (that is, managing editors, duty editors, senior news managers) with substantial discretion over that image flow. Those core numbers had not massively increased by 2010, but the surviving television agencies had become substantially integrated parts of the two leading global news agencies.

In the field, both WTN and Visnews had developed close alliances with leading broadcasters, and these often influenced what news they covered and how they covered it; some of those alliances dated back to the 1950s and 1960s. Both, after all, maintained their duopolistic dominance of this industry sector through the consent of the largest corporations active in international journalism and broadcasting: the BBC, ITN (and its various owners), Reuters, NBC, ABC, CBS, CNN, Australia's Channel Nine Network, and others. In 1992, Tunstall observed that "The loose Reuters-Visnews-BBC alliance constitutes the strongest single news entity on the world scene." The television news agencies' relationships had broadly, though not exclusively, seen Visnews supported mostly by public broadcasters around the world, and UPITN/WTN, mostly by commercial ones (Harrison and Palmer, 1986).

The alliance Tunstall alluded to disappeared when Reuters consumed Visnews between 1992 and 1993, diminishing the longstanding BBC connection.[1] But the BBC-Visnews relationship wasn't without difficulty already: there was a perception in Visnews that the BBC expected some degree of control that Visnews editors weren't prepared to offer. One Visnews editor, Tim Arlott, told Harrison and Palmer (1986, 74):

> It's a slightly prickly relationship because they sometimes think that we are just a news gathering arm for them whereas we are constantly reminding them that we have 400 other customers. They phoned us up about the Royals in Nepal and we said we have absolutely zero interest in that; it's not a Visnews story, it's simply for the British. We have different news instincts, different goals and different audiences.

Indeed, the BBC actively sought to constrain expansion by Visnews that wasn't directly related to gathering stories the BBC might want. Visnews editor Ron Onions told Preston (1999, 103) that when Visnews looked to Reuters and the BBC to provide backing for their attempt, in the mid-1980s, to establish a pan-European rolling news channel,

The BBC began to get a bit sniffy about Visnews—which was always regarded as a bit of a retirement home for elderly BBC gentlemen—getting above itself. Its job was to run a syndication service and that's it. It should have no aspirations of going beyond that....There was quite a lot of to-ing and fro-ing....[BBC Director General Alistair] Milne sent a memo finally to Brian Quinn who was then Managing Director of Visnews telling Visnews to get back in its box...something like that, "perhaps the time has come for it to revert to its traditional function." So there was a bit of an atmosphere for some while.

The partnership between WTN and its co-owner, ITN, was no less rocky. ITN's Chief Executive Stewart Purvis explained to Preston (1999, 114) how its contract with WTN blocked it from potentially useful, and profitable, arrangements with other broadcasters:

The problem about WTN rights was that it stopped ITN having real partnerships with people like CNN and NBC. Why would they partner us [sic] if they could buy our material via WTN? So we then began a protracted process of extracting ourselves from WTN, in order to get rights back over our material.

The BBC entered a relationship with WTN in 1993: it had been content to take its flow of agency images from Visnews when through its part ownership it had a say over the agency's direction, but it was not comfortable with surrendering that control to Reuters—a profit-driven wire service and, primarily, a financial services company. The alternative was to make a deal with WTN's owner, Disney, but the BBC felt that with WTN and its immediate owner, the ABC network in the United States, it was still dealing with like-minded broadcasters. The deal was orchestrated by Chris Cramer of the BBC and Richard Wald of ABC, and it had numerous repercussions.

After the ABC deal, ITN could no longer work with ABC or WTN (even though it continued to own 10% of WTN), since WTN had, through the ABC arrangement, become allied to the BBC.[2] U.S. network NBC lost the ability to work with the BBC (which they had maintained since 1954) and use their material. A BBC executive told me in regard to NBC, it "was like a divorce." Visnews (then transitioning to Reuters Television) was being shut out by the BBC, but soon formed new alliances with ITN and Sky. CNN and U.S. network CBS benefited from a strengthened WTN that could offer BBC stories (although at a cost). A little-known element of all this was the falling out between Richard Wald and his long-time employer, NBC; he sought to make the most of his international connections when he joined its U.S. rival, ABC (taking advantage as well of the BBC's disquiet that its old newsgathering ally Visnews was, under Reuters management, making deals with BBC rivals such as Sky).

As Tunstall (1992, 98) pointed out, an alliance with the BBC offered any news organization many advantages. The BBC World Service has an enormous number of trusted radio correspondents around the world, able to quickly provide details (in English) and, importantly, logistical information for future coverage, of nearly any story within minutes. The BBC domestic radio and television services cover the United Kingdom and Northern Ireland extensively, constantly feeding information to London. And the BBC Monitoring Service, based in Caversham, near London, listens to radio broadcasts and monitors online and print media from around the world, so the BBC is likely to discover stories even when international reporters near the action are shut out. Also, like the news agencies themselves, the BBC is a broadcast service company whose provision of facilities for hire can itself influence whether—and how—the world's television media cover a story, so it is better to have it as friend than foe. In the former Yugoslavia, the BBC did a good business renting portable satellite uplinks. In 1995, it was charging other broadcasters $1,000 for ten-minute transmissions from these dishes.[3]

While clearly critical at the distribution (retail) level of international television, television news alliances also allow participants to increase newsgathering capabilities while reducing costs to each partner. The resulting *homogenization* of the news is rarely mentioned within the industry. Tunstall (1992), Weiner (1992), and Bell (1995) all allude to the alliances that dominate television coverage of major international stories. My interviews confirmed those accounts. During the 1980s and early 1990s—through that TV news watershed, the first Gulf War—the principal alliances were as Tunstall describes here, as he notes the way alliances determine relations between the news teams of various companies (1992, 89). He notes that there were, at the time,

> two leading groups of reporting teams. One is the Visnews-NBC-BBC-and-allies grouping. The second is the WTN-ABC-ITN-Channel 9 (Australia)-CNN group. Members of each group seek to occupy adjacent hotel rooms where they set up their temporary "dub city" (for video editing and tape copying) and within such a group reporting teams combine their own material with footage from the tapes of other cooperating news organizations....As with other competitive news situations, there are also some elements of cooperation. In some cases, satellite facilities, and even technicians, are shared. Editing cooperation can, after some days, be extended into newsgathering cooperation.

The contracts between the agency members and broadcaster members of each alliance make such sharing of videotape in the field possible and ensure that each member of each alliance—and all the clients of each agency in each alliance—get the best pictures and best interviews shot by any of several news crews covering the story. The sharing of resources and personnel has traditionally been more ad hoc, left in the hands of the producers on the scene, although contracts negotiated between corporations more recently (such as the ABC-BBC pact) standardize such cooperation.

It was such a set of alliances that allowed CNN and WTN to work together to dominate coverage from Iraq during the first Gulf War, thereby not only shutting out the BBC, NBC, and Visnews, but also bolstering the position of BBC rival ITN and NBC's rivals ABC and CBS (Bell, 1995; Weiner, 1992; Waite, 1992).[4] For their part, during the lead-up to the Gulf War, the BBC worked closely with Visnews, as it had on major international stories in the past—for instance, when Visnews cameraman Mohamed Amin uncovered the massive 1984 famine in Ethiopia, but the BBC's Michael Buerk fronted its powerful story, which set off a massive global relief operation. As the first Gulf War approached, Amin was called from Nairobi to work with the BBC's John Simpson to secure an early interview with Saddam Hussein and to attempt to get into Kuwait and gain other exclusives (Weiner, 1992).

ITN—the BBC's commercial rival in the U.K.—was perhaps even more dependent on its alliances. ITN executives were seeking additional funding from their ITV owner companies in Britain in 1990, as major news was taking place in Eastern Europe. ITN (having experienced major cutbacks of its own) was having trouble covering it all. CNN and WTN provided heavy coverage of the stories[5] which, combined with the extra effort ITN put into the story (while dropping coverage elsewhere), enabled ITN to launch a promotional campaign about what a wonderful job they (not allies CNN and WTN) were doing in Eastern Europe. That campaign convinced their owners to provide extra news funding (Butler, 1991; Tunstall, 1992).

But alliances in international broadcast news often have peculiar limitations. For example, in southern Africa in the late 1980s, the stringers for ITN and WTN would sometimes cooperate, but usually would compete for stories, although each would always compete with the single cameraman in Harare who served both the BBC and Visnews.[6] During the 1990s, ITN journalists produced programs for BBC radio—an example of outsourcing for programming that would have been unimaginable in the early decades of intensive competition between ITN and the BBC.[7] When the city of Knin in Bosnia fell to Croatian troops in 1995, an important turning point in the Yugoslav civil wars, ABC had exclusive footage and refused to share it with its news agency, WTN, for international distribution.

On fast-breaking news coverage, the decision to cooperate or to compete with another company is often taken by the people gathering the news in the field, and sometimes even by freelance photographers who have no loyalties and the vaguest idea of the latest alliances. My observation indicates that sometimes news managers in London and New York uphold the decisions of their field staff when they learn of them, and work out complications later; other times they may reprimand their people in the field and attempt to put a fast end to the cooperation.

Finally, for the television news agencies, the overall trend of the 1990s (though commencing, to a degree, in the 1980s) was aggressive diversification into new, related sectors of the industry in an effort to maximize profit from their well-established television newsgathering brands; this formed a key part of what Preston (1999) identifies as the broader *marketization of television news* during this period. Such activities took many forms: the provision of satellite services including, but often going well beyond, the provision of uplinks to broadcasters at news events; customized newsgathering at news events; the production of television and radio programming, including corporate video news release production and distribution, and production for government (as with British Satellite News, detailed below); financial news channels; sports channels; the provision of studio facilities; news footage libraries; and even taking over the entire newsgathering operation for large broadcasters, as with the Visnews/Reuters arrangement with Sky News.

By 2000 there seemed to be some acknowledgment within television news agency management and its corporate masters that such diversification stretched these small companies too thinly, damaging their ability to focus on the core goal of fast, first (to paraphrase an Associated Press slogan) television coverage of events that would otherwise be inaccessible to their hundreds of broadcast clients. In Chapter Eight I will return to the turbulent 1990s to review the nearly non-stop television news agency war coverage that comprised so much of their output in that decade. For now, though, I will pick up from the institutional histories of the preceding chapter and describe the most vital developments at each company—and the all-important European News Exchange—during the 1990s and after.

Reuters Television

During the last years of Visnews—the late 1980s through 1992—and in the early days of Reuters Television, the course of the company and its day-to-day news agenda was significantly directed by a few young, aggressive, and financially savvy managers. These people often came from professions outside of TV broadcasting or news agencies directly to their influential positions with the largest TV news agency (and the oldest non-American one).[8] They were widely credited with modernizing management of the company and making newsgathering more efficient and less costly, but they also had a role in fomenting discord in what was either an old company going through a management change, or an entirely new company, depending on one's perspective. This author has been chastised by Reuters for the suggestion of internal unhappiness in the early months of Reuters Television, but the message from extensive observation and interviewing, supported by accounts in the trade press, unequivocally revealed a difficult newsroom culture and the surprising loss of experienced Visnews staff. But as Reuters Television appeared to settle into a more stable period in the late 1990s, it was upstart APTN—with its aggressive absorption of WTN—that began to suffer from some internal turmoil.

In the preceding chapter, we saw the American network NBC invest in Visnews in 1988 to boost its foreign coverage, undergoing ruthless cuts from its new parent, the General Electric Corporation. NBC News president Michael Gartner assured the U.S. public that NBC's international coverage could still be depended upon because Visnews "has hired young, aggressive news people from the BBC and is becoming a stronger and stronger news gathering agency."[9] Despite Gartner's expression of approval, within Visnews and NBC there was the feeling that Visnews was not operating efficiently. Gartner was likely referring in particular to David Kogan, who came to Visnews from the BBC in 1988[10] and quickly rose through the ranks.

By 1989, Kogan was managing editor for Europe, Africa & the Middle East, and had a substantial influence over the full daily intake and output of Visnews.[11] With Reuters Editor-in-Chief Mark Wood, Kogan had a key role in the absorption of Visnews into Reuters Plc and the layoffs of Visnews staffers that resulted (variously reported as about one-third to one-half of Visnews employees). Visnews people were angered and convinced that with no experience in television, Reuters management would destroy their reputation. Public critiques are rare, but the company's best-known employee, the late Kenyan journalist Mohamed Amin, had no qualms about telling me a few years after the takeover that Reuters Television is "being run by print people. They haven't done any good to the company at all." Reuters may have been stung by such criticism, because for a brief period in the mid-1990s it replaced Kogan as senior news manager with David Feingold, CNN's former London bureau chief (Deans, 1996; and interviews).

Tony Donovan, an American, had started as an accountant at NBC from Touche Ross, a consulting firm well connected with major U.S. and British broadcasters. NBC moved him to its London bureau to ensure cost reductions in its international coverage. According to a senior Reuters journalist, Donovan had been the "hatchet-man for NBC"—answering to NBC President Wright, and responsible for the substantial layoffs of news coverage staff.[12] He would then be installed as editorial operations manager at Visnews by NBC in order to bring about the same efficiencies; intriguingly, though, he went on to substantially shape both the modern Reuters Television and its competitor, APTN. Soon after the full Reuters takeover of Visnews, Donovan jumped to the Associated Press to start APTV, following Visnews veteran manager Stephen Claypole (in operational charge of Reuters Television in its early days and the man who originally hired Kogan[13]). But Donovan rejoined Reuters Television a few years later, taking over from Feingold.

Reuters Television continued to benefit from the 1988 alliance of Visnews and News Corporation's Sky news channel. Sky renewed its contract after the Reuters takeover of Visnews, despite concerns by Sky's journalists that they were hamstrung by a contract that did not allow them to sell their news abroad or establish their own newsgathering operation (Preston, 1999). And there was broad concern in the industry that Reuters ties with one major broadcaster could disadvantage the rest, and that this compromised Reuters Television's position as a "neutral" supplier of news. In 1995, the British trade journal *Broadcast* (February 17, 15) ominously editorialized:

> Last November's launch of Associated Press Television left the agency business wondering whether the industry had a space for a third player alongside Reuters and Worldwide Television news. The intervening period seems to have answered that question, but not quite in the way most people anticipated. Reuters Television has taken a step away from its agency roots by climbing into bed with Rupert Murdoch. Although it will still act as a supplier, it is inextricably linked to Murdoch's empire....But where will Reuters TV move from here? Putting TV reporters in its bureaux and working closely with a single organization puts it in the position of a pseudo-broadcaster.

The Associated Press's sales division, then aggressively flogging its new television news service around the world, so enjoyed this editorial that it included it in promotional material sent to lure away Reuters Television's clients. The Sky contract eventually ended with a shakeup within Reuters Television and a series of legal disputes with Sky about what Reuters was, and was not, supposed to be providing (Preston, 1999). Reuters Television also produced a portion of the popular British breakfast-time program GMTV, as well as programs for Russian television and CNBC. It won a large contract from NBC Super Channel in 1995 to produce 35 hours of prime-time public affairs programming. The deal included two complete program series: "Frost's Century," a historical program drawing on Reuters television archives, and "Russia Now," which relied heavily on the Reuters Moscow bureau (Lamerton, 1995).

Another venture was the financial news television channel RFTV, operated by Reuters independently of the Reuters Television London newsroom, but often drawing on Reuters Television resources (part of an industry-wide shift toward financial news services, from which the highly successful Bloomberg agency arose; see Winseck, 1997). During my mid-1990s research, Reuters Television journalists worried about the service interfering with their news delivery. An example of this occurred when the news division of Reuters Television attempted to cut costs by using video of a press conference by then-U.S. President Clinton, which was delivered to London by RFTV staff. When the footage arrived, senior managers in the

television newsroom were dismayed because the RFTV logo had been su
at the bottom of the screen before it was fed to London. Reuters Televi̇
have no choice but to deliver Clinton's comments to its broadcaster clien
the world with the RFTV logo stamped on it.

A "clean feed" (lacking any superimposed graphics or brand identifiers) is a
major reason why broadcasters subscribe to agencies; it enables them to create the
illusion for their audience that they, not an intermediary company, were on the scene
of the news event. A newsroom manager complained, "This cannot happen. We are
suffering because of a small part of the company's business!" A second, "clean" feed,
had to be arranged, while outgoing stories to clients had to be reshaped with a
decreased emphasis on Clinton's comments (to what extent is unclear) in order to
minimize the use of the branded tape. At other times, I observed difficult negotiations between the news staff and RFTV offices for time on Reuters-leased satellite transponders: news occasionally had to beg RFTV to relinquish satellite time
it had booked so that the newsroom could deliver a story to its clients. The compression and digital delivery of video has now eliminated these sorts of problems,
but they illustrate the pressure that the rampant marketization of television news
caused in agency newsrooms in the 1990s.

Associated Press Television

At around the time of the first Gulf War, the management of the Associated Press
in New York saw the enormous appetite for video news and the likelihood that its
principal rival, Reuters, would soon dominate the international television news
agency business (with its imminent takeover of Visnews). Such a foothold might
allow Reuters to dominate multimedia news delivery into the next century. Having
competed successfully with Reuters for 130 years, AP took up the challenge and
began exploring the creation of its own international television news agency. As put
by APTV's founding chief executive, Stephen Claypole, in 1995, "the (video)
agency sector has expanded by about 50% in the last five years, now producing
annual revenues of about $250 million." He added that "The Associated Press
believes that its future in the next century depends on the ability to provide all the
components of multi-media, video especially."

The APTV project was originally dismissed by many in the industry for its
naive expectation that equipping existing AP journalists around the world with
cheap Hi-8 video cameras would create a product that could compete in quality and
quantity with Visnews and WTN. The plan anticipated deploying professional
Betacam cameras to only 25 locations around the world, several "Hub Bureaus" and

various additional regional centers. The early AP plan depicts a graph showing CNN, Visnews, and WTN each with less than 20 international bureaus, and APTV with over 80. The plan neglected to explain to the AP board the substantial difference between a stringer with a Hi-8 camera and a fully equipped and well-staffed television news bureau, with professional newsgathering equipment and permanent communications links. Satellite costs were also downplayed due to the expectation that video compression would be available when the service started, reducing satellite bandwidth requirements and cost. When APTV did start in late 1994, widespread use of compression was still several years away.[14]

APTV backed away from its initial low-cost approach to newsgathering and purchased 179 Betacams for deployment around the world (Rathbun, 1994, 44). AP's total investment in APTV was reported to be approximately $400 million, with the expectation of breaking even after five years.[15] The AP has not reported whether or not that expectation was met. APTV was built by "poaching" a few carefully selected senior people from Reuters Television—Stephen Claypole, Tony Donovan, and later Nigel Hancock[16]—and then allowing those key managers to hire their key subordinates, mostly former colleagues from Reuters, WTN, the BBC, and ITN. An initial staff of about 150 was assembled, mostly in London and Washington (Rathbun, op. cit.). Highly regarded videographers and producers, especially in Bosnia, were also hired away from Reuters and WTN.

There were widespread accounts that some staff from the existing two television news agencies worked to complicate APTV's start. Informants from APTV and other companies tell of "disinformation, [and] misinformation" circulated in regard to APTV and its stories; of Reuters and WTN refusing to pool resources with APTV or "common" (share) stories with APTV on the Eurovision news exchange; and even occasional dirty tricks at satellite feedpoints in the field, affecting AP's ability to transmit a promised story.[17] By the time of AP's purchase of WTN, sources within each agency emphasized that this sort of thing had stopped and played down its severity. It is impossible to independently confirm such accounts. As this comment from WTN's last managing editor indicated in 1995, AP's investment in APTV quickly made it a formidable competitor:

> They've got a long way to go to catch up to the other two, but they have Associated Press behind them so they shouldn't be taken lightly. And they're doing…a little bit better than we thought they were going to do at this stage of the competition. They are a distant third, but they…can be legitimately called a third player as opposed to being completely dismissed. (Lowndes Lipscomb, interview, 1995)

APTV was remarkably successful at signing WTN and Reuters customers, or persuading news customers to drop the other agencies. U.S. networks CBS, NBC, and

CNN all added APTV in 1995, as did the BBC and ITN in Britain, but each of these networks maintained existing contracts with one or both of the other agencies. It was the first time that NBC and CBS had subscribed to a second international newsgathering service.[18] APTV's prospects were also boosted in mid-1995 by deals with Japanese broadcasters Fuji TV, TV Asahi, and others,[19] and an agreement was made with Japanese public broadcaster NHK to distribute NHK pictures.[20] The deals forced WTN and Reuters to strengthen their own resources in Asia or ally themselves with less-powerful broadcasters in the region. They used a no-cost, three-month trial to sell many of their new clients on their service.[21] By October 1995, APTV was claiming to supply 100 of the 450 broadcasters around the world it viewed as potential clients.[22] Now it supplies most of those.

In the early 1990s, the European Broadcasting Union offered WTN and Reuters a fixed period of time daily to put on the Eurovision network any stories they wished to distribute to clients in Europe but that had not been included in a regular Eurovision exchange that day. Both agencies were happy with the current system and had no wish to offer European clients another reason not to subscribe to feeds directly from them, so both rejected the offer. However, Tony Donovan was aware of the offer while a senior manager at Reuters Television, shortly after its takeover of Visnews. One of his first tasks when he took over as head of news at APTV was to remind the EBU of its offer, and to inform it that APTV was interested in using this "agency window" on Eurovision. With typical fair-mindedness, the EBU agreed (Tony Donovan, interview, 1995).

APTV used the 30-minute "window" on Eurovision every afternoon to great advantage, often saving its best stories (either most unique or most visual) to display there for the first time, even if they were produced hours earlier. In this way, European broadcasters, most of the world's wealthiest broadcasters generally, and the other agencies would see (on their newsroom Eurovision monitors) eye-catching stories every day from the new agency on the block. Using the Eurovision window, APTV was not only able to highlight its differences from the other agencies for potential subscribers, but to exaggerate them. WTN and Reuters may have had equally strong stories, but not as many of these were seen throughout the Eurovision network, because each competes for access to the news exchange with the other agencies and because such stories often go on agency satellite feeds only, not Eurovision. Donovan credited the window with increasing acceptance of APTV stories on the Eurovision news exchanges, claiming that originally, APTV stories were rarely accepted because few EBU members were APTV clients (and would not, therefore, have the right to use the APTV stories). As more broadcasters saw APTV in the window and subscribed, Eurovision News Editors were more likely to treat their story offers equally with those of Reuters and WTN and accept them on the exchange. (The exchange is described further in the next chapter.)

APTV pursued other strategies to differentiate itself from its competitors, apparently to good effect. Editorially longer, more in-depth feature stories than were usual for television news agencies were occasionally sent to clients. Stories were also packaged for broadcast to a greater extent than television news agencies traditionally did. Instead of giving a general description of a story and basic background information, APTV scripts transmitted with each story took the form of a newscast script, with words carefully matched to the edited pictures. Smaller broadcasters who chose to could read the AP script with the pictures, avoiding any research or writing of their own. APTN has since moved away from this format, reverting back to the classic television news agency "dope sheet" giving a basic description of a story and list of the pictures and interviews provided. APTV also tried to give more input to regional experts in editorial decision making and coverage decisions.

APTV could also claim to be spending its clients' money strictly on television newsgathering, rather than the many ancillary businesses its competitors were involved in, but of course APTN, with its acquisition of WTN in 1997, inherited many such ventures and started others of its own. At the time of the WTN takeover, APTV was reported to be losing the Associated Press about $30 million each year (Gapper, 1998), but by the early 2000s APTN was earning a profit. Richard Wald of ABC, who sold WTN to AP, said that he understood that AP made back the approximately $50 million it invested in WTN within three years of the purchase, and had gone on to "make a ton of money" selling video to news websites.

The early days of APTV were heady and invigorating as a cadre of inexperienced young journalists, overseen by an unlikely team of experienced managers, took on the Reuters/WTN duopoly; but the years following the WTN takeover were less happy, despite the agency's steady growth and eventual attainment of more clients than Reuters Television had. A series of executives to oversee APTN came and left, with employees craving a long-term strategy and steady leadership. One of those executives left under a cloud amid a no-confidence vote by staff, and he was to be replaced by others—picked by AP's management in New York and sometimes lacking experience in international television news (the same complaint leveled against Reuters by Visnews veterans a decade earlier). The APTN's senior journalists, Nigel Baker and Sandy MacIntyre, who had been instrumental in the growth of the company from its start as APTV, along with a few other managers from the APTV days and some transplanted from WTN, did provide a measure of consistency, but found themselves on the defensive. Baker told a trade magazine in 2000,[23] "Any merger is difficult for any organization to come through. There are bound to be problems and differences of opinion, but in news morale is good. Our latest research shows we're market leaders." My recent observation and discussion with staff at both agencies generally confirms that these days of turmoil are in the past.

The Demise of Worldwide Television News

As APTV matured and started to take major clients from WTN and Reuters, along with many of the key staff from both, people both within the agencies and within the larger TV news industry would often speculate that the industry could not support three agencies for much longer. And broadcasters were overwhelmed by the cost of up to three agencies, and by the deluge of pictures the agencies provided. This was "Picture Flood"—a term perhaps coined, but certainly brought to the fore, by BBC Head of Newsgathering Chris Cramer. In 1995 he complained to an industry conference:

> The sheer volume of news pictures flooding in through our front doors these days is already impossible to handle. 110 feeds a day at the BBC, six or seven hundred a week, and growing all the time. The choice of agencies and other picture sources is already a headache for most of our newsrooms and news managers.
>
> The picture flood, as I call it, is a real tribute to the three international news agencies— WTN, Reuters, and the fledgling APTV—but it can cloud our collective news judgments. It can also drown us in copyright management when we should be spending our time producing the best news programs. One tank rolling down a street looks a little like another. Agencies shouldn't be squabbling over the rights to this basic news material. They need to find the time to work out a sensible way around this tedious issue.[24]

The picture flood was causing concern among veteran broadcasters. There was the perception that the news was now lazily stitched together from the voluminous feeds coming into newsrooms, with little firsthand knowledge of overseas stories. Veteran Channel Four journalist Jon Snow told Preston (1999, 97) in 1991:

> When I started here 15 years ago, you would go out on a story with a camera, and you were dependent on generating all the material yourself, and you'd come back and that would be that. Now, you'll come back and they'll say "Listen, I've seen some material come in that ABC has shot for American consumption. Also WTN have shot something, so could you weave all that into your piece." And again you're diluting what used to be the skill, which was sending one person and one camera to observe one incident and then report to the viewer, and I think what happens now is that as a result you...don't get a distinctive angle on the story in any way. All you get is almost a wallpaper job of all the pictures that are available on this incident.

But despite industry prediction that there was one agency too many, WTN executives stayed optimistic. Terry O'Reilly, WTN's vice president responsible for news coverage and distribution in "the Americas," told a reporter (Prato, 1994):

> WTN will survive because we're a broadcasting company owned and run by broadcasters and we can do what we have done best for 40 years....History teaches us that diver-

sity in journalism leads us to better journalism. If the AP produces the quality of service it promises, then the public will benefit.

As noted in the previous chapter, at both WTN and Visnews/Reuters Television,
news operations were subsidized by various commercial services for broadcasters,
corporations, and (in WTN's case) governments. WTN reportedly made exactly half
of its revenues on television news, and half on ancillary services (Westcott, 1995a).
Journalists at each agency provided a mixed assessment of the role of the commercial services in relation to newsgathering, but my research suggested that news decisions often were influenced by the commercial possibilities of coverage—such as the
chance to rent satellite uplink time to broadcasters[25]—or by the use of their satellite capability to distribute public relations material or other commercial products
to newsrooms around the world. In some cases, the impact of an agency's ancillary
commercial activities on the news product was obvious.

By way of example, at WTN, output producers were permitted to use only fifteen seconds of library footage in their stories. The purpose of the restriction was
to force broadcasters to buy library video from the archive, rather than receiving it
in their regular news feeds. The restriction forced WTN to avoid stories that could
not be illustrated with new video, as might often happen (as with the death of a
newsworthy figure, away from any cameras). As noted earlier, without agency coverage of an international story, broadcasters often don't run the story, or they give
it short shrift: television news agency diversification did have direct impacts on the
global television news agenda.

Television news agencies distribute public relations material, sometimes "unofficially," as when a news event staged by a public relations company, corporation,
or government (see Chapter Six) is distributed as "news," and "officially," when they
simply sell time on their satellite channel into the world's television newsrooms
between their scheduled news feeds for corporations to broadcast product launches,
press conferences, or "video news releases." I observed an example of such an "unof-
ficial" PR event in a two-day sample of agency output from 1995, when APTV distributed a story about George Bush (Sr.) visiting Vietnam. Much of the video of
the story was not from an APTV camera crew, but from the Citibank Corporation,
which had flown the former U.S. president to Vietnam to inaugurate (and legit-
imize) its operations there.[26] However, with the footage smoothly integrated with
the rest of the story (but labeled in the agency's list of shots), a broadcaster would
have little reason to check its source, and would have difficulty re-editing the story
without the Citibank footage.

In a similar case, during my observation at WTN a wave-powered electricity
generating station was launched off the coast of Scotland. The best visuals of the

event had been provided by the company that owned the station; only a small amount of footage of lower quality was available from a Scottish broadcaster who had sent a camera crew. And yet a large part of the story of the station's launch had been major technical problems that had delayed it and threatened the proper set-up of the station. The video news release, unsurprisingly, showed none of this—just long shots of the impressive structure being taken out to sea. And these were the pictures WTN chose to use, neglecting the negative aspects of the story, for which it had illustration that was deemed insufficient. A senior WTN editor told me that they would strive to clearly label stories containing public relations material, but that this did not consistently happen. In these cases the news agency was not profiting from these stories, but simply using the useful images it had been provided (a classic "information subsidy"; Gandy, 1982).

In these ways WTN was undergoing the same process of marketization as was Reuters Television, albeit on a smaller scale, and it was well positioned to start supplying the growing new media market with video. The ABC executive nominally in charge of WTN, Richard Wald, told me that WTN was close to becoming very profitable by the mid-1990s, but profitability was not enough to save WTN in a three-agency environment. WTN became part of the Disney empire in July 1995, when the U.S. government approved the sale of Capital Cities (the owner of WTN's parent, ABC) to Disney. Newsroom staff joked about it, but one old hand wore a Mickey Mouse tee-shirt to the newsroom the next day, as if to remind his younger colleagues not to dismiss the event. As was evidenced in the case of UPITN coming under the control of the South African Information Ministry, journalists tend to believe in their autonomy from outside pressures, regardless of the nature of their employer. This belief is often manifest in the myth of the "firewall," often invoked by journalists in reference to the separation of editorial decisions in the newsroom from corporate priorities. While initially WTN heard little from Disney, a Disney executive was eventually assigned to London to oversee the global activities of Capital Cities-ABC, and while Disney expected its man to become the senior executive of WTN,[27] ABC executive Richard Wald maintains that he remained in ultimate control.

Reuters was more than an interested observer of the demise of WTN. Even within the TV news agencies, there was little recognition in the 1990s that Reuters already owned a piece of WTN. Until WTN's demise, ABC owned the majority of shares in WTN, but ITN, one of the original equity shareholders in WTN, continued to own 10%. And just under 20% of ITN was owned by a consortium including Reuters;[28] but there is no evidence of impact on the brutal competition between the two. In 1992, a *New York Times* writer reported that the two agencies "held merger talks" in 1991 (Waite, 1992). She added that neither the agencies nor their owners would disclose details, and no agency manager I have spoken with has acknowledged that such talks were held (or denied it). In 1995 Eric Braun—who would take over as chief of APTN in the mid-2000s—worked for the U.S. TV consulting company Frank Magid and Associates and was charged with presenting a report on global television news agency usage to the AP Board. He recalls that, by that time,

> APTV was firmly entrenched as number 3, WTN was number 2 but falling, and of course Reuters was the top mark....I recall somebody at that meeting said "what if AP was to buy WTN?.".....[W]e did some analysis and went back and said "it makes perfect sense, it's a good fit. You've got some duplicated bureaus and you've got a few duplicated clients but it actually marries up pretty well." (interview, 2008)

In 1996 an accounting executive installed at ABC by Disney approached Wald with the idea of selling WTN. Wald resisted and argued that "it doesn't make any money now but is just now getting into areas where there is going to be no additional cost and a lot of additional revenue." Wald correctly anticipated that television news agencies were on the verge of making windfall profits selling video to online news companies. But when Disney rejected a plan by ABC to start a rolling news channel in competition with CNN,[29] Wald's boss, Roone Arledge, told him that the value of WTN "is good, but not enormous, and there is no sense fighting with our new owners." Wald first offered to sell WTN to Reuters Editor-in-Chief Mark Wood. Wood was interested, but wanted ABC to remain as partner and part owner.[30] So, in 1998, the first bid for WTN came from Reuters, for somewhere between $40 and $50 million.[31]

In a meeting in London at which Wald expected to seal the deal, Disney's account executive—who had originally insisted on the WTN sale—unexpectedly demanded that Reuters buy 100%. An outraged Wald knew the deal was dead and contacted his fellow Associated Press board member and Associated Press president, Lou Boccardi—the man who had started APTV. Boccardi made an offer to Disney, which it quickly accepted. Agence France-Presse was also reported to be considering the WTN purchase (Gapper, 1998). ABC preferred to deal with its New York City neighbor, the Associated Press, and eventually Disney agreed to a price of about $55 million with the AP. ABC had invested $500,000 in UPITN in the early 1980s, and so saw about a hundred-fold return (for Disney) on its investment.

Within a few weeks, consultants and AP New York staff arrived at WTN's Camden offices to begin laying off staff, dismantling the operation, and shifting clients to APTV's services. Wald recalled that he was disgusted that the AP "sent some guy over to fire everyone." Even an AP staffer involved in shutting down WTN told me that it was handled "appallingly." When Wald complained to

Boccardi, "he saw that they stopped with the hobnail boots," and ABC provided some financial settlements to more-senior WTN staff who were dismissed. (AP veterans, however, report that satisfactory settlements came from AP as well, though many junior staff were left with nothing.) The new name for the combined operation of the two agencies, APTN, was announced in 1998, and a year later the company moved from its cramped central London offices into WTN's former headquarters in the Interchange Building in Camden, north London.

TVNewsWeb

Soon after the new millennium, for just over a year, the television news agency sector was once again a three-player game, as it had been briefly between 1994 and 1998. Pete Henderson was a former BBC and freelance television news cameraman and founder, during the turbulent early 1990s, of a Cyprus news services company called Newsforce. Newsforce had become a presence in covering conflict zones in the 1990s, selling its footage and supporting—primarily through the provision of satellite uplinks—both broadcasters and news agencies in doing so. Henderson was convinced that the potential for Internet delivery of news stories and his personal network of video journalists around the world gave him the necessary tools to take on the established TV news agency duopoly of Reuters and AP, and in 1999 he joined with former WTN editor Ken Heron—one of many left jobless by AP's buy-out—to give it a go.

With $7.5 million in venture capital funding, he started TVNewsWeb as an online broker for news video from around the world. Photographers could offer stories, his website would display them in "shop window" form, and subscribers could purchase the stories online and bring them in broadcast quality into their newsrooms. It was the first time that broadcasters could buy professional video from the world's news hot spots on a per-story basis, and it seemed the ideal recipe for putting the two established agencies out of business.

Television photographers who were not affiliated with the agencies or specific broadcasters found it to be a revelation. One French freelance journalist, Chantal Abouchar, told a newspaper (Lee, 2001), "What I liked was that it was in their interest to get as many sales of your footage as possible so they were working for you, almost as an agent. The agencies, on the other hand, just want to pay the lowest price. They already have their clients [the main broadcasters] and it made no difference to them to give them anything extra." Television stations liked it as well; they might normally get little more than £200 ($290) for giving Reuters or APTN the rights to distribute their pictures (if their agency contract didn't require them to supply the agency without remuneration), but TVNewsWeb gave them the chance to sell their pictures around the world. The company would typically sell stories to broadcasters for about $600 to $750 per story (Henderson, interview, 2001). Soon after TVNewsWeb's launch, ZBC—the Zimbabwean state channel—captured images of Democratic Republic of Congo President Laurent Kabila after he had been assassinated. They made £12,000 ($17,300) through TVNewsWeb.

The promise was that this would be done cheaply via the Internet, but the technology of the time couldn't support Henderson's concept. A proprietary, satellite-based delivery system was developed at far greater cost than originally envisioned. In just over a year of operation as a news agency, TVNewsWeb came to been seen by Reuters Television and APTN as an authentic challenger (despite a fair amount of initial dismissiveness about its prospects). But it never exceeded the market share of either.[32] The company's budget, already struggling under technical challenges, was hurt even more by poaching—at inflated salaries—some key staff from Reuters Television and APTN, as was very much the tradition in the television industry. In May 2001, it signed a prestigious deal with the BBC to sell BBC stories, but Henderson and Heron's anonymous investors pulled out weeks later, unhappy with the returns they were seeing, despite the obvious impact and phenomenal growth their investment was seeing.

Eurovision

It would be useful to conclude this two-chapter history of the wholesale television news sector with an overview of the important cooperative exchange of television news pictures between the large and influential publicly funded broadcasters of Europe: the Eurovision News Exchange. In 1967, the commercial newsfilm agencies Visnews and UPITN began contributing news stories to the Eurovision exchange, a frequent trading process of television news stories among the big public broadcasting companies of Europe, conducted by cable and satellite links.[33] By 1976, Visnews contributed 27% of all Eurovision items and was "the largest single contributor."[34] The amount of agency contribution to Eurovision steadily increased each year, and the agencies continue to make up the bulk of Eurovision news items. A 1987 study noted that

> about 50% of the items on the EVN actually come from the three newsfilm agencies (Visnews, Worldwide Television News [WTN] and CBS Newsfilm), most of them from areas outside Europe, either shot by agency staffers or stringers or bought from local broadcasters. (Lansipuro, 1987)

Hjarvard (1995a) found that 66.5% of Eurovision items came from WTN and Visnews during a 1.5-month survey period in 1990, and Eurovision figures for 1994 show 48.3% of all items were from agencies (Cohen et al., 1996). My own analysis demonstrated how this number skyrockets during an international crisis: during a constructed week in 1995, during the Bosnian civil war, the major morning satellite feed of Eurovision, EVNO, consisted of 84% news agency items (not untypical that year). In recent years, European broadcasters have become far more dependent on agencies and less so on the EBU for provision of their news video, since new and less costly satellite delivery options have made the agency feeds more accessible.

The Eurovision News Exchange does some international newsgathering of its own. For example, the EBU operates U.S. bureaus that not only pull material from U.S. broadcasters, but contract local newsgathering crews. And the EBU dispatches satellite uplinks and producers to major news stories around the world, if there is sufficient demand from members.[35] They were a major presence, for example, in Haiti following the 2010 earthquake (European Broadcasting Union, 2010). Agencies may use Eurovision video from EBU member stations, but must reimburse European broadcasters through the EBU for any they distribute to their clients. A WTN document explained that this costs an average of $300 per story, and it discouraged producers from using such material.

During the 1980s and 1990s, the international television news agencies competed with each other and structured their coverage to have their stories selected by EBU news editors for inclusion in regular Eurovision news exchanges. In this way, European broadcasters (or, rather, the mass of European citizens who involuntarily fund those broadcasters) were paying the cost of transmitting the agency's story from the field, even though the agency would go on to profit from the news video by redistributing it in its own unilateral feeds to clients. Agency clients who were EBU members could choose to pay the agencies a lower subscription fee, entitling them to use any agency material that appeared on a Eurovision exchange, but not entitling them to receive the more comprehensive scheduled news feeds directly from the agency. Thus, Eurovision served the agency as a two-way delivery system: moving video from its own crews in the field to its London headquarters, and moving its stories to its European clients either directly from the field or from London headquarters.

The decision of what stories—either from EBU member broadcasters or from agencies—appear on each exchange is that of the Eurovision news editor (formerly called "news coordinator"). This person was a senior journalist from a member broadcaster, serving on the exchange for a fixed period before being replaced by another European broadcaster, based on a rotation published by Eurovision in advance.[36] An editor in each international television news agency monitors a "four-wire" or "squawk-box" communications system throughout the day, offering agency stories to the EVN news editor and determining European broadcasters' interests.[37] It was apparent that many Eurovision member journalists have always sought to encourage such inter-agency competition in the belief that it will get the best footage owned by the agencies into the Eurovision exchange. Wallis and Baran (1990, 56) pointed to the mixed blessing of the system:

> This extraordinary self-regulating system assures that everyone is happy, provides interesting opportunities for Visnews and WTN to play poker at the Eurovision table, and adds to the general streamlining and homogenizing effects readily evident when comparing...different television news programmes.

The number of stories each agency put on Eurovision each day was a matter of pride and professional rivalry between the two (and, in the 1990s, three) agencies. Competition would drive much of the daily routine both in the London newsrooms and in the field. An internal email between editors in one television news agency one morning read: "We're kicking Reuters' butts today aren't we?" That editor chuckled and typed back "yup." An EVN editor, referring to the day's participation in the Eurovision exchange, made a comment typical of each agency's afternoon meeting: "I think we competed pretty well." Stories run by other agencies on Eurovision were called "losses" by management, and the EVN editors were expected to explain why their company failed to get the story first. The competitive nature of the agency role in the Eurovision news exchange was put bluntly by one WTN manager:

> A lot of people get a bit overly enthusiastic about what we do, but it's a commodity isn't it? Every morning on Eurovision you're flogging a commodity. Some people are in the City of London flogging cocoa beans saying "mine is bigger than yours"; we're flogging news footage saying "mine is more exciting than yours."

APTV Chief Executive Stephen Claypole (1995) wrote of one unidentified commentator who once said "that if television was the global village, then the agency sector was a gang-fight in a global alleyway." The importance of Eurovision to the news agencies has declined markedly over the past decade. Both agencies still have a dedicated editor providing stories to Eurovision. But with low-cost digital video delivery options into the London newsroom and from the newsroom to clients, there is little need now to use EBU facilities to uplink agency stories from the field (as was so often the case with stories from the Yugoslav civil war). And within both agencies the culture of "beating" the other on Eurovision lives on only in the memories of veteran staffers—the current generation of newsroom staff is unaware of the raucous celebrations that once ensued in the newsroom in the event of a Eurovision "victory." But news managers still do boast when a story of theirs is popular on

Eurovision, and still do keep an eye on what European broadcasters are interested in, and in what the competition is doing, by using the exchange.

Notes

1. At the end of 1995, the Reuters contract with the BBC ended, and ABC subsidiary WTN became the sole agency allowed to distribute BBC material.
2. Baker (1994). ITN would subscribe again to WTN, though, a few years after this re-alignment. One senior WTN journalist told me the practical effects of the ABC/BBC alliance were, in fact, minimal, given the difference in newsgathering deadlines, corporate cultures, and pressure to have exclusives. For example, ABC would not want the BBC breaking a big U.S. story of theirs before they could do so on their main evening news bulletin. But over a decade later (interviews, 2008) a BBC executive insisted to me that the two companies are "best friends" and collaborate extensively.
3. From a news agency editorial meeting, 1995.
4. See Weiner (1992) for a detailed account of CNN's coverage from Iraq.
5. Weiner (1992), and interviews.
6. Based on my ethnographic research in Harare, Zimbabwe, in 1990. Mohamed Amin of Visnews/Reuters (in Tetley, 1988) reports his frequent competition for stories with BBC or NBC crews, despite the close alliance and picture flow between Visnews and those broadcasters.
7. *Broadcast*, July 21, 1995, 6.
8. The new Reuters managers were dubbed the "Young Turks" by many in the industry, and two in particular fit this profile. Each joined Visnews in the late 1980s and moved quickly up the management ladder of Reuters Television after the takeover. They are David Kogan, appointed at 37 years old as the new managing director of Reuters Television (*Financial Times*, March 7, 1995), and Ralph Nicholson, even younger than Kogan and managing editor during the period of my research.
9. Quoted in Goldman (1985).
10. There is some disagreement among sources as to exactly when Kogan came to Visnews, but this appears to be the most reliable date.
11. I interviewed Kogan in this capacity in December 1989.
12. Various interview sources and interview with Tony Donovan, APTV (1995).
13. Busfield (1995c).
14. I am grateful to APTV in London for providing me with the original proprietary plan for APTV, created in 1992 and/or 1993 by the new Associated Press Broadcast Services division in Washington. Associated Press Internal Document: *AP Television International Service*.
15. See, for example, Busfield (1994b).
16. Hancock spent most of his career with ITN before moving to Reuters Television. He left Reuters in early 1994 to briefly head up a UPI attempt to re-enter the international television news agency business. With that effort doomed in the face of AP's major investment in television, Hancock joined his former colleagues from Reuters in the senior manage-

ment of APTV. *Broadcast*, April 1, 1994; May 13, 1994; and interviews. Claypole's background is detailed in Busfield (1995c).

17. Such dirty tricks have a long history in the television news world; former Visnews bureau chief and NBC correspondent Martin Fletcher provides examples from his Visnews days (Fletcher, 2008). The most common seemed to be simply letting the air out of the tires of a competitor photographer on the way to a story, or to a satellite feed point to transmit a story. A former senior WTN editor told me: "everybody knew three agencies was going to be too much: APTV's arrival threatened the livelihoods of RTV and WTN people...."

18. APTV Signs Up Four New Clients, *UK Press Gazette*, October 16, 1995, 13; *Broadcast*, January 27, 1995, 2; and other sources.

19. APTV Signs Japan Deals, *Broadcast*, June 30, 1995, 5.

20. From a WTN editorial meeting. This arrangement exemplified the limitations of ownership ties and alliances: ABC had a long-term cooperative agreement with NHK that included cooperation in newsgathering, yet NHK's deal with APTV was a blow to ABC's main international news supplier and subsidiary, WTN (Layne, 1994).

21. APTV Lands Three Year Deal With CBC, *Broadcast*, October 20, 1995, 2; Fuller (1995, 65); and interviews.

22. APTV Signs..., op. cit.

23. APTV founding Managing Director Stephen Claypole left the agency around the time of the WTN takeover. APTN chief executive Derek Taylor resigned in May 2000 following a staff no-confidence vote. Ian Ritchie, who has spent most of his career with regional broadcasters in the U.K., followed until 2003 when he moved to another role in Associated Press. Several others have filled the senior role at APTN since.

24. Chris Cramer, Address to the Montreux International Television Symposium, June 13, 1995, provided by the BBC.

25. The process is straightforward: if enough broadcasters promise to hire an agency's crews, cameras, editing equipment, and satellite uplinks at a news event, the commercial services division will cover the cost of putting those resources in place with the expectation of considerable profit. The news division, then, has limited use of those resources to tape and transmit to London the occasional story for agency clients.

26. APTV's shot list, provided to clients, identifies the source as Citibank.

27. Disney press release.

28. See Preston (1999) for analysis of the variety of conflicts of interest that this situation created.

29. According to Wald, Disney executives in 1996 "thought there was only room for one 24 hour [news] channel."

30. Wald recalls that Reuters liked both the idea of keeping AP away from WTN, and the idea of taking over WTN's newsgathering infrastructure and its London facilities.

31. Gapper (1998) reports that $50 million was offered by Reuters, but Wald of ABC, who was conducting the negotiations, told me the sale to AP was for about $45 million, in addition to perhaps $10 million worth of services, including several years of APTN feeds. He says the Reuters offer was for less, but Reuters wanted some continued investment from ABC.

32. Interviews by the author with Henderson and Heron (weeks after their London offices

closed in 2001); Lee (2001). http://www.guardian.co.uk/technology/2001/jul/09/internet-news.mondaymediasection.

33. Visnews chronology in an advertisement from *EBU Review*, 1978.

34. Ibid.

35. EBU North American operations are detailed in Naets (1987); and interviews.

36. One senior WTN duty editor complained that many Eurovision news editors are not journalists at all, but are from a broadcaster's international relations department, and thus have inadequate news judgment. He suggests stations are unwilling to "squander" their best journalists, requiring them to sit by the EVN circuit all day for days. However, it was rare that any agency intake editor had a favorable opinion of a Eurovision news editor. In the late 1990s, EVN began a simpler system of control from its Geneva headquarters, but still based on the judgment of members.

37. For a full explanation of this process, see Cohen et al. (1996, 13–15) and Hjarvard (1993, 1995a).

5

The Newsgatherers

W e turn from the history of the television news agencies to an examination of how they go about creating the source images of global television news. The wholesale news duopoly of APTN and Reuters Television must continuously provide a flow of images to allow broadcasters to create the illusion of reporting on the world, and this pressure has intensified with the rapid growth of the rolling (24-hour) news channels and the Internet and mobile service news providers, all of which depend so heavily on news agency images. We begin with the news production processes at both leading television news agencies and WTN (which ceased operation in 1997). These reveal consistencies with the very beginnings of the business, described in Chapter Three, but also many dramatic re-inventions of the process that owe much to the Internet, the explosion of cheap digital storage, and industrial inclinations toward "convergence," in the newsroom and "the field."[1] We start, in this chapter, with an overview of how "the news" is captured by the widespread newsgathering personnel of the television news agencies, before moving in the next chapter to the London newsrooms that are at the core of their work.

Both television news agencies have several dozen large bureaus around the world and many smaller ones, giving them at least a semi-permanent presence in hundreds of places around the world. The list below inventories the current bureaus of one of the two agencies (APTN);[2] a current list for Reuters Television was not available, but comparison with Reuters Television lists obtained during earlier research suggests a similar geographic distribution. The following are those presented by APTN as key ones (and my observation confirms that these contribute frequently to their news product):

Afghanistan, Kabul	Guatemala, Guatemala City	Peru, Lima
Argentina, Buenos Aires	Honduras, Tegucigalpa	Philippines, Manila
Australia, Sydney	Hong Kong, Hong Kong	Romania, Bucharest
Belgium, Brussels	India, New Delhi	Russia, Moscow
Bolivia, La Paz	Indonesia, Jakarta	Serbia, Belgrade
Bosnia and Herzegovina,	Iran, Tehran	South Africa, Johannesburg
Sarajevo	Iraq, Baghdad	South Korea, Seoul
Brazil, Rio de Janeiro	Israel, Jerusalem	Spain, Madrid
Bulgaria, Sofia	Israel, Tel Aviv	Syria, Damascus
Chile, Santiago	Japan, Tokyo	Taiwan, Taipei
China, Shanghai	Jordan, Amman	Thailand, Bangkok
China, Beijing	Kenya, Nairobi	Turkey, Istanbul
Colombia, Bogota	Kosovo, Pristina	United Kingdom, London
Costa Rica, San Jose	Lebanon, Beirut	United States of America, New
Cuba, Havana	Malaysia, Kuala Lumpur	York
Czech Republic, Prague	Mexico, Mexico City	United States of America,
Egypt, Cairo	Nicaragua, Managua	Washington D.C.
El Salvador, San Salvador	Northern Ireland, Belfast	United States of America, Los
France, Paris	Pakistan, Islamabad	Angeles
Germany, Berlin	Palestinian Authority,	Venezuela, Caracas
Germany, Frankfurt	Ramallah	Vietnam, Hanoi
Greece, Athens	Palestinian Authority, Gaza	

Television news agency bureaus have a variety of origins. Many have been created by the television news agencies in recent decades to reflect current news priorities; Shanghai, for example, would not have been a news hub thirty years ago, but it is now. Others exist in cities where there is currently war, or has recently been war. Belgrade, for example, remains important to the agencies despite the current absence of conflict in the Balkans. Some key bureaus exist because they have been an important office of the parent wire service, and this made a convenient home for the sister television news agency (and the two have increasingly co-located even when they previously had separate presences in a city, in order to facilitate cooperation between the two arms of each agency).

Boyd-Barrett (1980, 153) linked the location of news agency bureaus to these principal factors: *historical* ones, based on the legacy of imperial interests and the presence of (19th-century) cable links; *logistical* factors, based on the utility of an office as a base to cover a broader region (which, in turn, depends on the proximity of an international airport with frequent regional links and on communications infrastructure such as broadband, high-capacity data lines, and the legality and availability of satellite dishes); *political* factors, involving the presence or absence of restrictions on travel and the practice of journalism; *commercial* factors revolving around the local market for agency news; and *temporary* factors, such as the presence of bureaus in "hot spots" like Kabul, where a current conflict transforms the area into an international story.

Some key bureaus suggest strategic trade-offs of some of these factors against others, as with the large and important presence in Beijing of both agencies. Despite political restrictions that may limit what a news agency can do and say, the news value of the Chinese capital, its utility as a base for Chinese coverage, the exploding Chinese media market, and the emergence of Beijing as a global financial center have all been deemed more important. A WTN journalist admitted to me that the agencies are unlikely to challenge political restrictions on their work in China or provoke the government there, since their presence is so vital to their business:

> [I]f we go out and make some fancy feature about repression in Chinese jails and get slung out, that's our business. All the broadcasters employ us in parts of the world like Beijing and Baghdad because they know that they'll still get the pictures even after they've been slung out—you have to be fairly cozy. With a broadcaster you can afford to be sensationalist to boost your ratings even if you're going to take a hit by having that particular office closed down for six months. What your business is, is boosting ratings. Ours isn't boosting ratings. Ours is keeping our clients happy, and that isn't going to happen if you get slung out.

For television news agencies it is especially vital that bureaus that have few other bureaus close by be capable of serving as "firebases" (television news parlance for a location from which newsgathering crews can be quickly dispatched to cover stories throughout a wider region). Mohammed Amin, for example, working for Visnews essentially as a stringer rather than a bureau, covered nearly the entire African continent for them from his Nairobi office. Others have linked bureau locations even more directly to the specific financial and military interests of the United States, and (to a far lesser degree), other international powers. Schiff (1996, 9) concluded that "The distribution of the AP press corps is highly correlated with both [U.S. government] diplomatic staff allocation and total [U.S.] corporate investments." Since the 1960s, the main business of Reuters has been the reporting of financial news and the processing of stock trades, and so news bureaus have piggybacked onto the considerable infrastructure and investment by the company in major global financial centers, such as London, Frankfurt, New York, Bangkok, and Tokyo.

Interestingly, some important, but smaller, news agency bureaus now exist despite a lack of frequent international news, but more as strategic investments by news agencies so as to be in the right place at the right time because globally important stories are considered likely. The Associated Press went to great lengths to establish small bureaus in the capitals of two small and very poor countries: the kind of countries typically ignored by the international media. But both of these are consistently newsworthy for being on the receiving end of American government hostility, making them interesting to American journalists in particular. One of these bureaus was in Havana, established in 1998, and the other was set up by APTN in Pyongyang, North Korea, in 2006. Nigel Baker of APTN, with an APTN producer from their Beijing bureau, scored an industry coup in negotiating permission for an APTN Pyongyang bureau, to be run in collaboration with the state broadcaster.[3]

The bureau has provided the only images of events that have received international attention, such as the surprise visit in 2009 by former U.S. President Clinton to secure the release of two American journalists imprisoned there. The North Korean government originally permitted a one-year trial, but it was sufficiently pleased with the APTN presence to extend the permission for additional years. But the bureau's value for AP has stretched beyond the utility of having exclusive rights to video from a secretive, yet newsworthy, location. The New York Philharmonic orchestra went to Pyongyang in 2008 in a rare cultural exchange, and AP was the exclusive source for the story for American broadcasters. That led to numerous requests from other broadcasters around the world to cover their own links with the reclusive country.

Agency bureau chiefs (who are also often producers or videographers) strive to obtain television pictures of interest to London news editors by whatever means possible. Ideally, this means having a staff photographer at the scene, but when this is impossible, or the television news agency has been denied access to the scene, the bureau chief must try to obtain pictures through other means. This may involve hiring a freelance crew, giving a small and cheap camera to someone close to the action, such as a soldier (a practice that was reported to have occurred frequently during the Yugoslav civil wars[4]), or buying pictures shot by a local broadcaster or a "citizen-journalist." Such exceptional costs must normally be approved by the duty editor in London, who will usually do so in consultation with more senior managers, but it is apparent that occasionally field staff obtain pictures on their own initiative when circumstances make consultation with London impossible.[5]

The key to television news agency newsgathering (and that of broadcasters) is access to places where news is happening, and that often involves bribes (though few agency staff would publicly characterize such expenses in this way). Former Visnews editor Andrew Ailes told me that this rarely meant more than a few packs of cigarettes in the 1960s and 1970s, but it was common during the 1990s for producers leaving London for developing stories to be furnished with thousands of U.S. dollars to use at their discretion (but always with a full accounting to their editors). If not used to secure access to an otherwise inaccessible place, such funds might be spent on securing the balcony of some local's apartment in order to get the ideal camera position for a story.

Videographers, field producers, and other bureau staff are expected to keep London, and local colleagues, informed of their movements, particularly in dangerous areas. They have considerable motivation to do so, despite the rush of deadline pressures. Not only does it reassure London that they are always on the move earning their keep, but it ensures that London can react quickly if they do not report in when expected. Such intervention from London may not save an agency staffer from prolonged captivity, as with John McCarthy (of WTN) in Beirut, or Tony Liddle (WTN) and Gavin Johnstone-Robinson (Visnews)[6] in Zimbabwe, but urgent inquiries from the headquarters of an international news agency, and possibly the British government, may save a journalist from an even worse fate than incarceration.

In addition to each bureau, which typically has a bureau chief who is senior producer, and one or more camera crews, each company pays dozens of stringers in smaller cities around the world. Some, like those in Kenya or Zimbabwe, might produce stories for the agencies a few times a month. Others, like the one-time Visnews stringer in Lusaka, Zambia,[7] might go years without an agency story. But the agencies may pay retaining fees to keep the most remote stringers on duty should they ever be needed, although it appears there are now far fewer such occasional staff on the news agencies' payrolls than was the case a few decades ago. Editors in London have the contact details of stringers, allies, or potential freelancers in countries and cities around the globe, and at the suggestion of a potential story (out of range of a staff photographer), they will get on the telephone to the one with the best prospects of obtaining images for them (or will ask the nearest bureau chief to do so).

But sending a videographer to the scene of a story isn't enough. Provision also needs to be made to get the video to London as soon as it is shot, and so the company database also provides details of potential satellite uplinks or other transmission means. But for locations without broadband connections, or satellite uplinks an agency can hire, or frequent flights to a regional center from which a story can be transmitted, duty editors will have to consider if the images are valuable enough to come to London with a considerable delay. They will often decide they are not, and accept the reputational damage of not covering a story, as opposed to covering it late. I recently observed one television news agency come across its competition's coverage of a story from Kigali, Rwanda, find a videographer of its own to obtain pictures, and then abandon the story for lack of an easy transmission option.

Often, a stringer or bureau chief has to work to "sell" a story to the duty editor in the agency newsroom, especially on an otherwise busy news day; or to sell an idea for a future story to the editor overseeing their region, or the London planning editor, charged with assembling the "diaries" of upcoming stories. My observation and interviews suggested that television news agency workers in the field rarely have the opportunity to develop and discover new stories, that is, to do *entrepreneurial journalism*. An agency editor complained to me that he felt far too much coverage was "reactive and not pro-active." Many agency workers in London told me that their bureaus rarely discover and research stories on their own, since the pressure to cover the news of their area (as determined in London), and deliver it quickly to London, is all consuming. But APTN chief Nigel Baker (2004, 70) recounts a notable exception, when an APTN editor speculated that Afghans caught between Taliban troops and invading American forces in September 2001 might be trapped in remote areas without food. A camera crew that was dispatched to the Afghan mountains found local people surviving only by eating grass, and the story became a prominent one.

Agency bureau chiefs are not only responsible for coverage of their region, but are also expected to be the primary marketing and customer service liaison between agency headquarters and broadcasters in their area—and this might be a difficult balance when the demands of one broadcaster have to be weighed against the needs of 400 other agency clients worldwide. In large regional bureaus like New York and Hong Kong, the emphasis is on making sure clients in the region are happy, and signing up new ones. In many smaller bureaus, like Kabul or Jerusalem, the focus is entirely upon daily news delivery and beating the competition. One agency journalist explained how a Frankfurt bureau chief fulfilled this role:

> [S]he had a very close relationship with German broadcasters and knew exactly what they wanted...and could say [to the London newsroom] "look, the edits are too short for the Germans and Europeans, they want longer cuts and much looser cuts as well," so she had a very clear idea. . . .

Since at least the 1970s, and to some extent from their inception in the 1950s, the international television news agencies have danced around the problem of whether they wish to offer many carefully tailored regional news services or a single, global news service. Through that history, they have sought a compromise position between those two poles. They are forever plagued with the accusation that from their flood of images each broadcaster can only pick out a tiny selection of stories that are relevant and interesting to their local audience, unless, of course, broadcasters give in completely to the idea of a single, homogenous, and global conception of news (discussed in Chapter Two). Broadcasters everywhere have always asked the agencies to send more news from their respective regions of the globe. The big American networks NBC, and then ABC, bought heavily into the television news agencies because they were dissatisfied with asking for coverage that better suited them, and preferred to control the agenda directly; and BCINA, the predecessor of Reuters Television, was created by the BBC specifically to counter the early American influence on syndicated television news pictures.

In recent decades, both contemporary agencies have debated the value of decentralizing their news production operations. This could allow for greater efficiency as news stories only of interest to East Asia, for example, stay in East Asia, and those only of interest in the Americas stay there. It would diffuse the criticism that both are Anglo-American services with Anglo-American agendas, and it would allow editors with close ties to broadcasters in their region to control the flow of news to that region. In 1989, prior to its absorption of Visnews, Reuters reorganized into geographic areas based upon time zones: Reuters Asia, Reuters America, and Reuters Europe–Middle East–Africa (Taylor, 1991). Individual Reuters Television regions, revolving around bureaus, are (in theory) financially independent from the London newsroom. This structure influences the management of global television and text news services, and there seemed to be something of a power struggle underway between centralized global control from London and the regional headquarters during my 1990s research. In the 1990s Reuters experimented with far greater decentralization of its international television operations but seemed to refrain from surrendering the overall control held by the London newsroom.

Now both agencies appear to have found a compromise by (generally) managing European, Middle Eastern, and African news coverage from London as well as maintaining an overview of global news operations from there; managing most news coverage for Asia and Oceania from a large Asian bureau; and managing news coverage for the Americas from New York or Washington. Editors in London speak to senior editors in the other regions during the day, and the main news feeds for each region are produced in each region, instead of all in London, as had been the case previously.

Historically, the television news agency day moves around the world to coincide with the major evening news bulletins of broadcasters around the world. Thus a main East Asian news feed is delivered in the East Asian afternoon, the main European news feed during Europe's afternoon, and the main one for the Americas in their afternoon, which is London's evening. So when operations were more centralized in London, staff would work through a 24-hour cycle in London producing feeds for the world. Now a minimal night staff stays on in London to monitor events and keep in contact with the other regional hubs, but the key feeds for broadcasters in other parts of the world are produced in those parts of the world. But live, rolling news and the non-stop provision of news to online and mobile services has also diminished the importance of theses deadlines.

If the *brain* of the television news agencies is made up of the central newsrooms in London (and I've met agency field staff who would debate that), then the *heart* is made up of the hundreds of television *photographers* who shoot images for them every week (along with the *producers*, who arrange the images, gather information, work with clients at the scene of stories, and ensure that everything gets to London on time and on budget). The rest of the system could not exist without the flow of images the photographers and producers provide—often at great personal risk.

Although most agency video shooting (or videography) is routine—even mundane—it is the photographers more than any other category of agency staff who are killed or maimed with distressing frequency. (More about this in Chapter Seven.) Some photographers (also often called "camera operators") will contribute frequently to their agencies' international distribution of pictures, while others might be called on only a few times a year, if even that. This book focuses more on the brain of these organizations and so provides too little emphasis on the vital work of agency photographers; indeed, there is little research and few modern accounts of such work to build such an understanding. But there are important exceptions, including Fletcher (2008); Colart and Venter (2004); Venter (2005); Bowden (1987); Tetley (1988); and Loyn (2005). I've recently encountered two research students interviewing agency photographers from conflict zones, including Mitra, cited below.

News agency staff photographers are usually people hired from local broadcasters in the countries, or regions, they are normally assigned to cover (though the best ones go on to cover the globe). There are many reasons for this. Cynics might argue that it allows the news agencies to pay lower salaries to locally hired photographers, rather then the going rate for television photographers based in the U.K., Europe, or North America; or that the cost of providing insurance to such photographers and other locally hired staff—if offered at all—might be lower (for detail, see Venter, 2005). In some cases, governments don't allow access to foreign journalists, and so hiring local staff is the only means of covering the story. Those factors may be influential, but probably not as much as the importance of local knowledge, relevant language skills, and ethnicity. In many violent situations the fact that a television photographer looks "local" may save his or her life; but in some cases, conversely, the superficial appearance of being from the international, as opposed to the local, media (that is, an expensive camera and white skin) might be what saves the photographer. (A local soldier with little regard for local lives might think twice about the trouble he could face for killing a foreigner.)

This raises the intriguing question of whether local understandings of events and local loyalties ever conflict with the established (globally oriented and London originated) story frames of the international news agencies. In journalism scholarship, framing "involves selection and salience. To frame is to select some aspects of a perceived reality and make them more salient…in such a way as to promote a particular…definition [or] causal interpretation" (Entman, 1993, 52; quoted in Pan, 2008), and I explore it further in the television news agency context in Paterson (2001). The research project described in chapter seven demonstrated how local "fixers" hired by international media might seek to steer the news coverage in ways they feel are more fair or relevant. An Indian photographer for one of the television news agencies, recently returned from Afghanistan, told Mitra (2010, 53):

> I like to make sure that I get that kind of pictures which would be interesting to a particular nation or region which has more clients—which would be a Western country in my case—and I will make sure that I have those pictures and that they are used since we are an agency. I think that is what any cameraperson or photographer would do. But I would definitely try to cater to the country or region with the high number of clients—major European countries are big clients. I will make sure that if I see a person from that country in the field, I would try to get their reaction and would offer it to my bosses in London saying this is what I have. Mostly when I am doing a vox pop [short interview] or interview, I try to get the interview in the local language catering to those countries.

Much more is said about the practical work of gathering news for the international television news agencies in Chapters Seven and Eight, but now we turn to how the news they gather is processed in London and how the overall operations of the television news agencies are planned and managed.

Notes

1. Many of the observations of news work reported in this chapter and the next are from my research with the now-defunct Worldwide Television News. These examples illustrate general processes that are still relevant within Reuters Television and Associated Press Television News, without the need for contemporary details that could be commercially sensitive for either organization.
2. As of November 2010, via APTN website: aptn.com.
3. Interviews, and Associated Press, 2006.
4. The ethical implications are substantial and troubling, for, if true, it suggests the possibility of deadly battles staged for international television. But to the best of my knowledge, neither combatants nor Western media people who may have knowledge of such practices have provided details, so this story remains unverifiable. This issue is discussed further in

Chapter Eight.

5. The fascinating story of how an APTV producer bought pictures of the sinking of the liner Achille Lauro off Somalia in 1994 from a passenger on the ship is recounted in Colart and Venter (2004, 221–225). Maass (2001) quotes Reuters Television News Editor Rodney Pinder, as reporting, "decisions relating to purchasing footage from freelancers are made 'eight times out of ten' by the Reuters team on the ground; superiors in London are contacted only if the price is unusually high or if the authenticity of the film is questioned."

6. McCarthy's five-year incarceration in Lebanon was the longest of any international television news agency staffer (McCarthy and Morrell, 1994); the Zimbabwe cases involved a few weeks of incarceration by a government and are not uncommon; these cases are detailed in Paterson (1992).

7. This was as of 1990.

6

The Television News Factories

The television news agency newsroom is an efficient information factory, taking in news in many forms (moving and still pictures, sounds, textual reports), processing and packaging it, and shipping it out, 24 hours each day, every day of the year. That it is also a manufacturing plant for "reality" (the reality that global television viewers perceive) rarely, if ever, enters the minds of the workers at this factory, concerned as they are only with the speedy processing of what they know as "news."

In 2005, Reuters Television moved from the ITN Building on Greys Inn Road in central London to the opulent new Reuters building in the heart of London's Canary Wharf financial area. APTN—and before it, WTN—chose an uncommon and eye-catching location for its headquarters, a refurbished 19th-century, red-brick warehouse alongside Camden Lock in north London; canal boats once supplied England with gin from that very building (an analogy to the stupefying power of television news would be too easy at this point).

AP took on the lease of the Interchange Building with the WTN takeover, and decided as it planned its converged London newsroom to stay on in the building and sign a new lease with the landlord, British Waterways. The Interchange Building is regarded as such a vital part of the U.K.'s industrial history that the country's historical preservation agency—British Heritage—had to approve every detail of AP's renovation of the building. AP sublets much of the second floor of the Interchange Building to (as of 2008) fourteen international broadcasters including China Central Television and Brazil's TV Globo.

Intake and Output

In each television news agency newsroom labor is broadly divided between two separate but highly interactive and complimentary areas: that of intake, and that of output. The division is not dissimilar to that of any news operation, for someone must always ensure that information is brought in, while someone else is charged with shaping that information into the news product. At television news agencies the division is crucial, for the product they market is not so much their skill in news processing and storytelling, but their ability to bring in stories others cannot, and to "turn around" those stories quickly—even instantly—for use by the world's broadcasters.

A portion of newsroom activity every day centers on the Eurovision News Exchange, and the decision about which stories to put on it and which to take off it for international distribution. This process and aspects of its evolution were described in Chapter Four. And while most of this chapter focuses on how the television news agencies plan and manage their own daily news coverage, it is vital to recall that a very large portion of what they bring into their newsroom for their client broadcasters are "up-picks": the television coverage of broadcasters from around the world. Some may be from clients, some not. This recycling of television content is discussed a bit more in Chapter One, but here I'll describe the overall editorial process within the television news agencies' central newsrooms.

While nominally responsible for output as well as intake, duty editors (or editors of the day—EoDs) usually leave output decisions—what story goes on what feed, and how those stories are told—to others[1] and focus almost exclusively on determining what is to be covered, and then bringing in that coverage. The structure requires a separation between information (and picture) *gathering* and *storytelling*, which doesn't work terribly well in practice. This is overcome in part by constant communications in the newsroom between input and output. But at busy times that communication can break down, with a variety of input and output staff simultaneously trying to contact the same few agency staff at the scene of a news event, only to realize hours later they were all seeking the same information. This may be attributable to the confusion inherent in any busy workplace, but might also indicate that a system like this—designed for speed as it is—may often work against the basic instincts of journalists. The system expects those charged with output (the storytelling element) to quickly assemble the agency's product from the ingredients provided by the input desk, but they are often unwilling or unable to do so and chase the details they need themselves.

Typically in the television news agencies the duty editor is not part of management (as the company designates its supervisory staff) but is considered the highest authority in the absence of management, and a voice of management in the newsroom. A duty editor is also considered the supreme journalist, the person most expected to be able to move beyond routine coverage decisions into the realm of the "sixth sense," the innate ability to smell a story before it develops and ensure that the company gets it. In my twenty years of occasional observation and interviewing, most EoDs I've met came from newsgathering roles with ITN or the BBC, or, only occasionally, other broadcasters.

The foremost task of a duty editor is deciding which news of the day is worth covering, and determining how the coverage will be brought in. Part of this process involves deciding which clients are worth extra effort. For example, after delivering a crucial Bosnia story, a duty editor asked an assistant, "Will you just check that CBS [the American network] are happy...got all they need?" And, as a duty editor of another agency explained in regard to a particular story at the time of our interview, they may be under considerable pressure from major clients to provide coverage from a location, even when they feel there is nothing happening there:

> I don't think it really is a story to be honest, but there is intense client interest, especially across the Atlantic. I have to persuade the people on the ground...who are saying "what is going on here? You know, "we don't really feel that anything is happening": I'm sorry but it's at the top of my wires, it's at the top of [client's TV news] bulletins...so you still have to try to do something, so go out and do something.

One television news agency worker told me that broadcast journalists (for example, from the BBC, ITN, ABC) regard the agencies as "sausage factories" and prefer to work for broadcasters, not the TV news agencies; and further, that journalists trained in broadcasting don't last long in agency jobs. A television news agency journalist explained how the work of the broadcast journalist is preferable:

> Agencies are like factories, really, because there are such different steps and it's all putting elements together and sending it off. And because you're not involved in the whole process, it's easy to feel a bit alienated from the whole thing, whereas if you're on the "intake" side at least you do feel like you're part of the news gathering.
> And actually, the gathering is more interesting in a news agency, I think, than the "output" side; whereas if you're working for a broadcaster, it's the other way round, you know, the "output" side...that's what people see, so that's much more rewarding.

Television news agency output editors must constantly judge which stories will interest which clients. A story about a diplomatic row between China and Taiwan might be of vital importance in Asia, but of limited interest in Latin America. Their decisions are substantially shaped by frequent phone and email conversations with the editors of client broadcasters. But sometimes they are also based on preconceived notions of what certain groups of broadcasters prefer.

Several journalists at WTN and Reuters were convinced of their clients' preferences regarding extreme violence on screen, for example.[2] Based upon his experience watching news in other countries, and to a lesser extent, upon client requests, a WTN manager concluded:

> It's very interesting to see how natural characteristics come out in terms of TV. In America, for instance, most of the national channels won't show a sniff of the blood that the Germans will gleefully show. The Germans love blood and guts all over the place...the German stations are very blood and gore oriented—they love a good shoot out, whereas in America a lot of it's cleaned up very much by the time it hits the viewers....Italians love "mother and baby" stories, you know, "pregnant grandmothers in Chile"—give it to them. The Russians like scientific stories.

The taste for celebrity pictures provides another example. An editor told me,

> we're aware, for example, that our American clients will take anything with, sort of, Hugh Grant, Liz Hurley, and the Royal Family on it, so things like that become almost self-evident.

It is reasonable to hypothesize that such stereotypes are self-perpetuating and naturalized within the newsroom. Intake obtains Liz Hurley (substitute any contemporary celebrity) pictures knowing the audiences in the United States will want them, output puts Liz Hurley on the U.S. feed because it is routine to do so, and management does not question these actions because everyone understands that the audiences in the United States want those pictures. And of course the occasional (though rare, it seems) call from a U.S. network asking about such footage, where a U.S. network employee in London may be making assumptions about what his or her supervisors in New York want, perpetuate such otherwise unfounded stereotypes.[3] We do know from research done independently of the television industry that news audiences actually want more detailed and contextualized information about international political stories (Philo, 2004), but television news agencies typically argue that they only respond to broadcaster demand. In 1995, then-APTV Head of News Tony Donovan (who would later take charge of the Reuters Television newsroom) suggested more self-reflexive examples, perhaps signifying a welcome and overdue rejection of such stereotypes:

> I've grown up, while I've been in agencies, with listening to people in newsrooms in London saying "they'll love this in Asia" or "the Asians are very interested in this," and a lot of the time that's a guess, that's a guess on the part of people who are probably taking stereotypical attitudes to the whole thing. "The Japanese," if there's a catastrophe, an accident, a train crash, a plane crash, a car crash, stereotypically we say that, "the Japanese will show all the gore." I don't think there's any evidence for that whatsoever.

It's become a deep-rooted and accepted fact now in most, certainly in all of the agency newsrooms that, you know, "don't worry about it, if there's severed limbs the Japanese love it." It's stereotypical, insulting, all of those things.

Planning

As Galtung and Ruge (1965) observed, most news, especially internationally, is expected and planned for: "news" are really "olds." Key to news agency coverage—to a greater extent than for other media—is "future" or "forward" planning (or, simply, "the diary"). This role is especially crucial at news agencies because other media use planning diaries circulated by their news agencies to plan their own world and national coverage. The bailiwick of agency future planners is what McManus (1994, 97) calls "minimally active discovery"—the compilation of future stories from possibilities conveniently put before them. Of course, some institutions are more successful at putting their story ideas (or spin on global affairs) on the news agenda than are many others, though I have written previously (Paterson, 1999) of how Greenpeace, in particular, exemplified a civil society organization skillfully squeezing itself onto the international news agenda on many occasions alongside the usual cast of major governments, big corporations, and celebrities.

"Future Planning" has historically been considered a fairly minor administrative position within each television news agency. This is remarkable, since it is actually a crucial determinant of what agencies cover and how they do so. At a more abstract level, it is the dominant means by which agency news workers assert their control over a very unpredictable world of news. There is considerable comfort to a news manager or EoD in having several neatly typed pages outlining "the news" over the course of the next day, week, or month (see, for example, Tuchman, 1978, 56–57). To the journalist in the newsroom that comfort stems from being empowered to deploy newsgathering resources logically, efficiently, and safely. To the manager that is important, but even more important is the ability to predict the costs of coverage of the world for the weeks ahead.

In the past decade much of the global planning responsibility has shifted—in both television news agencies—to regional editors, sometimes with a planning editor in London still compiling master diaries of upcoming events. Another aspect of television news agency planning is to be well prepared for predictable news events of international significance, such as the deaths of world leaders, in order to be able to instantly supply clients with footage and information when the event inevitably occurs. And as superficially distasteful as it seems, it is worth mentioning—as a vital part of agency planning—that I was aware at one agency of extensive (but very quiet) work to prepare footage and coverage plans for the eventual death of Nelson Mandela. Former APTN chief executive Eric Braun (interview, 2008) offered a similar example:

> [O]ur desire [is] to be ready to deploy quickly because clients are so reliant on us…in the first 24 hours of a breaking news story. We've been on "Castro watch" forever, since his operation: "how long is Fidel going to last and what happens after his passing." So we've got working plans for so many different contingences on world leaders, changes of government, what have you. . . .

Planning staff are deluged with information from agency bureaus and press releases from governments, organizations, and corporations, as well as tips from their company's text editors and reporters. Planning staff are expected to know the coverage plans of allied organizations that might share coverage costs with them, such as ABC, the BBC, or the EBU. Braun (interview, 2008) noted that agency clients also play a role in determining coverage plans, observing that "we get an awful lot of guidance from the clients and subscribers who will call us a week or a month ahead of time" about upcoming events in their region; for the clients this can ensure they don't duplicate, at extra cost, coverage their agency subscription might provide. It appears that only the wealthiest of agency clients routinely propose coverage to the agencies. From all of this, planning staff determine which stories to present to managers for consideration, what to discuss further with bureaus, what to put on the agency's coverage agenda without further consideration, and what to file away or discard. The plans of other agencies and broadcasters are taken into account where they are known.[4]

As McQuail (1987, 165) notes, there is some evidence in the journalism literature of news planners shaping the outcome of news events, through the provision of the means of reporting; this possibility is certainly relevant to the case study of television news agency work presented in the next chapter. An example I observed in 1995 was the violent pro-independence rioting that occurred in Tahiti (mentioned in Chapter Two), which commenced at the moment the television news agencies and some broadcasters had deployed on the island to cover French nuclear testing nearby (surely no coincidence). That there would be the means to cover civil unrest in Tahiti, virtually in real time, had been determined by agency planners over a month earlier.

On stories that are less than earth shattering, the extent to which forward planners or regional editors are positive about a story's prospects can make the difference in whether an event makes it to the newsrooms of the world or not. Managers can turn nasty when the planning staff fail to provide all the information they desire, but as one duty editor explained, "one bad TV assignment could cost thousands of dollars and seriously affect the ability to pay for better stories later."[5] Planning staff bring up ideas pitched to them by bureaus or other sources, and try to leave it to managers and senior editors to accept or reject. In one meeting, a senior manager quickly dismissed one such idea—coverage of parades for Singapore's "National Day" with "we don't care"; in other meetings, other stories were often dismissed with "let it go."

To a substantial degree, television news agency journalists "bringing in" the coverage each day are inclined to feel they have little autonomy, for they simply follow the coverage diary. WTN's forward planner explained to me that her job focuses on "timing" and "delivery": when something will happen, and how to get it. But this perception of the role is significant for what it neglects: the forward planner's *individual agency* is negated in favor of a view that implies a rote administrative role. That WTN staffer was an experienced journalist, but quick to dismiss the place of "news judgment." For her, the news is simply there; she merely lists it, extracts details, formulates coverage plans for it, and presents it to managers. The act of news selection (much less news definition or framing) is denied.

Some coverage planning is "protective": London staff don't anticipate using a story for international distribution, but they tell an agency crew nearby to cover the event anyway. If the event develops greater news significance, or if competitive pressure or client interest dictates that it should be distributed, the company is protected. Costs are minimal, since staff crews and bureau resources are already paid for. And the agencies have to think a step ahead of their clients, always anticipating what news coverage they might want. As then-APTN Director of Content Nigel Baker explained, "the broadcast clients might say they want time to think about whether they are interested in the story. By the time they decided they were, there would usually be no means of obtaining coverage if the agency had not taken a positive decision to react swiftly and cover the story immediately" (Baker, 2004, 65).

But scheduled events of marginal interest out of easy reach of staff crews present a problem. Protective coverage would be expensive. I saw little indication that this issue often emerges, though. A likely reason is that anyone scheduling a news event typically does so within easy reach of a television news agency bureau *and* that agency bureaus don't propose stories that they can't reach easily. The consequences, in terms of limited coverage of the developing world and more remote areas, are significant. The importance of planning at news agencies highlights the considerable power that news agency budgets have over what does and does not become the news of the world, and the considerable—probably dominant—role of pseudo-events (Boorstin, 1961; Dayan and Katz, 1992): the scheduled, staged media events of key international actors seeking to be the dominant voice on some issue of international importance (detailed in the next chapter).

Typically, the key central newsroom staff at each agency will have a morning meeting to discuss major coverage underway around the world for that day, and any substantial preparations for coverage the next day. While the editor of the day or duty editor conducts the meeting, the newsroom managing editor (or similar senior manager) will normally be present. That newsroom manager may change existing plans on the spur of the moment, request closer cooperation with other company journalists or departments, ask for cost reductions, or suggest other stories or other approaches to existing stories. The duty editor runs quickly through the leading stories of the day, to be followed by reports from regional editors and often entertainment, sports, business, and possibly other specialist editors. Any client interest in specific stories will be noted, along with what has been done to accommodate that interest. The manner in which the competitor agency is handling the stories of the day is sometimes discussed. If managers are uncomfortable with any perceived advantage another agency has on a story, they are quick to express this to editors.

There was rarely disagreement in the many television news agency editorial meetings I observed. Tuchman (1978, 35), observed that in meetings of journalists:

> To avoid discussion becoming quite heated, editors must maintain a careful equilibrium, for dissonance interferes with the daily accomplishment of the group's task.

But such an explanation is overly functional. It is also clear that the agency journalists I observed and interviewed share a common view of the news of the world; rarely did I hear disagreement with company editorial decisions, even in informal discussions well away from regular editorial meetings. The senior editor on duty at each agency's main Asian hub, and main North American hub, are also usually consulted in conference calls during these daily meetings. Each wants to know what of interest is coming up to their area and to describe stories in their area (most commonly, Washington) and the coverage they are planning, which will feed into the agency's international distribution (or live coverage) planning.

Decisions on whether to cover a story and how much to devote to it are couched in references to "developments" (what has recently happened to change a story); "coverage" (who has pictures and how do we get them), and "pegs" or "angles" (how the relevance of the story can be demonstrated). In one meeting, it was noted that pool (shared) pictures from the U.S. aircraft carrier Roosevelt (launching NATO warplanes) were expected, but an intake editor expressed concern that she didn't "think there's any real peg" that would justify the cost of delivering the story to London. Importantly, discussions of delivery costs are now almost entirely a thing of the past, since digital video files can now be delivered at virtually no cost via the Internet. The exception is where live coverage is needed or the scene of news coverage is remote, and far from broadband.

The potential for conflict substantially drives news coverage decisions. Stories without a clear potential for conflict, as well as stories without significant political or economic consequences for the world's major powers, tend to be marginalized. During one WTN forward planning meeting, coverage of a women's march in South Africa was proposed. When the planning editor explained that the march was designed as a celebration of the role of women in South Africa, rather than a protest with the potential for conflict, a senior manager concluded "that doesn't seem like it's worth doing."

Costing the News

At WTN it was routine for news managers to also hold frequent meetings with the company's accounting staff to discuss coverage costs and fill in budget details. When necessary, bureau chiefs around the world were telephoned from the meetings to explain specific costs. The discussion of costs in frequent meetings evidenced the considerable pressure on London agency journalists to account for every dollar spent. The very aggravation of doing so (pulling them away from traditional "journalism") might occasionally be reason enough to avoid coverage costs (costs that most often come with developing world coverage or coverage of non-news elite nations, that is, where the agencies do not have cheap or pre-paid coverage and delivery options). Venter (2005, 42) observed that in the event of massive and sudden stories, such as the 9/11 attacks in the United States, "when the daily news budget is quickly depleted, it is still covered and the deficit factored in over time."

Tight financial controls in the television news agencies can have potentially dramatic, even devastating, consequences in the real world of human tragedy; and the role of major international TV news providers in the making, or unmaking, of a major international story (or news personality) can be directly tied to their decision to allocate resources to such stories. In previous writing I have cited the example of a debate I witnessed within WTN in 1994 about whether or not to pay the high cost of dispatching a satellite uplink to a fast-developing crisis (the company owned dishes, but getting one and a crew to run it to the scene would likely have involved complex arrangements with expensive chartered aircraft). BBC and Channel 4 correspondent and editor Nick Gowing (1994, 3) observed that:

> The absence of a satellite dish usually means significantly less TV coverage of a crisis. Often no dish means no coverage. On the other hand, the presence of a dish creates news coverage because of a TV news manager's corporate obligation to justify its costly deployment.

Without the pictures, logistical support, and ability to transmit a live picture provided by the news agencies and, occasionally, other companies and organizations, the world's television broadcasters are able to provide their viewers with little coverage (at least, little with the necessary visual interest to be a prominent story). There is evidence that television coverage occasionally drives Western policy responses, which in turn drive further press interest in such stories (Gowing, 1994; Robinson, 2002). The story of the Rwandan refugee crisis in 1994 provides an interesting example. The sheer number of lives at stake has often failed to raise tragedies from that continent especially high on the news agenda, while, ironically, the occasional presence of major tragedies reinforced the impression that these are the only kind of African story (see, for example, Hawk, 1992). In 1995, a Reuters EoD was particularly frank about his decision process as he correlated the number of deaths to issues of proximity and ethnocentrism:

> It is a body count....I would guess that you would say obviously a story in Rwanda has to have a lot more bodies in it than a story in a Western country, a lot more....Certainly, this afternoon there's a South Africa bus crash, 19 dead, 55 seriously injured. 19 dead. 19 dead. Not enough. 55 seriously injured, we would go to move it, because the body count could go up. When you start talking about 30 people dead, then its starts to become a story to run outside the region.

In July 1994, as Rwandan refugees by the hundreds of thousands fled into Goma (near the Rwandan border of the Democratic Republic of Congo), aid agencies and wire service reporters at the scene sounded the alarm that a humanitarian disaster of unprecedented proportion loomed. For days, international television kept virtually silent, despite no shortage of information on the crisis and its implications (information, not pictures). Suddenly, the world's television newscasts came alive with news of the Goma tragedy—and estimates of up to ten thousand people dying daily—far too late to influence governments to try to reverse the exodus or to get supplies in place before the death toll soared. In an echo of the Ethiopian famine a decade earlier, wealthy governments and the United Nations reacted to pressure from the compelling television coverage, and moved quickly to help. In the meantime, similar, albeit smaller, disasters unfolded in other parts of the world, with a similar lack of attention from global television. So what key event made Goma so suddenly and thoroughly newsworthy, when it had until then been a non-story?

The creation of a Goma television story for the global TV audience was the result of a decision in the Geneva headquarters of the European Broadcasting Union, where managers had received a sufficient number of requests for coverage from member broadcasters (Europe's public broadcasting networks) to decide to allocate their own costly resources, in this case a "flyaway" satellite dish (a satellite dish transportable by plane) and the technicians to go with it, to the Goma story.[6]

Until then no other major TV news service had been willing to allocate such resources, despite the magnitude of the story and the difficulty in getting news pictures out by other means. For WTN, the cost of sending its own live transmission equipment at the end of a hectic and costly news month influenced the decision to let the world's broadcasters feed from the EBU's satellite dish, rather than immediately dispatch its own.[7] When the EBU's flyaway began to transmit, vivid pictures and live reports became available from the Goma camps, and television reporters from around the world began to converge on Goma because the ability to reach their audience live, at little cost to themselves, had now been provided. And when the EBU decided that the flyaway should fly away to another world hotspot, with it went the story of Goma's refugees. Medium became message in Goma, as the financial realities of television news overshadowed the Rwandan tragedy, and reinforced the world of fleeting and incomprehensible disaster that is the Western "reality" of Africa.

Apart from the constant pressure to account for every expense, television news agency journalists also must rigorously observe the legal restrictions that come with every image they process. The most innocuous failure to do so could result in a costly lawsuit and even more costly damage to their reputations. The agencies will always strive to illustrate stories with pictures from their own staff, because then they own the picture and can provide it to their clients without complication. But often they distribute images that were originally created by another company or organization, and then they must observe strict rules about how they can use those images and where they can be distributed, and pass on any relevant rules to each of their clients. This is called "sourcing" the images: providing precise details of who owns every picture. For example, in the 1990s the BBC, like other regional and global broadcasters, attempted to provide limited "international syndication" of its news footage and stories, but at the same time it had an alliance with WTN and its parent, ABC. The copyright issues became complex. News manager Lowndes Lipscomb of WTN (interview, 1995) offered an example:

> If the BBC included Reuters material in a Nine O'clock News spot, WTN has access to the BBC, the BBC foreign desk has got to know that they're Reuters pictures which we can't have and vice versa....[R]ight now both WTN and Reuters have access to BBC pictures....[T]here is an element of copyright pollution which forces the desk people to be able to source their materials.

The Iconic Image and the Story of the Day

As stated by APTN's senior editor Nigel Baker in Chapter Two, an essential part of television news agency work concerns the "televisual impact of a story," and to those ends, newsroom staff and field staff collaborate through the day both on the logistics of getting pictures and on the aesthetics of the story: what few pictures will powerfully represent what they perceive as the crux of the story. Schlesinger (1980) wrote that the ethnographic observations of moments of crisis in the television newsroom are revealing for their insights into how journalists revise their framing of news; but in an agency the frames are so self-evident (and the types of stories so few) that such need for revision is rare. The standard visual grammar for the telling of a Yugoslavia war story was so routine that a few hours before the important city of Knin was about to be overrun by Croatian troops, and well before any pictures had been shot, a WTN journalist confidently told me,

> The story today is the offensive [to capture] Knin, so we want [video of] the flag above Knin—that will be the picture—we want to have Croatian troops in Knin securing the place; you want to have the Krijina Serbs surrendering, retreating, or whatever, battle tanks burning, and that sort of thing, to tell the story.

Interestingly, Fletcher (2008, 5) recalls his early days as a Visnews photographer sent to capture the raising of the British flag at the headquarters of the European Community (when the U.K. first joined). He arrived late and missed it, so he asked them to do it again. Getting the vital, iconic image (by any means) launched his career. When leading stories are determined in morning editorial meetings, the EoD or a regional editor will contact bureaus to request specific kinds of coverage and to determine what images can be obtained. At this stage, concepts of "iconic" images for the day emerge.

On a day during some recent observation in an agency newsroom, when Russia was expected to interrupt the flow of gas to the Ukraine in a diplomatic row, an example emerged. There was an eagerness among London editors for camera crews in the Ukraine to find a Ukraine family watching in disappointment and fear as the gas stopped flowing into their home. After hours of effort, it was determined that no such image would be possible, and alternatives were sought. The story of the day must be visual, and the visuals ideally should be stronger than earlier visuals. A WTN manager commented in an editorial meeting that Reuters pictures out of Bosnia "didn't look very strong" because they were "not even burning houses," but "burning woodpiles next door to houses."

It is the television journalist's appetite for the single powerful visual image that enables those who wish to influence the news agenda to do so with ease, as public relations companies and politicians know well. Examples of corporate efforts to feed the television news agencies the perfect image were recounted in Chapter Four as an aspect of the marketization of news in the 1990s.

Live News

As CNN promoted the myth of "live news" during the first Gulf War[8] (MacGregor, 1997; Semati, 2001), news agencies began to think about ways to provide live images in addition to their standard "raw footage" of global events, and so we move now to review their increasing focus on live news. Few broadcasters, even the largest among them, can provide extensive and continuous live news coverage of events far from where they are based, but the two television news agencies do so frequently. All but the largest broadcasters and many of the larger regional rolling news channels, which typically have only a very limited newsgathering capability, depend heavily on the live coverage the two commercial television news agencies provide (and for European public broadcasters, on occasional live news coverage from the European Broadcasting Union as well). The APTN's Sandy MacIntyre explained that the second Gulf War, commencing in 2003, was the point at which the focus of the television news agencies became live coverage. In the first weeks of the war, the agencies fed a nearly continuous stream of pictures to their clients consisting of just-arrived videotaped footage from around the region and live images from wherever they were available (often including roof-top cameras pre-installed in Baghdad).

APTN now offers a separate full-time satellite channel to clients who pay extra for it, exclusively to carry live pictures as they become available. Eric Braun of APTN told me (interview, 2008), "you can pretty much wager that anybody who has a 24 news channel does subscribe to us and probably Reuters too and also has us on speed dial...they want to know 'when are you going live' with whatever is next in the daybook." Reuters Television provides a great deal of live video as well on its one existing satellite channel. What remains unclear is the extent to which the increasing focus on live news shifts television news agency resources away from more hidden or complex stories that don't lend themselves to such coverage. In a recent contribution to Cushion and Lewis's (2010) useful overview of the growth of rolling news, I outlined (Paterson, 2010, 105–107) the key types of television news agencies' live coverage:

1. Scheduled live video feeds from government or corporate news conferences, speeches from the United Nations (usually provided by the UN's own television production wing), military briefings, rocket

launches, meetings, and the like. They can be planned for and announced to clients well in advance, and are often available to the news agency to redistribute at no cost. They might also be feeds of images from pool arrangements an agency has made with other agencies and broadcasters, such as a visit by a dignitary to a school where officials want only a single camera present to minimize disruption.

2. The second type consists of often elaborate live productions, sometimes using multiple cameras overlooking an unfolding news event. Such coverage can be staged when the agencies anticipate a significant story with visual interest and a clear, fixed location. But they must also be able to have ample time to station cameras around that location safely, along with the transmission equipment to feed those pictures to a satellite uplink. If the events don't unfold as planned the agencies lose a costly gamble, but the value of such coverage to their rolling news clients is immense. The case study in the next chapter provides an example.[9]

3. A third type is the rebroadcast of live television coverage from a broadcaster somewhere in the world—normally a client or ally of the agency. The broadcast will be targeting only their local audience, but when a local agency bureau notifies their company's London duty editor that the images are powerful enough to warrant international distribution, a relay of the pictures to London will be rapidly established. Examples might be an unfolding hostage drama or a celebrity death (as with the extensive coverage of Michael Jackson's death by U.S. stations, relayed globally by the agencies). The agencies may have to pay high fees to the broadcasters involved for using their coverage in this way.

4. I'll include here a fourth use of such "live" feeds, which are not live at all. This is when other news is dropped to transmit to clients in real time the rushes—or unedited video straight from the camera—from the scene of unfolding events. When clients are eager to air pictures before their competition, the agencies might abandon their normal processes of taking in the pictures shot by their videographers, listing the shots and transcribing the interviews, and editing only the best portions for their scheduled feeds to clients. Instead, they will put the incoming pictures out to clients as they arrive, straight from the camera, at the considerable risk of surrendering editorial control and exposing the public to footage they normally would not see due to gore or violence (if broadcasters, in turn, broadcast what they receive as it comes in).

The final practice is curious, since the agencies often insist that it is their editorial judgment and integrity that adds value to the words and images they provide. But in sending to clients video footage their editors haven't previewed, they surrender that control for the sake of immediacy. The APTN's MacIntyre defended the practice, saying "we allow people [client broadcasters] to take it off the satellite in real time…[but] the London newsroom are in control of what goes up on the satellite." Reuters's Editor-in-Chief David Schlesinger told the trade press (Broadcast, 2006), "We're finding great demand for live material, we're putting many more live shots up than we ever used to before and I think that underlines the point that all broadcasters are feeling they have to get that immediate 24-hour coverage."

The Urge to Converge

The last ten years have brought considerable technological and organizational change to the television news agencies, all under the broad—but ill-defined—rubric of "convergence." The core activity of both companies, moving video images from all parts of the world to London for processing and distribution, began to become significantly cheaper and easier from the late 1990s on. One of the innovators, curiously, was Greenpeace, which used a video compression system of its own design in 1995 to send the news agencies television pictures of its attempts to block French nuclear testing in the South Pacific (Paterson, 1999). Greenpeace realized that a few minutes of video could be converted to digital form and slowly transmitted over the narrow bandwidth of a maritime satellite telephone line, received at its London office, and recorded back to videotape for delivery to the agencies. Soon such video compression technology was commercially available, and its use by broadcasters and the news agencies became widespread.

By around 1998, such devices, commonly called TOKO boxes (for the U.S. company that developed them) or simply "squishers," were used to send video reports from around the world, but especially from the most remote locations where satellite dishes could not easily or safely be deployed. But the use of the Inmarsat satellite phone connections was still expensive. A minute of video took a half hour to transmit, and so for video of fairly poor quality and a cost of about $150 per minute, the technology was considered a useful option but not one for frequent use. Since the 1990s satellite television news transmissions have also increasingly used compressed digital video, resulting in a drop in satellite costs by a factor of ten or more. That decrease in cost—and increase in demand due to the multitude of rolling news channels—accounts for the agency's eagerness to provide live pictures whenever possible.

Much of what television news agency field producers do has little to do with the fact-gathering of journalism; instead, it involves establishing a comfortable base for client broadcasters at the scene of a story, and providing them the means to "report from the scene" for their various television networks around the world using the TOKO, or, on larger stories, a flyaway satellite uplink. Khalid Kazziha, an APTN senior producer in Africa, explained in a 2001 interview:

> We line up our clients—CNN, BBC, MBC, Al-Jazeera, one stand-upper after the next—and they all use the same pictures [provided by APTN's photographer at the scene]. Which means the initiative of the correspondent can be limited sometimes by the fact that they don't have the ability to get their pictures out on breaking stories—but they always want to make sure they have presence on the ground, and that's what the TOKO allows them to do. In the initial phases of any disaster or conflict they need to show that they are there, even though they're cooperating with the agencies. (Transnational Broadcasting Studies, 2001)

The TOKO evolved into the more sophisticated satellite video telephone technology known as B-GAN (Broadband Global Area Network). The system used existing Inmarsat satellites, but through the use of small transmitting antennas that fold out of briefcases and more sophisticated video compression, they enable a good quality of live transmission or a slower transmission of full-quality video. The technology has permitted live coverage—and more coverage—from difficult-to-access locations around the world. Since the live picture is below standard broadcast quality, broadcasters will often use the pictures in a small form surrounded by graphic images or pictures from other locations so that the audience doesn't notice. But it surpasses both the satellite telephone video of only a few years prior, and the Internet-transmitted live video that broadcasters now occasionally use to limit costs.

With the introduction of digital video servers in the agency newsrooms from the late 1990s into the early 2000s, far fewer staff were needed as the reliance on videotape—and videotape editing—rapidly died out. It wasn't just that a large staff of professional videotape editors lost their jobs, but there was also less work for many more junior staff as stacks of videotapes no longer needed shifting from one department or desk to another, and videotape libraries were gradually converted to digital form that required far less human intervention. For example, the trade press reported that forty Reuters Television staff—fully a third of those working in the central newsroom—were due to be let go as a direct result of moving away from videotape (Broadcast, 1999).

Now stories often arrive in the newsroom in the form of a digital file, whether by satellite or Internet (ftp: file transfer protocol); or, if in analog form, arriving stories are instantly recorded as digital files. Since the files are sent via the Internet or the company's own leased data lines, the cost is minimal. These arriving stories are immediately available to all staff to work with at their desks. Normally, as soon as pictures come in, London output staff will begin editing news images (using editing software on their own computers) into updated versions of ongoing stories, to be delivered within the next scheduled newsfeed. More urgent pictures might be fed out to clients within minutes of arriving, and sometimes pictures go out to clients instantly as they arrive in London (and, increasingly, directly to the public via news websites and mobile services).

From the early 1990s through the present, each company, as with the rest of the news industry, has been pushing for "multi-skilling": the gradual erosion of traditional highly specialized work roles in favor of a more flexible work force capable of completing a wider range of tasks. The result of this process is that many news production employees can move with little retraining in and out of a variety of newsroom posts, and that some specialized technical roles have vanished. But it is worth noting that through the 1980s, the international image of the television news agencies was very much manifest in the exacting nature of the editing of the video output. With the de-professionalization and digitalization of this task, video is now edited quickly by some of the least-experienced newsroom staff. Television news agency professional editors also possessed the ability to recognize in an instant a multitude of key people in the news stories of the day, and thereby rapidly identify and cut into place the most valuable images from a large amount of incoming video. Clearly, the future belongs to the "multi-skilled" journalist, but research into the impact of this trend on the overall nature of news would be valuable.

As the technology to move video images was rapidly improving, the news agencies were working to combine their vast operations across a variety of different media (photo, video, radio, and print) into more efficient "converged" operations that could more easily share information and the raw sounds and images coming in from around the world. The Associated Press opened a substantially converged, multimedia newsroom in New York in 2004 and followed that in 2008 in London for its Europe, Africa, and Asia coverage (Edmunds 2006; interview, Eric Braun, AP vice president of international television, 2008). Abandoning Fleet Street, Reuters opened its multimedia newsroom in London's new Canary Wharf financial district in 2005 (just before this became the very heart of the global financial meltdown).

Both news agencies adopted similar physical arrangements for their converged newsrooms. In each, those news workers processing video—what once was known as the television news agency part of the company (a terminology now out of favor despite the title of this book)—occupy what seems the most central part of the newsroom, with typically larger text operations and the similarly sized photo operations adjoining at one or both sides. Reuters Television's input journalists sit directly behind (and close enough to shout to) their master control technicians, who manage the flow of video in and out of the building. In both companies, television output desks are located within a few meters of those managing input, and regional editors for television are also nearby, but a further distance from the prominent video walls displaying incoming video feeds, television output, and the output of selected major broadcasters. A newsroom manager explained that this is because regional editors are meant to be looking ahead, rather than focusing on news of the moment.

Everyone is connected by desktop messaging systems and email, and so shouts or mad dashes across a newsroom—once commonplace—are now rare. At the AP, a morning editorial meeting among senior editors for text, photos, and television takes place to briefly summarize coverage plans for the big stories of the moment from across the world, and for major stories anticipated later in the day. Less daily interaction between the television and print (or photo) journalists was evident in the Reuters newsroom. (I dare not speculate on which system works better, though both approaches seem now to work well for each.)

The AP, especially, has pushed its staff toward "multimedia" story production—seeking ways to combine the still and video images, sounds, and text output of the agency into web-based stories exploiting the features of each. Similarly, they encourage staff from the various types of media to collaborate and share resources, and will often assign specialized "cross format coordinators" to major stories to encourage collaboration and multimedia storytelling (Sandy MacIntyre, interview, 2010). While Reuters has announced similar initiatives, my recent observation in its London newsroom suggests that, in general, the different media channels are left to pursue stories in their own way, and collaborate only on occasion. Reuters's head of news, Lloyd Watson, told me that multimedia production "is not what our clients are screaming for" (interview, 2010).

In the digital age, television news agencies need to be alert to any potential source of images as they begin their coverage of a big story, and often that means aggressively chasing the "citizen journalist." When news of the underground (subway) and bus bombings in London in July 2005 began to appear on British news broadcasts, the London newsrooms of AP and Reuters sent all the staff they could muster into the street. APTN's Director of News, Sandy MacIntyre, urged his staff to question bystanders for any mobile phone video they might have. He told a trade magazine, "it is standard-operating-practice to chase amateur video, because no matter how quickly we get to the scene, we can't get footage as quickly as those who are already there" (Romano and Kerschbaumer, 2005). (APTN, along with Sky and ITN, distributed the mobile phone video of the incident.) And sometimes stories fall into an agency's lap. When an enormous section of the world-famous Camden markets in London went up in flames in 2008, APTN staff pointed a camera out the window of their senior executive's office and fed live pictures to their British broadcaster clients and the rest of the world.

Notes

1. "Output" typically consists of producers assembling each scheduled "feed" to clients and more junior workers assisting them in the writing of scripts to accompany the stories and the editing of video, all overseen by a senior output editor. At APTN the separate "live" channel is another aspect of output, constantly seeking some live image from somewhere in the world to feed to the world's rolling news channels.
2. Aspects of agency distribution to broadcasters of images of blood and gore are elaborated upon in Chapter Eight.
3. There is certainly some broadcaster demand for such material, which contributes to the creation of agency stereotypes and institutionalizes the production of such news product. Extensive content analysis of agency output with broadcaster output in conjunction with production research in both environments might yield a clearer understanding of this feedback process.
4. That is, when such plans are officially known. At WTN this was when another agency or broadcaster had told WTN what it was doing for the sake of coordination. The plans of other agencies or broadcasters were often known unofficially (usually because WTN's people in the field had picked up hints from another company's people in the field), but such knowledge would not go into planning documents, but would be discussed in meetings.
5. At two agencies, this researcher's presence in planning meetings was highly valued by planning staff; they believed management were gentler with them than usual with my tape recorder running (or my notepad open).
6. This account of television coverage of Goma results from my pilot ethnographic research in the WTN London newsroom in 1994. This dish may have been a unique one necessitated by Goma's location, and operated by the BBC for the EBU, according to Covault, 1994.
7. A senior WTN editor who contributed extensively to this research countered that "agencies have nothing to apologize for," citing the numerous times the agencies have provided coverage of some of the most dangerous and challenging stories in Africa when other media have been ignoring them. This is an important counter to the Goma example offered here.
8. A myth because the realities of war cannot be televised in real time.
9. A further example from my research is provided in Paterson, 2010:
    > In April, 2006 French university students, at times in conjunction with labor unions, organized a series of protests over changes to labor laws, and these appeared to news agency editors to be getting increasingly more confrontational. With a major protest expected to culminate in a large square in Paris, both news agencies saw an opportunity and rented balconies in different positions overlooking the square. They placed cameras in them and established live feeds from each. Broadcasters around the world were able to show live, from multiple camera angles, what seemed like a spontaneous, breaking news story.

7

A Year in the Life of an International News Story

As noted in the previous chapter, an increasingly common type of agency journalism is the elaborate, multiple-camera live production of scheduled (or predicted) news events. This is a perilous and costly form of coverage, but it is valued by rolling news channels because it enables those channels to broadcast live pictures of faraway events for extended periods, with no expense beyond the agency subscription they have already paid for. This chapter presents a case study of television news agency coverage of a single large, internationally significant story. But it was not a major story, such as the ongoing wars in Iraq and Afghanistan. It was a story for about a week, and live coverage for international rolling news channels was provided for little more than one weekend afternoon. And so from the evidence in this chapter of the massive planning that went into a story like this, one can deduce the far more extensive planning and investment that goes into those mega-stories. It is the mega-stories and the multi-day live events on which television news agencies spend most of their revenue. For example, a substantial amount in the last decade has gone toward maintaining heavily fortified bureaus in Baghdad and Kabul.

The focus of this chapter is what might be seen as a very typical midsized television news agency story (in the sense of being especially well suited to coverage by these organizations). This was the 2008 declaration of independence by the Balkan state of Kosovo—until then a province of Serbia, and before that, Yugoslavia. While by 2008 Kosovo had been nearly forgotten by most broadcasters, the news

agencies viewed the province as a potential flashpoint and maintained significant bureaus there. By mid-2007, diplomatic processes closely monitored by the news agencies suggested that a unilateral declaration of Kosovo's independence from Serbia—with the blessing of the United States and Europe—could soon come. At APTN, intricate coverage plans were developed, and these offer a useful example of how every larger story on international television gestates in the planning emails of television news agencies for months before the global public sees such "live," "instant," "breaking" news on its screens.

The description below draws from ethnographic observation in both London and Kosovo, analysis of reams of internal electronic communications, analysis of content, and interviews to explore the television news agency role in the manufacture of an international news event. This project was conducted by this author with two other researchers, Kenneth Andresen and Abit Hoxha. Our joint findings are described in a forthcoming research article (Paterson et al., forthcoming), and here I focus just on the television news agency portion of the project, which I conducted in the U.K. No such inside look at the making of live global news exists in the literature, and never before have the internal emails, budgets, resource lists, and client communications of a television news agency (or, quite possibly, any global news organization) been made so comprehensively available for independent analysis. So with the generous assistance of the Associated Press, I offer here a rare look into the planning process of a television news agency.

This story is also an example of how Boorstin's (1961) concept of the "pseudo-event" plays out in the context of contemporary geo-politics and rolling television news. Clarke—whose 2003 case study of an international story this project mirrored—followed Boorstin in observing that "key to the success of pseudo-events is that journalists are willing to report them." We expect them to be more dramatic, less complex, and so easier to explain to audiences, and—vital for the sake of television coverage—easier to plan news coverage around. The purpose of this manufactured event was clear: if you declare yourself a country, you can be a country—with two stipulations. The world's media need to pay attention, and some powerful countries need to agree. If powerful countries disagree, this also helps ensure that the world's media will pay attention. And it is interesting to speculate whether the birth of a country less proximate to Europe or without the same ability to manufacture a "pseudo-event" would have received similar news coverage. A case in point is East Timor.[1]

On February 17, 2008, television channels around the world and, most predominately, around Europe, offered their audiences live television coverage of the independence declaration from Prishtina, Kosovo. But at APTN, planning for the coverage of Kosovo's independence had been progressing steadily for nearly a year (alongside dozens of other planned stories every month requiring more than a single report).[2] The local police reported that "about 1200 international media teams" had descended on Prishtina (Paterson, ibid.), but despite that large number, most television media doing international reporting elected to depend on news agency coverage of the event, and even those sending their own staff often did so to provide the image of their reporter on the scene, to be integrated with the live and taped images from the news agencies. Most of these journalists had come from media outlets in the Kosovo region.

Since the Balkans are far from the newsrooms of leading international media outlets, they have long been the near-exclusive domain of the news agencies. This is all the more the case, because during the long Yugoslav civil war and later Kosovo conflict, the news agencies built up considerable bureaus in the region with large numbers of battle-hardened local staff who could be deployed to other hotspots around the world as needed. These bureaus were maintained long after most other media left. From the 1990s to the present day, the news agencies became the international "prime definers" of news from the region (Paterson, 1998, 2007; van Ginneken, 1998, 114), as most media contentedly surrendered day-to-day coverage to them.[3] And so as Kosovo's independence approached, the assumption that it would be an "agency story" held within the agencies and across news media generally. But it is also significant that the London editors and Balkans bureau staff who organized this coverage were deeply involved as young journalists in either the Yugoslav civil war or the Kosovo conflict of 1999, or both. While the world had forgotten Kosovo over the subsequent decade, for them this was the logical climax of a story they had invested much of their lives in (and many had seen friends lose their lives in that earlier coverage). As one APTN editor told me, it was "the endgame."

While much of my observation of news agency planning coverage meetings revealed heated exchanges and the brutal dismissal of coverage proposals from agency staff around the world, the internal planning for Kosovo's independence announcement at APTN was conducted with striking harmony: the significance of the story, the potential outcomes of the story, and the basic expectations for coverage of the story were mutually understood from the outset (among the bureaus involved, key editors in London, news managers, and client broadcasters).

In 2007, when U.N. mediator Martti Ahtisaari recommended "supervised independence," APTN journalists in Serbia and Kosovo began to negotiate coverage with London editors seeking to stretch their news budget across myriad ongoing and anticipated global news stories. The pace of planning increased when, by the end of 2007, there was no international agreement on independence, and Kosovo's elected leaders began to speak of unilateral independence. Serbia had warned that moves toward independence would endanger the region's stability.[4] The problem for AP, and everyone else, was whether or not that should be taken as a threat of war.

In May 2007, APTN's Europe editor, in frequent email communication with Kosovo bureau staff, set up a conference call between London editors and the Prishtina and Belgrade bureaus to discuss plans for an independence announcement. They speculated on the possibility of Russia and the United States reaching an agreement about Kosovo's status at the G8 meeting about to take place (though it would soon become clear that any independence announcement would come much later), and about a sudden U.N. Security Council resolution in support of independence.

A comprehensive plan was circulated by the Belgrade bureau, based largely on well-informed guesswork about how the diplomacy would play out in the coming months (AP internal document, May 25, 2007).[5] It stated that if the U.N. security council were to use the word "independent" in connection with Kosovo, a strong reaction in Serbia could be expected, including an urgent session of Parliament in which "right-wingers" would push for sending troops.

But AP in Belgrade also predicted that an attack by Serbia would be unlikely, since the country was seeking improved relations with the United States. It asked for an extra camera crew in Belgrade to cover diplomatic moves and "demos"—agency slang for public protest demonstrations. Mitrovica, in northern Kosovo, was identified at this early point as the likely trouble spot, and where two camera crews and a satellite uplink should be deployed. AP staff did not want to be caught by a sudden mass movement of refugees out of Kosovo and no cameras in place to capture it. But the Belgrade bureau also noted that Serb officials were telling them that they expected Russia to block any such U.N. resolution (evidencing the role of agency bureau chiefs and producers in maintaining an ongoing dialogue with local officials, wherever they are).

Plans were put in place to move extra staff to Kosovo in case of a rapid announcement after the G8. When Kosovo's prime minister mentioned during the summer that an independence announcement could come as soon as late November, APTN's clients were informed, and the agency's output desk in London produced a video news feature entitled "What's Next for Kosovo?" Kosovo would have been well off the radar of most journalists around the world at this point, and so the feature—even if it wasn't aired by broadcasters—would have helped to prepare client newsrooms for the flow of stories from Kosovo that were on the way in subsequent months. Reminding the world about Kosovo might also have helped justify to APTN's clients and to AP management the considerable investment in the story already underway.

In Chapter Six I commented on the prevalence of a "picture of the day" mentality in television news agency newsrooms—a determination early in the development of a story that a particular picture is needed to tell that story to the world. This was again evident in the early stages of APTN's planning for Kosovo's independence, as the following passage from an email of May 2007 (nearly a year before the independence announcement) suggests. The email summarized an initial planning conference call and was written by a producer at APTN's Prishtina bureau (APTN internal communications, May 24, 2007). The producer wrote that "there are 2 pictures that are 'key' to the Kosovo story" and listed these as:

1. K.Albanians waving their black/red flag, people crying from happiness.

2. The other pictures will be the first K.Serb refugees leaving their homes. Live or ENG depends.

AP print and television journalists corresponded by email in early December ahead of a meeting of the United States, EU, and Russia (called the Troika) to present the United Nations with a report on the positions of the two sides in regard to Kosovo's future status. In the final days of 2007, APTN kept journalists based in Serbia and Kosovo on standby to react quickly to violence that might come from the increasing talk of independence from Serbia, or to unannounced moves by the Kosovo government toward independence. In January, Kosovo's politicians began to speak more openly about a unilateral declaration of independence, and news agency journalists began more complex planning. AP provided coverage of the Kosovo Parliament voting to approve the new pro-independence Prime Minister, Hashim Thaci.

APTN's Europe editor in London, along with the heads of relevant bureaus, kept a close eye on any diplomatic moves that might signal a green light to Kosovo. When a visit by French president Sarkozy to Romania was rumoured (it didn't happen) in mid-January, he suspected an effort to get Romania—an opponent of Kosovan independence—on board with the EU old guard, which was beginning to actively mobilize support for independence. The Paris bureau was asked to seek information on Sarkozy's intentions.

It is important to remember that nearly constant planning and negotiation was going on within the news agency at a time when there was almost no news about Kosovo circulating internationally. News agencies would not have been alone in undertaking such planning; other large broadcasters and newspapers with international coverage would have been giving thought to the story by this time as well. But the television news agencies had the burden of requiring costly and complex resources to be in place well before they were needed, so links could be tested, plans rehearsed, and clients informed. The goal was to be able to feed the world's broadcasters video reports from around the region and live coverage from key locations—not at the moment of the independence announcement, but in the weeks before it.

For a news agency to do that, it has to predict events well and gamble on deploying its resources to cover those events long before other media do. The agencies knew that as the event approached, broadcasters would be clamoring for images and story angles, and reporters would be descending on Kosovo seeking news agency help with their reports.

On February 1, senior APTN staff and the bureaus involved were sent a detailed "deployment email" from the Europe Desk telling them where to go, and when. The key moment was identified as the presidential elections occurring in Serbia on February 3, from which the agency thought any number of scenarios might unfold. They predicted that if an ultra-nationalist candidate won (he did not), Kosovo would move quickly and declare independence on Sunday, February 10. If the "pro-Western" candidate were to win (he did), they predicted an independence announcement on Sunday, February 17. In the end, they were precisely right. Intriguingly, these predictions were being circulated internally at APTN while Kosovan officials were still staying silent about dates. The email warned that "there is [a] chance events will unravel more quickly after the election results," so staff were told to be prepared to travel on the fourth or fifth of February. All staff being temporary redeployed to Prishtina or Belgrade were told to be there by the eighth of February.

The "deployment email" listed an "expected succession of events"—essentially the script for the big day (again, well before a public announcement of plans from Kosovo's government). The script included: (1) the announcement from Kosovo's Parliament building "prompting around one million people to take to the streets in celebration"; (2) a closing of the border with Serbia; (3) international security forces moving to protect Serb enclaves; (4) and "possible clashes" in Mitrovica, possibly with North Mitrovica declaring itself part of Serbia; (5) a possible flow of refugees; and (6) (the only imprecise prediction) an "unclear" reaction of some kind from Serbia.

Multiple-camera coverage would be set up at the Parliament building, feeding an AP satellite van with a link to London. Cameras would be set up outside to cover any celebrations. A microwave link would be established between the bureau offices and the satellite van, so reports from roving ENG cameras could be edited in the bureau and transmitted instantly to London via the van (minor television news agency bureaus like Prishtina do not have their own satellite uplink facilities). ENG crews would also roam the border areas and outlying villages. Another AP satellite van would be sent to Mitrovica (detailed below), and a third would be hired from a private company to transmit breaking news from Belgrade. Crews would be sent to the Serb side of the border. All staff being brought in to assist in the coverage were reminded "to bring flak jackets and helmets." APTN built its small Prishtina staff up to eleven or more people, joining about twenty other AP staff who registered with the Kosovo Press Center.[6]

APTN asked a senior producer from its large Belgrade bureau to relocate to the Prishtina bureau to help coordinate the coverage. Photographers and technicians were sent to Mitrovica, in northern Kosovo on the border with Serbia, on February 1. Staff in the region predicted that if there were to be any flash point for violence at the time of an independence declaration, it would be at the bridge in the center of the city that divides the ethnic-Serb part of the city from the ethnic-Albanian part. The bridge had been the scene of violent clashes in 2004, and it was the job of regional bureau staff and editors in London to remember that. AP's plan was to discreetly place a satellite uplink van on the southern side of the bridge, with various video cables feeding into the van that would uplink its signal by digital Ku band satellite link to APTN's master control in its London newsroom.

One of the feeds would come from a camera operator in high position with a good camera shot of the bridge (an apartment with a balcony is typically rented at a generous rate by a news agency for such a purpose); another would come from a camera at street level; and the third from a wireless microwave link to another camera position—in a similar high position—on the other side of the bridge. The southern (Albanian) side of the bridge was considered marginally safer in the event of violence (the anger would be in the north), and so the valuable satellite van was placed there.

Efforts were made for the photographers to be local people with the "right" ethnic backgrounds for each side, just in case the crowds turned on them. The north Mitrovica crew also had laptop computers that could send their video out via ftp on a broadband Internet connection in case the microwave link across the bridge broke down; they also gave them the ability to independently edit video they shot before sending it to London. As a further backup they also brought a B-GAN in from their Moscow bureau—a satellite telephone used for transmitting video. All together, eleven APTN staff camped in rented apartments and hotels on both sides of Mitrovica, waiting for a confrontation that never came.

In the beginning of February, APTN moved personnel and equipment to Prishtina, other parts of Kosovo, and Belgrade, from London, Berlin, Jerusalem, Rome, Sarajevo, Brussels, Paris, Moscow, Pale (Bosnia and Herzegovina), and Bucharest, and brought in their own equipment as well as additional hired cameras, satellite uplinks, and microwave transmitting gear. The Associated Press's Vienna Bureau chief—responsible for directing news coverage for eastern Europe—emailed

APTN and other international desks in the agency with an assessment of "independence timing, staffing and story planning." Like APTN staff, they predicted the declaration on Sunday, February 17, but they advanced the speculation about hidden diplomatic moves even further than APTN's communications had by suggesting that a meeting between President Bush and U.N. Secretary General Ban Ki-moon, scheduled for that Friday, was significant, and that an immediate confirmation of the independence timing might follow. The email mentioned that AP writers were working on an Independence Day story analyzing the U.S. role in Kosovo's independence.

On February 13, government sources in Prishtina told AP staff that they had reason to expect "the United States will be one of 5 nations that will definitely recognize Kosovo one hour after the declaration of independence" (AP internal communication). AP editors could then plan—days ahead—to include in their Independence Day coverage a feed of a U.S. State Department statement on Kosovo about one hour after the declaration. This is fine example of a little-commented-on aspect of international journalism: *knowing the story*. As this planning process illustrates, early in the coverage planning, senior editors at news agencies—and, one can only suspect, given the lack of relevant research, within other large international news media—*imagine a set of potential outcomes and plan the telling of the story accordingly*. All the relevant international actors—in this case, the U.S. Department of State, the EU, the Russian Foreign Ministry, and the Serbian President's Office—were expected to behave in a decidedly predictable fashion and thereby play out the imagined script accordingly.

An international agency journalist covering the world must understand its affairs, and their meaning, intimately. That is probably impossible, but the global minutiae displayed by agency editors and writers is often staggering. They can often identify places or people in incoming television pictures before the details are given by the bureau sending them. And their identification of people sometimes extends to secondary government officials (or opposition figures) around the world—people who would often only be known to political elites within their own nation. The pressure to report such details accurately to clients every day ensures that only those who master this sacred knowledge rise to positions of influence in the editorial process.

Knowledge of the world enables agency journalists to do their jobs well, but *certainty* of their knowledge is what enables them to do their jobs at all. Without being convinced of their own ability to make sense of the world, their work would be overwhelming and confusing indeed. The certainty of world understanding sometimes extends to a confident interpretation of the subtext of the discourse of world leaders, and its future implications. Ironically, Gans concluded that in U.S. journalistic professional culture, "...the rules of news judgement call for ignoring story impli-cations" (Gans, 1985; quoted in Herman and Chomsky, 1988, 31). But international television agency news production requires prediction of major news in order to maximize cost effectiveness. News coverage cannot happen without planning, and planning is far easier with a script. The news agencies shape their coverage plans according to their internal predictions of what will happen.

And it is perhaps even more important that they warn their client broadcast-ers of what they expect to happen, and when (though, as this case study illustrates, those external warnings are far more conservative than the detailed internal predic-tions). The process of "knowing the story" means that the global news discourse of an event—the story told to the public—in one sense gets written by the knowledge-able few long before it actually occurs. Of course, journalists can only make edu-cated guesses—and they must, for the logistics of news coverage to function—but the question of how those guesses shape the story that is told is a vital one, and an under-researched one. Returning to the example of this case study, it could well be argued that the strings behind Kosovo's announcement were being pulled in Washington. But the journalists described here decided the story was in Belgrade, Mitrovica, and, to a lesser degree, Prishtina. And that was the story that was told.

On Thursday, February 14, APTN's output desk sent a message to clients that at 11:30 the following day their Global Video Wire (their supplementary satellite channel for live news) would send a special bulletin on Kosovo with a series of taped reports that APTN had produced during the past week. The range of topics of these reports (when there still remained no definitive news about an independence dec-laration) is instructive of the manner in which a television news agency seeks to cater to client broadcasters seeking different angles on a story: diplomacy, protest, vio-lence, peace efforts, celebration, and historical importance. It is unlikely that any broadcaster would have aired parts of all the AP reports. They had to choose at this point what their angle was going to be and use the AP material that illustrated that. The list of AP stories was as follows:

All packages are AP Television—AP Clients, except where stated.

1. Kosovo Backgrounder—A look at the defining moments over the past 20 years that have led towards a historic declaration of indepen-dence for the province. Source: Various—AP Clients Only
2. Kosovo Return—Exiles arrive to celebrate Kosovo's independence.
3. Kosovo Hospitals—Hospitals stock up on first aid as independence appears close.
4. Kosovo Enclaves—Serb areas worry about future as independence looms.

5. Kosovo Declaration—Museum hopes to display independence documents.
6. Kosovo Train—Train service which breaks down ethnic differences.
7. Kosovo Water—Fear of blockades of water, electricity by Serbia.

While APTN had been preparing for a February 17 announcement since the beginning of the month, they still used caution in the stream of advice they sent to their broadcaster clients. As late as February 14, APTN still told clients that the date of the announcement couldn't be determined. When the Kosovar prime minister called a news conference on Friday, February 15, APTN—and local journalists—downplayed its significance. But the BBC and CNN prepared to provide their own live coverage of the "presser," just in case it was the independence announcement and the BBC did transmit a portion of it live. In the end it was a minor announcement. A local journalist told Hoxha (in Paterson et al., forthcoming) that "He managed to get a free advertisement (for the independence announcement to follow) in BBC and CNN," but another local journalist speculated that the U.S. government intervened to ensure the announcement would come on that Sunday. Or could the press conference have simply been a test by the organizers of this pseudo-event to ensure that the world's media were ready?

The AP's internal communications told staff that the 17th was likely, since a Sunday announcement would prevent Russia from calling an emergency meeting of the U.N. Security Council. The news agency was sufficiently confident of its understanding of the Kosovo government's secret intention to deploy its staff accordingly, but not quite willing to advise its client media of that judgment.[7]

The news agencies' investment in television coverage of this news event was substantial. Staff who were involved felt it was well justified: APTN's Europe editor told me it was "the main set piece news event of the first half of [2008]." This was, in fact, a fairly predictable, highly manufactured, and fully packaged story in the sense that it came with its own international video coverage—that of Kosovo's national broadcaster—provided internationally by way of the European Broadcasting Union. So APTN worked hard to provide broadcasters with something more.

And APTN did what television news agencies have always specialized in doing: they gambled on violence. When violence occurs, it is globally newsworthy. The news agency without the pictures loses (literally, in the sense of lost subscriptions when disappointed clients are due to renew). APTN prepared for Kosovo to explode, and it did not. In a one-month period leading up to and including the week of the independence declaration, APTN spent U.S. $250,000, according to APTN's director of news, who approved that expenditure. He candidly told me, in 2009, that in hindsight, though "it played well in Europe, it did not really resonate [in other parts of the world]....[W]e spent too much on it."

Despite this massive overall expenditure on a single story, the meticulous, dollar-by-dollar cost accounting described in the last chapter prevailed even as this coverage reached its climax. Early in the independence week, at APTN in London, the Europe editor and senior EoD decided not to pay for coverage of a mid-week press conference due to the cost of doing so; they were confident that no news of importance would take place until the weekend and were concerned about the mounting costs. Editors in London asked their journalists arriving in Prishtina only for images of "streets getting cleaned up."

On Independence Day, APTN staff were pleased, seeing their pictures on the screens of major broadcasters around Europe. Especially popular were sweeping pictures of celebrating crowds outside the Parliament building, made possible because the Prishtina bureau had gone to the extra expense of hiring a giant camera boom (unusual for news coverage) to sweep over the crowds. In Paterson et al. (forthcoming) we address the further question of how such coverage—more visually reminiscent of concert or sports events than news events—might unwittingly contribute to the very purpose of the organizers of the pseudo-event: to show that an historical, irrefutable, joyous, and momentous event has occurred. From the point of view of the television news agency, it is simply doing the hard work, and spending the hard cash, to chase the iconic image on behalf of its clients.

Notes

1. Former television news agency producer John Jirik observed (correspondence, 2000) that as Indonesian troops handed over control of East Timor to the United Nations in preparation for independence, international television journalists left in mass, citing a concern about security and leaving the story largely unreported.

2. While the author conducted some limited observation at Reuters Television during the period and an interview concerning that coverage, this case study focuses on APTN both because the author spent more time observing it in the week prior to the independence announcement and because AP agreed to support the research project through further interviews and the provision of extensive documentation. It is reasonable to assume that Reuters Television conducted a similar planning process and provided similar news coverage, although there are indications that they did not invest as heavily as AP.

3. This is not to imply that many large media organizations did not maintain a considerable presence of their own through much of this period. Thussu (2000) cites Gibson (1999) reporting that at the height of the conflict CNN had seventy staff in the region and was spending $150,000 each day.

4. AP news report of November 19, 2007, referenced in AP internal communication.

5. All Associated Press internal documents quoted in this chapter are quoted with the permission of APTN.
6. Email to journalists from the Kosovo Press Center, February 21, 2008.
7. A far more dramatic case of news agency "internal knowledge" occurred in the months preceding the U.S. bombing of Baghdad, at the start of the second Gulf War. News agencies, along with major broadcasters, spent millions of dollars and months of effort quietly preparing for coverage of a war that, in terms of what they were communicating to the public, was not a strong possibility, given U.S. insistence that diplomacy was being pursued.

Producing the Crisis

The Business of Reporting Conflict

The story of how Associated Press Television News went about covering Kosovo's independence, which I provided in the preceding chapter, was made possible largely by the generous assistance of a senior APTN producer who lived and worked in Kosovo. She is a Kosovo native and a veteran of covering its recent turbulent past for APTN. A few years earlier she had married a young British APTN producer, Kerem Lawton, who had arrived in Kosovo after covering conflict and disaster for the agency in Turkey, Iraq, Albania, and China. The two were expecting a child. In March 2001, Lawton raced to Kosovo's border following American and British peacekeeping troops trying to quell shooting between Macedonian troops and an Albanian rebel group. Seconds after the cameraman with whom Lawton was travelling went to get pictures of local villagers fleeing the violence, a mortar shell struck the APTN car, killing Lawton.

He was the first of seven APTN employees killed in the last decade while covering news for the world's broadcasters.[1] Nine Reuters Television staff were killed in the same period.[2] They are among nearly 1,000 journalists killed in the last twenty years, but their stories make clear the often perilous nature of the profession that makes possible the international television news coverage of the world's broadcasters. Many of the television news photographers who have been considered the best conflict photographers of their generation have died violently doing their work. Such tragedies take a considerable emotional toll on the fairly small and close-knit employees of the television news agencies, where headquarters staff are in constant contact with field staff, and field staff move frequently in and out of roles in the London newsroom and so are often well known there.

As Chapter Two detailed, the bread-and-butter coverage of the television news agencies consists of politics, diplomacy, and conflict. Most broadcasters can cover the politics and diplomacy on their own—or manage without the fairly mundane visuals of it. But they are much more reluctant to wade into war zones, especially for the long term. Former APTN Vice President Eric Braun told me (interview, 2008) that

> a lot of the consumers of television news, particularly in the USA when they are watching any of the networks—CNN, NBC, Fox...little do they realize that most of the most dangerous pictures are actually taken by the agency photographers, not by the people who work for the branded networks.

This chapter explores the role of the television news agencies in manufacturing their major product: the world's image of war and conflict. The focus on conflict is rooted in the editorial priorities of the newsreels—the predecessors of the television news agencies. In the mid-1940s, for example, 77% of Paramount News newsreel film was devoted to war news;[3] it was the height of World War II, but this set a precedent that the television news agencies never strayed from. Television news agencies are the only entities that provide our day-to-day television coverage of major and minor conflicts around the world, long after major broadcasters have packed up their satellite dishes and gone home. But in doing so, their journalists and editors have often become targets both in a rhetorical and literal sense, and many have paid the ultimate price.[4]

By necessity, the television news industry creates a simplified televisual story about actual happenings, a story that corresponds to television news producers' perceptions—which are, of course, constrained by the logistics of television coverage, the organizational pressures on those journalists, and the vast range of factors influencing journalistic work. The public is especially dependent upon the story provided by television news in moments of rapidly developing international crisis, when other media cannot provide information with the speed or excitement provided by television. In such instances, television news workers come under extreme pressure to understand a story sufficiently to tell it, and then to tell it visually, as they understand it. They must comprehend a story, or believe they do, with little information, and then craft a brief visual version of the story. If the story is non-visual, or if the most relevant images are unavailable, they must improvise to provide visual evidence of the crisis they perceive. The story they tell—the story of the "crisis"—emerges from many influences far removed from either the desire to accurately depict the various facets of the conflict or from traditional news values.

The turbulent 1990s, described in industrial terms in Chapter Four, saw a shift in focus for the television news agencies from an overview of most of the world (but always with little attention to Latin America and Africa and a focus on Europe and the United States) to a fairly narrow focus on Eastern Europe, and then the Middle East. The fall of the East Bloc and the Balkan wars, and the "event-oriented" stories they generated, made up a substantial portion of the news agencies' output, diverting their resources from the developing world and from less conflictual, more "process-oriented" stories. For example, in 1989, Visnews's then-Managing Editor David Kogan told me, "Once Nelson Mandela is released...I will probably be taking resources out of Johannesburg and putting those into Eastern Europe."

At the time, those Johannesburg crews and equipment covered not only South Africa, but much of the continent. That the Balkans and Eastern Europe (followed later by the Middle East) should replace the developing world (and, generally, southern hemisphere nations) on the global television news agenda could be seen symbolically as reflecting the transference of the object of European and U.S. pity and scorn—the Other (see Dahlgren and Chakrapani, 1982)—to a more proximate, and thus more relevant and threatening, locus. It is certainly a more cost-effective locus for the Anglo-American providers of the world's news. If the West needs barbarians at the gates, and the Cold War "gate" fell in 1989 (the Berlin Wall), the threat to Europe and the United States had to be reconstructed, even at the expense of coverage of the rest of the world. The diversion of resources to war coverage resists quantification, for staff and equipment movements within the television news agencies are rarely discussed, difficult to track, and subject to constant change. But during the 1990s, agency concentration on the first Gulf War, then the war in Bosnia, and to a far lesser degree Chechnya, was considerable, comprising the vast majority of agency contributions to Eurovision.

The Balkans

The Balkan wars, in particular, were the television news agency preoccupation of the 1990s, and before the ongoing Iraq war, probably the longest—and most dangerous—continuing conflict story for the modern television news agencies. The agencies' coverage of the bloody breakup of the former Yugoslavia itself resembled a military campaign.[5] To construct the "war" in Bosnia seen by international television viewers around the world, alliances were discarded in an instant and re-established when convenient. The soldiers in this strange war ran on adrenaline for years, bemoaning the futility of the battles they waged, but always determined to strike the definitive blow. They risked their lives daily and fought fiercely. Winning was everything; no rules of engagement applied. Many had never played this vicious game before, but when recruited for their local expertise soon rose to positions of command. Others had played the game elsewhere; for some it was even a way of life. The liberation battles of South Africa were the training ground for several. Commanders spoke of the need to reduce casualties but gloated when their troops risked all. Principles held high to inspire these troops would be discarded easily for economic gain. Many careers were ended by bullets or shrapnel.

The forces I describe are not armies but international television news agencies; the people not soldiers but producers, photographers, and other agency field staff and freelancers, and their editors and managers in London. These are the people at the front lines of the creation of the televised "War in Bosnia": they created a war not with guns and shells but with their cameras, notebooks, and satellite dishes. Without them there would have been an actual war in Bosnia, but little of it would exist in the global consciousness, so it would have mattered little on the world stage. The agencies devoted massive resources to covering the wars of the former Yugoslavia, sometimes putting close to one hundred staff and freelance workers in the area (Westcott, 1995b).

The challenges of covering South Africa on the brink of civil war through the 1970s and 1980s and the Soviet occupation of Afghanistan gave rise to a few groups of extraordinary combat videographers who went on to routinely compete against and work for the television news agencies, as staff or freelancers. The fascinating stories of several of them—especially Rory Peck,[6] Peter Jouvenal, Nicholas della Casa and Vaughan Smith (who went on to start the Frontline Club for journalists in London)—are told in BBC journalist David Loyn's epic 2005 book *Frontline*. Their company (called "Frontline") began with coverage of South Africa, as did another company that went on to be based in Cyprus: Newsforce. From the late 1980s until the early 2000s, and especially during the period of the Yugoslav civil wars, these small news companies specializing in television war coverage became prominent. Where Frontline focused on obtaining pictures of conflict that other companies could not or would not obtain, Newsforce specialized in making the apparatus of TV news coverage available in conflict zones and other inaccessible locations. Lowndes Lipscomb of WTN told me (interview, 1995):

They're not a news coverage company. They're more a supplier of dishes, satellite dishes, and field producers to companies who want them, so we might hire [them]. ABC hires Newsforce a lot. We occasionally will use them when all of (our) dishes are deployed....They...look around for people like us, Reuters, and ABC, the American networks, and set up special operations for them. That's what they do....They're very good at war zones, and a lot of the American networks might be more (accepting of) the notion of putting Newsforce into a Goražde or...Sarajevo...than setting up their own operation which might be more vulnerable. These people, the Newsforce people, are pretty well war trained, and are more used to operating in that kind of environment.

Major broadcasters came and went in the Balkans. A few, such as the BBC and—to an extent—CNN, stuck it out for the duration. The print press, if anything, was more fickle; the presence of a print reporter at the battle front carries little weight with readers. But neither the print nor television news agencies could leave, for their mandate was to be where no one in their right mind would be, to provide a never-ending stream of accurate information and exceptional pictures from a war that permitted neither. As APTV Chief Executive Stephen Claypole put it (1995), "Even the oldest organizations, which are justifiably proud of their news traditions, admit that stories like the agony of Bosnia are dominated by the agencies."

But that unique position, that privileged place as chronicler of the war, embraced a paradox. The war was what the news agencies—print and television—told their clients it was, and few other international journalists were there to argue. And the war was what the agencies could report it to be, but news agencies could report only a small portion of the Bosnian civil war, those portions involving dramatic events occurring within the reach of agency journalists. But that war of singular, seemingly unconnected, dramas in a few locations became the war known to the world, the war the world reacted to, and thus the war the journalists themselves would continue to focus their efforts upon despite the knowledge of a larger, much more complex, all-but-unknown war underway just out of their reach.[7] The role of television is crucial. Without television pictures, broadcasters don't welcome a story, audiences don't react, and policies don't change. The international television news agencies told this story well and trusted that it represented accurately the terrible reality of Bosnia. They created the dominant image of the Bosnian civil war, an image highly distorted by structural constraints inherent in television news agency coverage routines. Further, the coverage shaped by those constraints had an agenda-setting impact across all media, making the distorted image (for example, a focus on the besieged city of Sarajevo with Serbs as sole aggressors), the guide for coverage by all media.

In August 1995, the agencies started to gear up for a new outbreak of all-out fighting, expecting the Croatian Army to enter the conflict in a massive way. Eventually it did, but it scored quick and decisive victories, apparently with little loss of life. Some in the agencies had been expecting the outbreak of World War III. Agencies and broadcasters filled all available hotel space in Split and Zagreb. Reuters and WTN shipped satellite dishes to those cities and did good business renting them out to broadcasters converging on the story. For over three years—and due largely to pressure from the BBC and its Sarajevo correspondent Martin Bell—Reuters and WTN had pooled their Sarajevo and Pale resources, meaning that they would share their satellite uplinks, armored vehicles, and crews, along with the images both obtained, in order to minimize the number of people going into dangerous situations and to maximize their safety. Reuters wrote to WTN in June 1995 demanding to dismantle the pool (Busfield, 1995a), and the arrangement ended on the first of August, 1995.[8] A WTN editor told the trade press:

> The pool was set up because we did not want WTN and Reuters both sending crews to dangerous situations and competing for the best angle and then running back for an artificial deadline [to compete with the other agency on Eurovision]. Reuters decided unilaterally to withdraw from the pool arrangement. (quoted in Busfield, 1995a)

But WTN would change its story a few weeks later, placing the blame on APTV for the pool's breakup. Its newsroom chief, Lowndes Lipscomb, said the AP's decision to compete against the pool instead of join it forced Reuters to withdraw. But APTV responded that it had not been invited to join the pool, and saw no reason to do so.[9] Before the breakup, BBC Head of News Gathering Chris Cramer called Managing Editor Mark Wood of Reuters to express his concern, and Cramer and a senior ITN executive wrote to Reuters and WTN to urge them to maintain the pool.[10] It had been a rare and intelligent period of cooperation in an otherwise hugely competitive period for the agencies. Had the parent corporations of each agency declared competition to be irrelevant in war zones (which would not have been unreasonable given the meager profitability of the television agencies at the time), lives might have been saved, news coverage might have been more comprehensive, and the long-running row over the pool arrangement—which embarrassed each of the agencies—would have been avoided. As it was, a television news agency photographer told Venter (2005, 86): "I've known a lot of people that have lost their lives trying to get the story first."

The news agencies and broadcasters were severely restricted by whatever access the various armies chose to offer them. Regarding access to one remote battle area, a WTN manager, in an editorial meeting, reported that Reuters and APTV

> have gone in without the permissions…we have taken the decision on the ground [at the bureau level] to adhere to the Serb Army [sic]…it will hit us right now, but in the long term its not worth pissing off the Serb commanders which apparently the opposition have done.

A company executive at the meeting requested that local staff be instructed to inform the Serb Army of the presence of the other companies in the restricted area, to "make sure it's known—to fan the flames." WTN need not have bothered. Sources inside and outside of Reuters told me that their agency had historically had more difficulty with access in the former Yugoslavia, and particularly with access to Bosnian Serb-held areas. At Reuters, I was told that Reuters wire-service reports early in the war were seen to be hostile to Bosnian Serb ambitions, and thus all Reuters's employees were targeted for exclusion. As put by one senior Reuters Television journalist, "The fact that nobody likes us prevents us from getting things the other bad guys [APTV and WTN] seem to be able to get quite easily." Another said of the Bosnian Serb and Croatian authorities: "These people have very long memories." Such access issues led to forms of self-censorship, both for the safety of staff on the ground and for the preservation of access. I observed a senior Reuters editor decline to use an unflattering story about Bosnian Serb commander Radovan Karadzic because of "the damage to our already fragile communications with the other side" (the Bosnia Serbs); using the story would be "far too dangerous."

During this period, broadcasters and agency journalists spoke off the record about the practice of paying combatants to videotape battle scenes as an alternative to putting staff photographers too close to battle. This was a little-known aspect of getting "bang-bang"—exciting pictures of wartime action. Occasionally the agency pool would purchase Hi-8 video images from freelancers or "camera-soldiers" when the material promised to be especially dramatic, or the three television news agencies would try to outbid each other for the best such images.[11] During the summer of 1995, I was informed that WTN was frequently outbidding the other agencies for such pictures offered in Bosnia; but agency journalists interviewed by Venter (2005, 86) also said such arrangements may occur without the knowledge or agreement of London editors. Senior agency informants confirmed to me that this practice occurred in the Yugoslav wars; this history is certainly worthy of further investigation. Venter provides this remarkable admission from one seasoned television news agency photographer of "how he would train non-journalists, such as soldiers, to use a video camera and to film the conflict on his behalf, in order to avoid putting himself in danger." The photographer chillingly explained to Venter,

> I can actually recruit people on the ground to go out and do the things that I wouldn't do. Uninsured, non-professionals, unskilled, untrained who can go out there and get those images. That's one of my tactics to survive. If I have to go into a minefield, my fixer goes first. He dies before I do, for $100 a day. (Venter, 2005, 86, fn35)

A principal mandate of the international television news agencies is to get the first and best pictures of any conflict, anywhere, for the world's broadcasters, and to stay on the scene of a lingering conflict long after the broadcasters go home. That mandate carries a high cost for agency personnel. Many have died, many more have been wounded, and many have spent long periods incarcerated, most notably WTN's Beirut Bureau Chief John McCarthy. Journalists, and especially television journalists, were often deliberately targeted in the former Yugoslavia. The London Independent reported, "Many reporters have been shot, very deliberately, by snipers while driving cars clearly marked with 'TV'—the sign of a press car."[12]

Getting television pictures of a war is an especially dangerous activity. Over 50 journalists died covering the war in the former Yugoslavia (Walpole, 1995), although one London newspaper put the total at 75 (Simpson, 1995). Largely following the example of the BBC, the television news agencies began to invest in safety equipment for their crews. In Bosnia, WTN shared the rental of an armored car for about $13,000 per month, and spent heavily on helmets and flak jackets. During my observation at each of the three TV news agencies, crew safety in the former Yugoslavia was a major concern, and at each agency a senior manager focused almost exclusively on safety issues.

Most journalists who enter conflict zones do so with full appreciation of the risk, and while most will embrace the credo "no story is worth dying for," there is surely no shortage of "adrenaline junkies" among media personnel who too frequently push the "edge of the envelope" to obtain a story—or more often, an image—that exposes them to too much risk (that is, their chances of dying or being seriously injured as a result of undertaking the task are high).[13] News agency photographers—video and still—are legendary (one might say notorious) for their willingness to risk all to obtain the image no one else has. Although news agency managers deny it, it is clearly a qualification for the job. The television news agencies have been condemned for encouraging the competitive ethos that might inspire staff to take unnecessary or unwise risks in order to obtain pictures or interviews the competition doesn't have. News agency managers and editors are in the immensely difficult position of balancing safety against their core business: obtaining the images broadcasters can't get for themselves. It is unclear if their industry could function any other way, but anger in the industry persists. One former Reuters Television producer told me that

> the shooters/journalists are very aware they are being exploited. But they have families to feed. As a profession they are also insanely proud of the risks they take for the "shot," which makes it easy for management to rationalize the danger it puts journalists in. . .

The New Focus on Safety

Television news agencies have a mixed record on the protection of field personnel. They are defensive about the safety of their newsgathering personnel, due in part to an essay by journalist Peter Maass in 2001 accusing Associated Press Television News of pressuring its top photographer, Miguel Gil Moreno de Mora, to take unnecessary risks in order to match pictures the Reuters agency was providing of the simmering war in Sierra Leone. In 2000, Gil Moreno was killed in an ambush with one of Reuters's best-known correspondents, Kurt Schork. BBC correspondent Jeremy Bowen had narrowly escaped death the day before when an Israeli army shell killed his colleague Abed Takkoush. He wrote: "Three friends dead in two days on different continents. I still wonder how news stories can ever be worth such losses" (in Colart and Venter, 2004, 125). Gil Moreno de Mora, once a corporate lawyer in Barcelona before falling in love with news photography,[14] had been APTN's star videographer in the Balkans, constantly gaining remarkable images others could not (he would go on to do the same from Chechnya and numerous other war zones). A biography at the website of the foundation established in his name observes that "his images were the only window to the world that the Chechens managed to open during the five years of war."[15]

Maass claimed he was told by several of Gil Moreno de Mora's colleagues that he had been pressured because the BBC had complained to the news agency about its coverage of the story, but both the BBC and APTN denied this. Returning to the tragic story of APTN producer Kerem Lawton at the beginning of this chapter, Lawton's father, John Lawton, himself a distinguished wire service correspondent, charged (Colart and Venter, 2004, 264–265) that, as London editors sent his son toward the fighting at the Macedonian border, they suggested as well that his pregnant wife might go along to interview the guerrilla fighters. But he also writes, "Kerem's colleagues, who I meet regularly in the field say the pressures from London have eased significantly since Kerem's death." It must also be noted that while my own more recent observation within the television agencies has been less extensive than in the 1990s, I have witnessed in the London newsrooms a considerable focus now on the safety of staff in the field, and less interest in what the other television news agency was doing at any given moment. These are indications that it is now rarer for competition to lead to unnecessary risk. However, while the decrease in the importance of daily competition on the Eurovision news exchange (see Chapter Four) may have tempered interagency competition slightly, there is still a potentially dangerous drive to be seen by the world's broadcasters to be getting the difficult stories and the inaccessible images.

In 2000, under pressure from the family of Gil Moreno de Mora, the two leading agencies again collaborated with each other and other television companies[16] to agree a set of safety standards called the "Joint code of practice for journalists working in conflict areas." The roots of the collaboration stretched back to the agency pool of the early 1990s. Venter notes (2005, 39) that even before this agreement "the agencies had their own mix of formal and informal policies on safety...[and] had already begun sending journalists on safety training courses." The policy consisted of these main points (published online by the Freedom Forum, in Venter, 2005, 48):

1. The preservation of human life and safety is paramount. Staff and free-lancers should be made aware that unwarranted risks in pursuit of a

story are unacceptable and must be strongly discouraged. Assignments to war zones or hostile environments must be voluntary and should only involve experienced newsgatherers and those under their direct supervision.

2. All staff and freelancers asked to work in hostile environments must have access to appropriate safety training and retraining. Employers are encouraged to make this mandatory.

3. Employers must provide efficient safety equipment to all staff and free-lancers assigned to hazardous locations.

4. All staff and freelancers should be afforded personal insurance while working in hostile areas, including coverage against death and personal injury.

5. Employers are to provide and encourage the use of voluntary and confidential counseling for all staff and freelancers returning from hostile areas or after the coverage of distressing events.

6. Media companies and their representatives are neutral observers. No member[s] of the media should carry a firearm in the course of their work.

7. We will work together to establish a databank of safety information, including the exchange of up-to-date safety assessments of hostile and dangerous areas.

8. We will work with other broadcasters and organizations to safeguard journalists in the field.

South African journalist and one-time APTV producer Sahm Venter provided a well-researched examination of the application of those safety guidelines. Venter's interviews and survey of a significant sample of active television news agency photographers suggested that while the news agencies were routinely sending field staff on (very costly) week-long, safety-training courses, they did not seem to be fulfilling a commitment to routine refresher safety courses, and few of the journalists in Venter's sample knew their companies had promised to do so. Most journalists felt the safety courses to be valuable, although both experienced journalists and journalism researchers have warned of an over-reliance on such courses and the possibility that they are used to excuse dangerous newsgathering. A few companies started and run by ex-soldiers have made a good business of media safety courses since the 1990s. (Centurion is one of the best known.) But one of Venter's journalist respondents told her:

> The world has changed and in war zones, journalists are targets. In the Iraq war the number of journalists killed by friendly bombing was huge. Journalists are taken hostage, killed

and beaten. I think the dangers facing journalists in certain areas are greater and more unpredictable than any Centurion course could prevent. (Venter, 2005, 82)

Few journalists say they were consulted when managers devised their company's safety policy, although managers Venter interviewed insisted otherwise. Venter found that journalists were occasionally using their right to refuse assignments and were doing so without repercussions from management; but some journalists still stated that they felt they needed to lie or make excuses to avoid dangerous assignments or finish one earlier than planned: "just over half of the journalists interviewed said they or someone they knew had done so" (Venter, 2005, 85). One particular interview response powerfully captures the combat journalist's dilemma:

One journalist admitted that he and others "often have to lie to London" and said, by way of an example, that he had once told his editors he was en route to a story in a dangerous zone when he was not and that he had then lied again by saying his car had broken down. He gave another example where he had lied to his editors when he told them that the military had prevented him from continuing along a road to a story. These were some of the tactics he said he employed to "do whatever I need to do to remain safe." (Venter, 2005, 85)

The survey found broad agreement that competitive pressure "encouraged by head office staff, and fuelled by younger, less experienced journalists" limits their ability to observe safety precautions. Journalists and agency managers disagreed on the amount of support given to freelancers, drivers, fixers, and other local staff hired on an ad hoc basis during the coverage of a story. Some respondents said they occasionally don't use safety equipment, like helmets or flak jackets, when either the local staff travelling with them or personnel from other broadcasters they are travelling with don't have such gear, or when they feel that doing so makes them more of a target.

Terry Leonard, an AP writer and news manager (later the AP's Southern Africa bureau chief), told Venter (2005, 52) that many agency staff should not be sent into dangerous situations simply because they are willing to, or feel the experience will be career enhancing:

There are two kinds of people...who definitely should not be in war zones...people who are not secure enough in their own judgment to make their own decisions, who will go because the crowd's going, who will go because their desk editor wants them to go. The other kind that's really a disaster is what we would call a "war junkie," somebody who feeds off the adrenalin of covering a war and who will take risks that are absolutely absurd because he loves what he's doing. These are people who get to the point where they cannot tell the difference between acceptable and ridiculous risk.

As the work of the DART Center for Journalism and Trauma well documents,[17] journalism safety is not just about staying alive in combat zones, but also about how journalists exposed to extraordinarily stressful events cope psychologically. The important survey of journalists by Feinstein in 2000, which included many television news agency journalists, found that "war journalists had significantly more post traumatic stress disorder (PTSD), depression, and psychological distress. Moreover, the rate of PTSD in the war group over the course of their working lives far exceeded that in traumatized firefighters and police officers, and approximated that recorded in combat veterans" (Feinstein and Owen, 2002; also see Brayne, 2004).

A final point might be made in regard to psychological harm in television news agencies, in this case, concerning the flood of images of violence and gore that agency newsroom workers are exposed to. Such images often characterize the kind of news coverage broadcasters most depend upon the agencies to provide—war coverage and developing world coverage. Sensitive readers should avoid the next sentence, in which I describe what I mean: my intent is not to shock but to make clear the intense and brutal nature of images that comprise a routine aspect of international television news agency production. In my few weeks of observation in agency newsrooms, I witnessed the gory aftermath of a shelling in Sarajevo, much of it shot by the agency photographer in the operating room and morgue, the result of a car bomb, where only the intestines and lower torso of the victim remained, and the scene immediately after a bus bombing where a female passenger, her head blown away in the explosion, remained seated in the burned-out bus.

With a massacre, a bombing, a shelling, or other carnage occurring almost daily in some part of the world, the television news agency newsrooms see it all and see it first. With better resources than local television stations, agency pictures of such horror often reach London television news agency newsrooms before they get to broadcasters in the area where the event occurred. Such stories are fast breaking, and agency photographers are under pressure to deliver pictures to London before the competition does. The result is that photographers arrive at the scene of the disaster and start recording continuously as they walk through the carnage, taking little time to record a variety of angles or trying to capture more subtle pictures that indicate the violence without the gore. They might return to get those later. After just a few minutes of recording, those photographers (or often, a motorcycle courier working with them) race to a satellite uplink and send the pictures to London without editing them.

Thus the most graphic images of the immediate aftermath of a violent event, usually a powerful explosion of some kind, are constantly seen in London. Crucially, no one else sees such images on a routine basis. Photographers do not—most cover such a story only occasionally, and only the most dedicated specialist combat photographers stay in war zones for long.[18] Journalists in the newsrooms of broadcast stations around the world do not, for the agencies often edit out the goriest material they receive before sending it to clients. Further, not every story goes to every client, and the typical journalist in a broadcast newsroom will see only a portion of the agency output his or her station does receive. And television audiences do not see anything like this, for most broadcasters heavily edit such material before showing it to their viewers. [19] Editors at the Finish broadcaster YLE told me they get too many images of carnage from agencies and feel that their audience had little appetite for gore. When one such agency story was received, a YLE editor remarked,

> Such grim pictures. You cannot use them. Where you only have the bodies, you cannot illustrate the wire copy very well.

Prolonged exposure to such images is tempered only by the agency shift system of days on, days off; but it is clear that over months or years in an agency newsroom, the exposure to such images is considerable. What is the effect of such exposure to so many gory images? How do agency journalists cope? The literature provides few answers, and the journalists themselves downplay the significance of such images. I have observed one consistent reaction in agency newsrooms to such material expressed as an unnaturally exaggerated detachment. Typically, a dark joke may be made amid a few uncomfortable laughs, and news workers then move on quickly to another task. It is a worthy topic for further research, and there have been indications in recent years that news agency managers are concerned about the issue.[20]

But the issue has implications for general representation of the world conveyed by television news agencies, as discussed in Chapter Two. If the portrayal of a non-Western world consisting mostly of carnage is accepted as natural (not shocking, extraordinary, or disturbing), the use of such images to illustrate global stories becomes routine, at the expense of alternative representations and story frames. Because the job forces these journalists to cope with such stressful images, it also facilitates the routine processing of such images and the perception of such scenes—in the agency newsroom—as ordinary. This might have the unfortunate side effect of causing agencies not to question such brutal images or seek alternative representations, contributing to the creation of the violent and chaotic global "reality" presented by television news.

Returning once again to threats to agency journalists in the field, we should note that in covering the current conflict in Iraq and Afghanistan the trauma of the work for the television news agency journalists has been compounded by the magnitude of threats against them: bounties on the heads of Western journalists by some insurgent groups and an astounding degree of threat from the military forces of the United States, whom Western journalists once commonly counted on for protection.

The New Threats

As put by BBC and Channel 4 journalist Nick Gowing "the new insidious development is that because of the impact of our real time capability to bear witness immediately, we are being actively targeted by warriors, warlords, and forces of even the most highly developed governments who do not want us to see what they are doing" (Gowing, 2003, 233). He and other commentators blame the increasing threat to journalists' safety in part on new technologies that permit journalists, especially those reporting for television, to get closer to combat for longer periods than ever before; but it is notable that analyses of journalists' safety have been making that argument for some time. Writing in 1986, Kirby and Jackson contended that "the new technology has increased at once the influence and the vulnerability of the journalist." According to one Associated Press editor, Nick Tatro, reporting from a dangerous area "used to be more hit-and-run…you look, you leave." But newer technology now allows transmission from the scene, and "sometimes we stay for hours or days on end in that environment."[21]

Disturbingly, one of the leading threats to television journalists in the Iraq conflict has been the very governmental power nominally in control of the country: the U.S. military. The killing of Reuters videographer Taras Protsyuk and a Spanish journalist by a U.S. tank crew, as they took pictures from their Baghdad hotel in 2003, was thoroughly described by veteran journalists—dozens of whom were present—and has been the subject of a public battle waged by Reuters and the journalists' families to hold the U.S. military to account. As with every other incident involving journalists, the U.S. military exonerated itself, although it offered at least three differing accounts of what happened in the months following the incident. But the presence of the world's media in the hotel was well known to military commanders, leading to the suspicion that the killing wasn't accidental. Several thorough investigations have been conducted since, and each has condemned the military explanations as farcical (Gopsill, 2004; Campagna and Roumani, 2003; Knightley, 2003; TeleCinco, 2004), but several have said that the main fault lay not with the tank crew who killed the journalists, but with the upper levels of command, who failed to pass on their knowledge that the hotel was a media center to troops on the ground.

Several other Reuters Television journalists have also died this decade, including some killed by U.S. forces in Iraq. The many journalists with top Reuters Television photographer Mazen Dana unanimously claimed that their reporting work in the area was clearly known to the U.S. tank crew that killed him (Wilson, 2003).[22] Reuters still photographers Dhia Najim and Namir Noor-Eldeen and staff member Saeed Chmagh were also killed by U.S. troops (they are commemorated by their Reuters colleagues at www.thebaron.info). The brutal killing of Noor-Eldeen and Chmagh in 2007 by a U.S. military helicopter crew was revealed to the world in 2010 when Wikileaks posted previously secret helicopter gun camera video of the attack,[23] leading Reuters to renew its call for investigation. Despite the damning visual evidence, to date there has been no new investigation or apology by the U.S. government to Reuters or the journalists' families.

In 2004, three Reuters journalists, along with an employee of the U.S. television network NBC, were abducted and tortured in the same manner as those at the Abu Ghraib prison by U.S. military personnel (Parenti, 2004; Wolper, 2004). Reuters has made complaints to the highest levels of the Pentagon. Its Global managing editor complained that U.S. military conduct is spiraling "out of control" (Regan, 2005). The U.S. military's only response to Reuters's requests for investigation following the abduction and torture of their journalists was a threatening demand that they drop their complaint (Harding, 2004). The Associated Press also complained to the U.S. military, stating that U.S. troops had been harassing and detaining journalists (Jurkowitz, 2003). Reuters was encouraged in March 2006 when the U.S. military announced new policies to protect journalists in Iraq, including a commitment to treat detainees claiming to be journalists as "unique" cases to be referred quickly up the chain of command, and a commitment to investigate allegations of abuse of detainees, including "a beating in custody that left a Reuters cameraman unconscious." U.S. Major General Jack Gardner also told Reuters that "watching or filming combat or meeting insurgents were not in themselves grounds for arrest" (Macdonald, 2006).

The question of whether television news agency journalists have been deliberately targeted by all combatants in the Iraq War remains an open one. Television news agencies, and their parent companies, have done some important and vital work for the protection of journalists, but the nature of news agency work has also been blamed for the loss of many lives through its preoccupation with the visual and the violent. In a decade that has seen positive indications that the television news agencies are willing to exercise more caution and restraint than they have in the past to ensure the safety of their personnel covering conflict, the losses among their personnel and those of many other media organizations have still soared—in no small part because few combatants seem prepared to recognize the requirement under international law that "Journalists engaged in dangerous professional missions in areas of armed conflict shall be considered as civilians."[24] And television journalists, whether through ambition, courage, or organizational pressure, still strive to obtain pictures from the world's most dangerous places.

Notes

1. These details are from a poignant article by the Associated Press (Associated Press, 2001) and are mentioned with the permission of the person concerned. I might note, since she writes about both in Colart and Venter (2004), that this APTN producer has the tragic distinction of losing two former partners to violence while they were working for AP.
2. I base these numbers on widely published accounts and tallies kept by press protection organizations like Reporters sans frontières.
3. Fielding (2006, 289), from Paramount News statement reported in *Motion Picture Herald*, February 3, 1945, 14.
4. This chapter describes that literal targeting, but instances of the rhetorical targeting include the rabid campaign against Reuters by American conservatives over their refusal to use the term "terrorist" in stories—mentioned in the notes to Chapter Two—and the internet-spread and incorrect accusation that a television news agency photographer incited a group of Palestinians to celebrate the 9/11 attacks in the United States.
5. The violent disintegration of the former Yugoslavia took place from 1990 until the Dayton Agreement of 1995. Violence in the region again flared in 1998 with about a year of conflict between Serbian forces and the Kosovo Liberation Army, followed by NATO's military intervention in 1999.
6. Peck's widow established a charity which continues to support and recognize freelance journalists: www.rorypecktrust.org.
7. Bell (1995) describes his nagging frustration at being unable to get at the war out of reach of television. BBC and (former) Channel 4 (U.K.) editor Nick Gowing recalled to a London seminar on journalism:

   > The problem is, it became very difficult to report in a very accurate way what was really going on—that quite often the Bosnian army were inciting the Bosnian Serbs into attacking the city and I saw this in the newsroom....I would see agency copy come through of say, 16 or 20 paragraphs sometimes, which would give the detail of what had happened which had to be subbed down for television...as "the Bosnian Serbs were shelling Sarajevo again." Quite often the layering that was often happening in the war simply was knocked out of the news cycle and I think in retrospect that is something which troubled...me; I was lucky enough working for a program where I was able to get 6, 7, 8 minutes on the air quite often which allowed us to put in...the more layered versions of this, but even then it got squeezed out...the war defied our ability to cover it.

   The seminar was recorded from CSPAN (U.S.) in the late 1990s, but I have not been able to determine its precise location and date. For analysis of when TV does and does not affect policy, also see Gowing (1994).
8. Some sources told me that Reuters was unhappy with the quality and quantity of coverage being provided by WTN crews in Sarajevo, believing it was hurting its reputation with clients.

9. Kelly (1995, 10); and interviews.

10. Disclosed by a WTN manager in an editorial meeting; also Busfield (1995b).

11. Interviews, and confirmed in correspondence with a former senior WTN journalist.

12. Helm and Daly (1995).

13. The risk culture of the war correspondent is well described in a considerable literature, most recently the extensive interview-based research of Tumber and colleagues (Tumber and Webster, 2004). A useful contemporary analysis of the psychology behind the phenomenon is Brayne (2003).

14. Interestingly, CNN's long-time sole correspondent/photographer for most of Africa, Gary Stryker, also went from a career as a lawyer into international newsgathering.

15. http://www.fundacionmiguelgilmoreno.com/en/biografia.html; also see Baker (2004, 68–69).

16. The five companies were Reuters, APTN, BBC, CNN, and ITN. Interestingly, Chris Cramer, who was himself a hostage early in his career, pushed the television companies and agencies into the Bosnia pool arrangement, led BBC efforts toward a comprehensive safety policy, was involved in the 2000 news safety agreement, and after a stint with CNN, is now an executive with Reuters.

17. See http://dartcenter.org.

18. I was occasionally told that scenes of horror involving civilian casualties in war zones are deliberately videotaped and transmitted in the most excessive and lurid way the videographer can muster. It is their opportunity to make a strong statement to the world, even if they realize much of their footage will not go beyond the London newsroom.

19. For broadcaster reactions to violence in Britain see, for example, BBC correspondent Martin Bell (1995), who describes letters to the BBC from the British viewing public urging less display of war violence and carnage. British broadcasters enacted strict censorship of violent footage to avoid regulation; war was thus made palatable. See also Frean (1995). Regardless of the inclinations of broadcasters, there is a substantial public appetite—of some sort—for violent images. According to a manager at WTN, in 1995, a small British production company produced a videotape entitled "Executions" for the consumer video rental and sales market, which was a compilation of gory scenes that had gone through WTN edit rooms but had generally been discarded as too gory and never sent to broadcasters. The tape became a best seller around the world. The producers, Still Movements Productions, claimed the tape was endorsed by Amnesty International, but that organization disavowed any connection with it. WTN does not know how the images were obtained, but it was apparent that its own editing staff were suspect. The fact that the images came from WTN was never disclosed in the media (*Newsweek*, July 3, 1995; *Times* [London], June 18, 1995; both via Lexis/Nexis).

20. APTN manager Nigel Baker recounts that his agency felt obliged to distribute the gruesome video images of the execution of an American who had been kidnapped in Iraq in 2004, with extensive warnings to its clients; and that "in house, the number of people who had to deal with it was kept to an absolute minimum" (2009, 49–50).

21. Trigoboff (2002, 20).

22. Dana had covered the Israeli-occupied territories for Reuters for fourteen years, surviving beatings and earlier shootings by Israeli forces. In light of a history of apparent Israeli efforts

to stop his work stretching over many years, his killing by U.S. troops, when none of the other journalists working with him were harmed, has been regarded by journalists' groups as suspicious (International Federation of Journalists, 2005, and others).

23. http://wikileaks.org/wiki/Collateral_Murder,_5_Apr_2010, accessed in April 2010, but the video seems to be off the Wikileaks website at the time of this writing.

24. Article 79 of the Protocol Additional to the Geneva Conventions.

Conclusion

Television News for the Few or the Many?

A concern in the 1970s was that five international news agencies based in the North had a virtual monopoly on the stories told about the South and that, in a more general sense, agencies—with their limited conceptions of news—dominated the international flow of news (i.e., MacBride, 1980; Nordenstreng, 1984). Today the news agency sector has decreased to just two dominant international players, and major international media are more dependent upon them than ever before as they cut newsgathering resources. Recalling Jonathan Dimbleby's 1980s prediction from the preface of this book that, as we find the capacity to be better informed, "we're at risk of becoming less and less informed by fewer and fewer people," a contemporary picture comes into focus of those few: shooting video of a meeting of diplomats or risking all to capture images of war; working the phones in London to coordinate the daily reaping of the news video harvest; laboring on the assembly line of television news agency output (to meet a deadline that is always just seconds away) to feed the ravenous appetites of television stations, websites, and mobile phone news junkies; and executives with their eyes always on one more subscription or one more breaking story transmitted a moment ahead of the competition. The global news agencies have in abundance the one thing almost no other media have in any form: new content.

The big shift now is from the old media to the new, and as broadcasters are squeezed by the proliferation of channels amid declining advertising, many will cut from two television news agencies to one, or strive to do without. In 2004 the BBC required journalists to go a week without Reuters Television and a week without

APTN to see if they could manage without either, and concluded that "for the scale of the operation that we run, we require two agencies—we couldn't be everywhere doing everything," according to the BBC executive who devised the scheme, speaking in 2008 (and requesting anonymity). The likely result will be even fiercer competition between the two agencies, bringing the risk of harm to news quality and breadth, and harm to journalists (as discussed in the preceding chapter). This may be offset by what seems the infinite expansion of appetite for news video through the Internet and mobile services. The television news agencies will gradually do less and less television, as they move further from their roots. In the 1990s the surviving television news agencies were wholly absorbed by the two leading wire services, diluting their unique cultures and leading them into the contemporary era, as the forces of news convergence now marginalize the distinctiveness of international television newsgathering at the wholesale level.

Are there prospects for a more diverse and "multi-perspectival" (Gans, 1980) view of the world on international television, either via challenges posed by new media, or more traditional competition to television news agencies from other news organizations? Perhaps the leading potential competitor to the current television news agencies is the very broadcaster they both helped to create, which itself has been lurking on the sidelines as potential competition in the wholesale market since the 1990s. Since 2008 CNN has suggested it wishes to operate as a full-service news agency, but the implications of that remain unclear. It ended its subscription to Reuters in 2007 and then further surprised the media world in 2010 by dropping the Associated Press and declaring that it could go it alone as a broadcaster and wholesale news provider. But it returned to Reuters for a small amount of "breaking" news.[1] CNN has saved millions of dollars annually by not taking full subscriptions with the two leading news agencies, but historically has not had the newsgathering and news distribution infrastructure of Reuters or AP (having about half the number of international bureaus as either agency and far fewer staff), and so commentators have regarded their decision as overly ambitious, if not self-destructive (i.e., Stone, 2007). A senior APTN executive estimated that, following the break with Reuters, 70% or more of CNN's international video content came from APTN.[2]

The problem for CNN is producing its own international news in sufficient quantity to satisfy the appetites of its various networks and websites in the United States and around the world. There are signs that CNN is investing heavily in building newsgathering infrastructure in regions where it has substantial programming investments. For instance, in Latin America, where CNN's Spanish-language channel has been successful (and it now owns a separate Chilean broadcaster), recent news events have seen a larger CNN presence than even that of the major Latin

American broadcasters, such as Brazil's Globo, or of either of the two international television news agencies. In the course of her research (presented in Chapter Two), Cleidejane Esperidião (2010, personal communication) observed that a week after the Haiti earthquake, CNN had eleven camera teams deployed, while APTN had ten.

Other potential competitors for the wholesale delivery of international television news pictures exist, albeit on a smaller scale. Their very existence suggests the possibility of a more fragmented market emerging. The news agency Bloomberg has grown rapidly but so far poses more of a challenge to the financial news services of Thomson-Reuters than to the video agencies. Baker (2009) reported that by 2007 the French news agency AFP had launched a TV news service with forty video journalists working from ten international bureaus outside of France. The domestic British news agency, the Press Association, has aggressively built a video newsgathering apparatus to supply video for the websites of British newspapers, but with the potential to expand internationally. The well-funded, commercial Ihlas News Agency from Turkey competes with the global television news agencies in the provision of news stories and in "broadcast service" support to broadcasters on Middle Eastern stories, and has grown substantially over the past decade. The wealthy and widespread Chinese state news agency, Xinuan, is another potential player in international television news distribution. But there is little indication that any of these would produce a substantially different kind of wholesale television news product than the existing industry leaders. The qualified international success of the rolling news channels Al Jazeera, Telesur, and Al Jazeera English, which profess a desire to challenge traditional story frames, does imply that there is a market need for a broader range of news at the wholesale level.

The news agencies have proud traditions of producing valuable journalism for over the past century and a half. The danger now is that the *brand image* of the truthteller becomes so institutionalized—from the corporate hierarchy down to every newsgatherer in the field—that the spirit of discovery, pursuit of justice, and holding the powerful to account is driven into the shadows and regarded as quaint, but wholly impractical, idealism. While our image of the world is constrained by the commercial imperatives of the news agencies, it is an image of many people and places—mostly in times of crisis—that might not exist at all were it not for these same agencies. Narrow definitions of news—as armed conflict, as American, as having global economic consequence—distort television's representation of our world. For most broadcasters, however, the representation of news would be far more distorted and sparser without their flow of news agency pictures. The television news wholesale system described in this book broadly works. It brings to the world television news pictures that would otherwise not exist; it brings profit to the companies that control it; and it contributes substantially to vital documentation of human history. On occasion, it exposes injustice and inspires the world to act. But I have sought to document how, despite all these positive characteristics, it is also a system substantially constrained by its commercial nature.

It may not be enough to simply ask the television news agencies to be what they are not. Perhaps referring to critiques by this author, the APTN's Nigel Baker wrote in 2004 (72), "there is a confusion in the minds of many that agencies perform the role of a public service broadcaster with a mission to cover stories of note wherever they happen in the world…agencies exist as a business to serve the needs of their customers. It should, therefore, be of no surprise that the agenda of the agencies is often swayed in favor of those customers." Just as the building blocks of human life—our air, our water, our food—are assumed to be so vital that no one or two private enterprises are given free rein over them, we could reasonably ask if the building blocks of *human consciousness* might deserve to be held in the same regard. One might struggle to find any other business so driven by competition, speed, and other commercial imperative *and* so directly caught up in the lives and deaths of the people who are both the producers and subjects of their product. Society usually finds merit in intervention to minimize the risk of harm when the profit motive and public good conflict, and so is public intervention needed here as well?

Television news shapes public understanding everywhere and has been known to distort that understanding in dangerous ways (as with the widespread and completely inaccurate perception in the United States of Iraq's involvement in the 9/11 attacks, most pronounced among viewers of one conservative television news network; Kull et al., 2002). And the constituent pieces of international news—in all its forms—are the product of the global news agencies, even if they have little to do with irresponsible (re)constructions of news by some media outlets. But, importantly, the television news agencies were not always constrained by a commercial agenda.

When Reuters took over majority control of Visnews in 1985 it ended *public control* of an international television news agency that had functioned with great success for over a quarter of a century. The control was public because the majority of shares in the agency were owned by public broadcasters, accountable to their national publics who paid for them, thus obligating them to follow a public service (as opposed to commercial) agenda in their editorial decisions. This didn't prevent Visnews from behaving in a very commercial manner at times, but it did ensure that commercial considerations rarely prevailed over the judgment of seasoned journalists, ultimately answerable to public organizations. In some regards, the Eurovision news exchange carries on this tradition. It has always been directly controlled by Europe's public broadcasters (not just the international few who happened to invest early in Visnews), but was not historically a newsgatherer in competition with agencies and broadcasters (Keune, 1991; Hjarvard, 1995b). It has come to play an increasingly journalistic role by providing the technical facilities for European broadcasters to use at the scene of major news stories all over the world.

National and transnational authorities (like the European Union) should recognize the threat to democracy posed by source concentration in mainstream journalism and take action to promote diversity (just as national governments—especially France—are seeing the need to subsidize national journalism). European policy during the 1990s did a great deal to bring about the current situation of commercial control over international news flow. It devastated European public broadcasters, which were the remaining counter to a commercially determined international television news agenda, and it spurred the growth of national and regional commercial broadcasters without placing journalistic criteria on them, so they naturally chose the cheapest and easiest means to provide news coverage: dependence on the agencies. Creating a larger, global role for the Eurovision news exchange would put leading public broadcasters (and this could expand to publicly controlled media everywhere) back at the forefront of shaping the news agenda, thus promoting a more democratic global public sphere.

European investment in Eurovision could enable it to compete internationally with commercial players as a news provider and orient the international television news agenda more toward a public, non-commercial, and non-American, ethos. If an independent, public-service, global wholesale television newsgatherer existed, what sort of news values might it have? To become globally relevant and challenge the worst aspects of mainstream television news framing, this new economic model should co-exist with a journalistic ethic focused on *humanity* (not power, politics, economics, or celebrity), and seek to balance resource allocation between threats to human life (and quality of life) everywhere and the story preferences of the broadcasters who participate. There is no need for less television news agency output to the world's broadcasters, but there is a need for a new option—a non-commercial option.

It is important to end this book by observing the pressing need for further research into the sources of news everywhere. Utopian dreams of media pluralism and access to a multitude of voices around the world have long since collapsed, and while the wealthiest media barons seek to dismantle what little is left of public media (Barnett, 2009), journalistic enterprise continues to decline as dependence on public relations and wholesale news increases (see Lewis et al., 2008; Paterson, 2007). Scholarship is struggling to catch up. The importance of collaborative research with media organizations increases as (genuinely independent) research access to those organizations becomes rarer. The wholesale and retail media must promote the broader view that media accountability and transparency are vital to a democratic public communications system (without which they are in as much danger from the disintegration of pluralist media as the rest of us). And future researchers of news agencies could do well to attend more than did this author to newsgathering in the field, among producers, videographers, and within bureaus. Much could be learned from such research, especially where it follows and accounts for the full news manufacturing process—from story discovery, to reporting processes, to processing and distribution, and even to consumption and redistribution (that is, through blogging and social media) by the public.

I hope my admiration for the television news agencies has been as clear as my concern about them. What they accomplish every day is impressive, but a focus on their everyday work obscures the problem that relaying a limited selection of information in a limited set of ways might limit public understanding, especially when so many people all over the world consume that same collection of audiovisual information every day. The television news agencies and the people who built them—many of whom I quote in this book—can be proud that they document history and often illuminate the worst of the human condition, when other global media turn away, or when powerful forces resist exposure. As put by the family of slain television news agency war photographer Miguel Gil Moreno, "his mission was to be the voice of justice of those who couldn't shout out, even though they were going through the worst experiences of their lives."[3] Our collective challenge now is to determine if we wish to continue to depend so heavily on the few commercial television news wholesalers for our image of the world, or to demand, from broadcasters, governments, and ourselves, a more representative and humane picture of our world.

Notes

1. Instructions to CNN staff to do so are provided in an internal CNN memo published by Reuters at http://blogs.reuters.com/blog/archives/9558. Also see Kenneth, 2007.
2. CNN's initial break with Reuters Television represented a curious return to its early days, when it depended on a cut-price contract with UPITN (which would become APTN) to build its reputation as an international news organization (see Chapter Three). Stone (2007) provides a detailed analysis linking the break to Reuters' marketization of the news product over the preceding decade or more, and specifically, Reuters' ever increasing protectiveness of the copyright of its images—an enormous complication and cost for an organization like CNN which strives to reuse its video stories over a vast range of channels and media platforms.
3. http://www.fundacionmiguelgilmoreno.com/en/biografia.html.

Bibliography

Ailes, A. (1994) *A brief history of the company's satellite achievements.* Reuters Television. Internal document.

Alleyne, M. D., and Wagner, J. (1993) Stability and change at the "big five" news agencies. *Journalism Quarterly,* 70(1), 40–50.

Althaus, S. (2010) The forgotten role of the global newsreel industry in the long transition from text to television. *International Journal of Press/Politics,* 15(2), 193–218.

Altschull, J. H. (1984) *Agents of power: the role of news media in human affairs.* New York: Longman.

Ang, I. (1996) *Living room wars: rethinking media audiences for a postmodern world.* London: Routledge.

Anon. (1947) Metro, INS linked to Telenews deal. *Variety,* December 17, 1, 24. Courtesy AP Archive.

Anon. (1949) Newsreels flop on tele, high costs, time lag are main factors, WPIX follows camel exit. *Billboard,* February 12, 15. Retrieved from: http://books.google .co.uk/books?id=M_YDAAAAMBAJ&pg=PA15&dq=%22Newsreels+Flop+On+ Tele%22#v=onepage&q=&f=false.

APTN.com (2010)

Archetti, C. (2008) News coverage of 9/11 and the demise of the media flows, globalization and localization hypotheses. *International Communication Gazette,* 70, 463–485.

Arnett, P. (1993) Journalists in peril: a view from the front lines. Paper for the Freedom Forum.

Associated Press (2001) Elegy for a news producer killed in Kosovo. March 30. *Freedom Forum.* Retrieved from: http://www.freedomforum.org/templates/document.asp? documentID=13562.

Associated Press (2006) Delicate negotiations lead to APTN bureau in North Korea. *AP World*, Summer, courtesy Associated Press.

Associated Press (2007) *Breaking news: how the Associated Press has covered war, peace, and everything else.* New York: Princeton Architectural Press,

Atwood, L. E. (1990) Old colonial ties and news coverage of Africa. Unpublished paper for the East-West Center, Honolulu.

Auletta, K. (1993) Raiding the global village. *New Yorker*, August 2, 25–30.

Ayish, M. (2010) Morality vs. politics in the public sphere: how the Al Jazeera satellite channel humanized a bloody political conflict in Gaza. In Cushion, S., and Lewis, J. (Eds.) *The rise of 24-hour news television: global perspectives.* New York: Peter Lang.

Baker, M. (1994) ITN opts to scrap WTN news contract early. *Broadcasting News*, March 25, 1.

Baker, N. (2004) Invisible giants, quiet revolution. In Paterson, C., and Sreberny, A. (Eds.) *International news in the twenty-first century*, 63–78. Eastleigh, U.K.: University of Luton/John Libbey.

Baker, N. (2009) Technology, timeliness and taste: the battlefronts for the twenty-first century news agency. In Owen, J., and Purdey, H. (Eds.) *International news reporting: frontlines and deadlines*, 38–54. Chichester: Wiley-Blackwell.

Bantz, C. R. (1985) News organizations: conflict as a crafted cultural norm. *Communication*, 8(2), 225–244.

Barnett, S. (2009) British broadcasting deserves better than Murdoch attack. Reuters, September 2. Retrieved from: http://blogs.reuters.com/great-debate-uk/2009/09/02/british-broadcasting-deserves-better-than-murdoch-attack/.

Barnouw, E. (1983) *Documentary.* New York: Oxford.

Barrett, L. C. (2010) Live from Chile: "This Media Event." *Columbia Journalism Review*, October 11. Retrieved from: http://www.cjr.org/the_kicker/live_from_chile _this_media_eve.php.

Bartram, J. (2003) News agency wars: the battle between Reuters and Bloomberg. *Journalism Studies*, 4(3), 387–399.

Batscha, R. (1975) *Foreign affairs news and the broadcast journalist.* New York: Praeger.

Becker, L., and Whitney, C. (1982) "Keeping the gates" for gatekeepers: the effects of wire news. *Journalism Quarterly*, 59, 60–65.

Behr, R. L., and Iyengar, S. (1985) Television news, real-world cues, and changes in the public agenda. *Public Opinion Quarterly*, 49, 38–57.

Bell, M. (1995) *In harm's way.* London: Hamish Hamilton.

Bell, M. (1998) The journalism of attachment. In M. Kieran (Ed.) *Media ethics.* London: Routledge.

Beltran, L. R. (1978) TV etchings in the minds of Latin Americans. *Gazette*, 61–85.

Berkowitz, D. (1990) Refining the gatekeeping metaphor for local television news. *Journal of Broadcasting and Electronic Media*, Winter, 55–68.

Bielsa, E., and Bassnett, S. (2009) *Translation in the global news*. London: Routledge.

Boorstin, D. J. (1961) *The image: a guide to pseudo-events in America*. New York: Atheneum.

Born, G. (2004) *Uncertain vision: Birt, Dyke and the reinvention of the BBC*. London: Secker & Warburg.

Bowden, T. (1987) *One crowded hour: Neil Davis combat cameraman 1943–1985*. North Ryde, Australia: Angus and Robertson.

Boyd-Barrett, O. (1977) Media imperialism: towards an international framework for the analysis of media systems. In J. Curran et al. (Eds.) *Mass Communication and Society*. London: Edward Arnold.

Boyd-Barrett, O. (1980) *The international news agencies*. London: Constable.

Boyd-Barrett, O. (2000) Constructing the local: news agencies re-present the world. In Malek, A., and Kavoori, A.P. (Eds.) *The global dynamics of news: studies in international news coverage and news agenda*. Stamford, CT: Ablex Publishing.

Boyd-Barrett, O., and Rantanen, T. (2004) New agencies news sources: a re-evaluation. In Paterson, C., and Sreberny, A. (Eds.) *International news in the twenty-first century*, 31–46. Eastleigh, U.K.: University of Luton/John Libbey.

Boyd-Barrett, O., and Thussu, K. (1992) *Contra-flow in global news*. London: John Libbey.

Brayne, M. (2003) Mainlining on war (book review). *British Journalism Review*, 14:1.

Brayne, M. (2004) Emotions, trauma and good journalism. In Paterson, C., and Sreberny, A. (Eds.) *International news in the twenty-first century*. Eastleigh, U.K.: University of Luton/John Libbey.

Breed, W. (1955) Social control in the newsroom: a functional analysis. *Social Forces*, 33, 326–335.

Broadcast (1993) industry news. May 28.

Broadcast (1994) Claypole joins rival. *Broadcast*, March 18, 4.

Broadcast (1999) Jobs on line at Reuters. January 29. Retrieved from: http://www.broadcastnow.co.uk/news/multi-platform/news/jobs-on-line-at-reuters/1208674.article

Broadcast (2000) Reuters TV may sue in Oz. August 25. Retrieved from: http://www.broadcastnow.co.uk/news/multi-platform/news/reuters-tv-may-sue-in-oz/1200271.article

Broadcast (2006) Reporting the world. April 27. Retrieved from: http://www.broadcastnow.co.uk/news/multi-platform/news/reporting-the-world/158070.article

Broadcasting (1996) Reuters journalists vote for strike action. *Broadcasting*, February 9, 2.

Broadcasting & Cable (1993) Filling changing needs and niches. Special report—news services. *Broadcasting & Cable*, May 31, 27–44.

Broadcasting & Cable (2005) The accidental journalist. *Broadcasting & Cable*, July 11.

Bromley, M. (2010) All the world's a stage: 24/7 news, newspapers, and the ages of media. In Cushion, S., and Lewis, J. (Eds.) *The rise of 24-hour news television: global perspectives*, 31–50. New York: Peter Lang.

Brosius, H., and Kepplinger, H. M. (1990) The agenda setting function of television news. *Communication Research*, 17, 183–211.

Browne, N. (1984) The political economy of the television (super) text. *Quarterly Review of Film Studies*, Summer, 9, 174–182.

Buckalew, J. (1970) News elements and selection by television news editors. *Journal of Broadcasting*, Winter, 47–54.

Busfield, Steve (1994a) Cramer vs. Cramer. *Broadcast*, June 30, 20.

Busfield, Steve (1994b) Agency provocateur. *Broadcast*, July 22, 18–19.

Busfield, Steve (1995a) Sarajevo pool close to the breaking point. *Broadcast*, June 9, 2.

Busfield, Steve (1995b) BBC and ITN express concern about ex-Yugoslavia news pool. *Broadcast*, June 16, 6.

Busfield, Steve (1995c) Gentleman player. *Broadcast*, November 10, 18.

Butler, D. (1991) UK: Hard news, hard times at ITN. March 1. *Management Today*. Retrieved from: http://www.managementtoday.co.uk/news/408724/UK-Hard-news-hard-times-ITN-1-3/?DCMP=ILC-SEARCH.

Campagna J., and Roumani, R. (2003) *Permission to fire*. New York: Committee to Protect Journalists.

Campbell, C. (1993) A myth of marginality: common sense, traditional racism and the news. Paper presented to the *Association for Education on Journalism and Mass Communications* meeting, Kansas City.

Carter, B. (1992) Networks cutting back on foreign coverage. *The New York Times*, June10, 10c, 18, via Lexis/Nexis.

Chase, S. (1947) Royal nuptials tip video's mitt on future news coverage. *Billboard*, November 29, 15. Retrieved from: http://books.google.co.uk/books?id= ASEEAAAAMBAJ&pg=PT14&dq=%22Royal+Nuptials+Tip+Video%E2%80%9 9s+Mitt+on+Future+News+Coverage%22v=onepage&q=%22Royal%20Nuptials% 20Tip%20Video%E2%80%99s%20Mitt%200n%20Future%20News%20Coverage %22&f=false.

Christian, H. (Ed.) (1980) *Sociology of the press and journalism*. Keele, England: University of Keele.

Clare, J. (1998) *Town criers in the global village*. Unpublished M.A. thesis, University of Leicester, U.K.

Clarke, J. (2003) How journalists judge the "reality" of an international "pseudo-event." *Journalism: Theory Practice and Criticism*, 4, 1.

Clarke, N., and Riddell, E. (1992) *The sky barons*. London: Methuen.

Clarke, S. (1995) London: international news capital. *Variety*, December 18.

Clausen, L. (2003) *Global news production*. Copenhagen: Copenhagen Business School.

Clausen, L. (2004) Localizing the global: "domestication" processes in international news production. *Media, Culture & Society*, 26(1), 25–44.

Claypole, S. (1995) The changing role of the news agencies. *EBU Review*, Autumn.

Cockburn, K. (1995) No accidental tourist. *BBC Worldwide*, November, 63–65.

Cohen, A., Levy, M., Roeh, I., and Gurevitch, M. (1996) *Global newsrooms, local audiences: a study of the Eurovision news exchange*. London: John Libbey.

Colart, C., and Venter, S. (Eds.) (2004) *Something to write home about*. Bellevue, South Africa: Jakana.

Collins, R. (1989) The language of advantage: satellite television in western Europe. *Media, Culture & Society*, 11, 351–371.

Conlan, T. (2000) News analysis—caught in the spotlight, May 26. Retrieved from: http://www.broadcastnow.co.uk/news/multi-platform/news/news-analysis-caught-in-the-spotlight/1195371.article.

Corner, J., Schlesinger, P., and Silverstone, R. (Eds.) (1997). *International media research: a critical survey*, 1–17. London: Routledge.

Cottle, S. (2007) Ethnography and journalism: new(s) departures in the field. *Sociology Compass*, 1(1), 1–16.

Cottle, S. (2009) Global crises and world news ecology. In Allan, S. (Ed.) *The Routledge companion to news and journalism studies*, 473–484. London: Routledge.

Covault, C. (1994) Satellite Earth stations. *Aviation Week and Space Technology*, 141(10), 120, via Lexis/Nexis.

Cox, G. (1997) Obituary: Kenneth Coyte. *Independent*, January 14. Retrieved from: http://www.independent.co.uk/news/people/obituary-kenneth-coyte-1283117.html

Curran, Sir C. (1979) Eurovision and the news agencies—a reply. *EBU Review*, 30(6), 30–32.

Cushion, S. (2010) Rolling service, market logic: the race to be "Britain's most watched news channel." In Cushion, S., and Lewis, J. (Eds.) *The rise of 24-hour news television: global perspectives*. New York: Peter Lang.

Cushion, S., and Lewis, J. (Eds.) (2010) *The rise of 24-hour news television: global perspectives*. New York: Peter Lang.

Dahlgren, P. (1995) *Television and the public sphere: citizenship, democracy and the media*. London: Sage.

Dahlgren, P., and Chakrapani, S. (1982) The third world on TV news: western ways of seeing the "other." In Adams, W.C. (Ed.) *Television coverage of international affairs*, 45–65. Norwood, NJ: Ablex.

Dahlgren, P., and Sparks, C. (Eds.) (1991) *Communications and citizenship: journalism and the public sphere in the new media age*. London: Routledge.

Dayan, D., and Katz, E. (1992) *Media events: the live broadcasting of history*. Cambridge, MA: Harvard University Press.

De Bens, E., Kelly, M., and Bakke, M. (1992) Television content: Dallasification of culture? In Siune, K., and Truetzschler, W. (Eds.) *Dynamics of media politics: broadcast and electronic media in Western Europe*, 75–100. London: Sage.

Deans, J. (1996) Kogan to leave after shake-up at Reuters. *Broadcast,* October 18.

Delano, A., and Henningham, J. (1995) Hacks: read all about 'em. *Guardian* (London), October 16, 14–15.

Diamond, E. (1988) Television's new fall lineup. *New York Magazine,* 22 August.

Dillinger, B. (1995) *Finnish views of CNN television news: a critical cross-cultural analysis of the American commercial discourse style.* Doctoral dissertation, University of Vaasa.

Dominick, J.R. (1988) The impact of budget cuts on CBS news. *Journalism Quarterly,* 65(2), Summer, 469–473.

Donohue, G., Tichenor, P., and Olien, C. (1972) Gatekeeping: mass media systems and information control. In Kline, G., and Tichenor, P. (Eds.) *Current perspectives in mass communication research,* 41–69. Beverly Hills, CA: Sage.

Dunning, J. H. (1995) The eclectic paradigm in an age of alliance capitalism. *Journal of International Business Studies,* 26(3), 461–487.

Edmonds, R. (2006) The new Associated Press: under construction. Retrieved from: http://www.poynter.org/content/content_view.asp?id=98708.

Elliott, L. (1993) Assessing U.S. television's media imperialism: an exercise in theory-building. Paper presented to the *Association for Education in Journalism and Mass Communication Conference,* Kansas City.

Engleberg, S. (1986) Publisher is cited as unregistered agent. *The New York Times,* November 1, via Lexis/Nexis.

Entman, R. (1992) Blacks in the news: television, modern racism, and cultural change. *Journalism Quarterly,* Summer, 341–361.

Entman, R. (1993) Framing: toward clarification of a fractured paradigm. *Journal of Communication,* 43 , 51–58.

Entman, R. (1994) Representation and reality in the portrayal of blacks on network television news. *Journalism Quarterly,* 71(3), 509–520.

Epstein, E. (1974) *News from nowhere.* New York: Vintage Books.

European Broadcasting Union (2010) Haiti. Retrieved from: http://www.ebu.ch/en/union/news/2009/tcm_6–67197.php.

Fair, J. E. (1992) Are we really the world? Coverage of U.S. food aid in Africa, 1980–1989. In Hawk, B. (Ed.) *Africa's media image.* New York: Praeger.

Featherstone, M. (Ed.) (1990) *Global culture: nationalism, globalization, and modernity.* London: Sage.

Feinstein, A., and Owen, J. (2002) War photographers and stress. *Columbia Journalism Review,* July/August, 51

Fenby, J. (1986) *The international news services, a Twentieth Century Fund report.* New York: Schocken Books.

Fielding, R. (2006) *The American newsreel; a complete history, 1911–1967.* 2nd ed. London; Jefferson, NC: McFarland & Co.

Fletcher, M. (2008) *Breaking news: a memoir.* New York: St. Martin's Press.

Flournoy, D. (1986) Emerging from the periphery: satellite news exchange in the developing nation. Paper presented to the *International Association for Mass Communications Research* meeting, New Delhi.

Foote, J. (1995) Structure and marketing of global television news. *Journal of Broadcasting and Electronic Media*, 39(1), 127–133.

Foy, H. (2007) *The global news agenda: are accusations of an imbalance between the developed and developing world justified?* Unpublished B.A. dissertation, University of Leeds.

Frank, R. (1991) *Out of thin air: the brief wonderful life of network news.* New York: Simon and Schuster.

Franklin D. G., Jr., and Iyengar, S. (2000) Prime suspects: the influence of local television news on the viewing public. *American Journal of Political Science*, 44(3), 560–573.

Frean, A. (1995) When violence must be cut. *Times* (London), April 12, 32.

Frederick, H. (1993) *Global communication and international relations.* Belmont, CA: Wadsworth.

Freedom Forum Media Studies Center. (1993) *The media and foreign policy in the post-cold war world.* Briefing paper. New York: Columbia University.

Friedland, L. (1992) Covering the world: international television news services. Paper for the Twentieth Century Fund.

Fuller, C. (1995) Elbowing for news room. *TV World*, October, 63–66.

Galtung, J., and Ruge, M. (1965) The structure of foreign news: the presentation of the Congo, Cuba and Cyprus crises in four Norwegian newspapers. *Journal of Peace Research*, 2, 64–91.

Gandy, O. H., Jr. (1982) *Beyond agenda setting: information subsidies and public policy.* Norwood, NJ: Ablex.

Gandy, O. (1994) From bad to worse, the media's framing of race and risk. *Freedom Forum Media Studies Journal*, Summer.

Gans, H. (1980) *Deciding what's news.* New York: Vintage Books.

Gans, H. (1985). Are U.S. journalists dangerously liberal? *Columbia Journalism Review*, November–December.

Gapper, J. (1998) ABC puts TV news agency up for sale. *New York Financial Times*, May 13, 18.

Garnham, N. (1979) Contribution to the political economy of communication. *Media, Culture & Society*, 1, 123–146.

Gaunt, P. (1990) *Choosing the news.* Westport, CT: Greenwood Press.

Geyer, G. (1996) Who killed the foreign correspondent? Red Smith lecture in journalism. Department of American Studies, University of Notre Dame.

Gibson, J. (1999) CNN counts costs of war. *The Guardian*, May 14, 4.

Giddens, A. (1991) *Modernity and self-identity: self and society in the late modern age.* Stanford, CA: Stanford University Press.

Gilliam, F., and Iyengar, S. (2000) Prime suspects: the influence of local television news on the viewing public. *American Journal of Political Science*, 44, 560–573.

Gitlin, T. (1980) *The whole world is watching: mass media in the making and unmaking of the New Left*. Berkeley: University of California Press.

Golding, P. (1979) Media professionalism in the developing nation: the transfer of an ideology. In Curran, J., Gurevitch, M., and Wollacott, J. (Eds.) *Mass communication and society*. London: Edward Arnold.

Golding, P., and Elliott, P. (1979) *Making the news*. New York: Longman.

Golding, P., and Harris, P. (Eds.) (1997) Introduction. *Beyond cultural imperialism: globalization, communication and the new international order*. London: Sage.

Goldman, K. (1985) *NBC News pulled questionable story*. Newsday, February 20, II, 9, via Lexis/Nexis.

Goldman, K. (1988) *NBC may buy part of Visnews*. Newsday. August 2, II, 11, via Lexis/Nexis.

Goldstein, I. (1994) Broadcasting international crisis: retrospect and prospects. *Journal of International Communications*, 1(1).

Gonzenbach, W., Arant, M., and Stevenson, R. (1991) The world of U.S. network television news: eighteen years of foreign news coverage. Paper presented to the *Association for Education on Journalism and Mass Communications* meeting, Boston.

Gopsill, T. (2004) Target the media. In Miller, D. (Ed.) *Tell me lies: propaganda and media distortion in the attack on Iraq*, 251–261. London: Pluto Press.

Gowing, N. (1994) *Real time television coverage of armed conflicts and diplomatic crises: does it pressure or distort foreign policy decisions?* Working paper 94–1, Joan Shorenstein Barone center, JFK School of Government, Harvard University.

Gowing, N. (2003) Aiming to stop the story? International News Safety Institute. Retrieved from: http://ics.leeds.ac.uk/papers/pmt/exhibits/1990/nikgowing.pdf.

Grabe, M. (1994) South African Broadcasting Corporation coverage of the 1987 and 1989 elections: the matter of visual bias. Paper presented to the *Association for Education on Journalism and Mass Communications* meeting, Atlanta.

Graber, D. (1990) Seeing is remembering: how visuals contribute to learning from television news. *Journal of Communication*, 40(3).

Griffin, M. (2002) *From cultural imperialism to transnational commercialization: shifting paradigms in international media studies*. Retrieved from: http://lass.calumet.purdue.edu/cca/gmj/OldSiteBackup/SubmittedDocuments/arc hivedpapers/fall2002/Griffin.htm.

Griffin, M., and Kagan, S. (1999) National autonomy and global news flows: CNN in Israel during the Gulf War. In Nordenstreng, K., and Griffin, M. (Eds.) *International Media Monitoring*, 73–94. Creskill, NJ: Hampton Press.

Grimes, T. (1990) Encoding TV news messages into memory. *Journalism Quarterly*, 67(4), 757–766.

Gunter, B. (1987) *Poor reception*. Hillsdale, NJ: Lawrence Erlbaum Associates.

Gunther, M. (1994) *The house that no one built: the inside story of ABC News*. Boston: Little, Brown.

Gurevitch, M. (1992) The globalization of electronic journalism. In Curran, J., and Gurevitch, M. (Eds.) *Mass media and society*, 178–193. London: Edward Arnold.

Gurevitch M., Levy, M., and Roeh, I. (1991) The global newsroom: convergences and diversities in the globalisation of television news. In Dahlgren, P., and Sparks, C. (Eds.) *Communications and citizenship: journalism and the public sphere in the new media age*. London: Routledge.

Hachten, W. (1981) *The world news prism: changing media, clashing ideologies*. Ames: The Iowa State University Press.

Hachten, W., and Beil, B. (1985) Bad news or no news? *Journalism Quarterly*, 62(3), 626–630.

Hall, S. (1988) The rediscovery of "ideology": return of the repressed in media studies. In Gurevitch, M., Bennett, T., Curran, J., and Woollacott, J. (Eds.) *Culture, society, and the media*, 56–90. London: Routledge.

Hall, S. (1992) Encoding, decoding. In During, S. (Ed.) *The cultural studies reader*, 90–103. London: Routledge.

Hallin, D. (1993) The passing of the "high modernism" of American journalism. Address to *The Old News, the New News, and the First Amendment Conference*. Murfreesboro: Middle Tennessee State University.

Hallin, D. (1994) *We keep America on top of the world: television journalism and the public sphere*. London: Routledge.

Hannerz, U. (1996) *Transnational connections: culture, people, places*. London: Routledge.

Harding, L. (2004) US military "brutalised" journalists. *Guardian*, January 13. Retrieved from: http://media.guardian.co.uk/broadcast/story/0,7493,1121995,00.html.

Harmon, M. (2010) Cheap video, bad journalism. *British Journalism Review*, September 21, 7–9.

Harrison, P., and Palmer, R. (1986) *News out of Africa: Biafra to Band Aid*. London: Hilary Shipman.

Hartman, P., and Husband, C. (1974) *Racism and the mass media*. London: Davis-Poynter.

Hawk, B. (1992) Metaphors of Africa coverage. In Hawk, B. (Ed.) *Africa's media image*, 3–14. New York: Praeger.

Heinderyckx, F. (1993) Television news programmes in Western Europe: a comparative study. *European Journal of Communication*, 8, 425–450.

Helland, K. (1995) *Public service and commercial news*. Doctoral dissertation, University of Bergen.

Helm, S., and Daly, E. (1995) Journalists death toll now stands at 56. *Independent* (London), August 11, 9.

Herman, E., and Chomsky, N. (1988) *Manufacturing consent*. New York: Pantheon.

Herman, E. S., and McChesney, R. W. (1997) *The global media: the new missionaries of corporate capitalism*. London: Cassell.

Hester, A. (1990) The collection and flow of world news. In Merrill, J. C. (Ed.) *Global journalism*, 29–50. New York: Longman.

Hjarvard, S. (1991) Americanization of European television: an aesthetic approach. In Nye, D., and Pedersen, C. (Eds.) *Consumption and American culture*. Amsterdam: VU University Press.

Hjarvard, S. (1993) Pan-European television news: towards a European political public sphere. In Drummond, P., Paterson, R., and Willis, J. (Eds.) *National identity and Europe: the television revolution*. London: British Film Institute.

Hjarvard, S. (1994) The Global Spread of a European Model: the Experiences of Regional News Exchange Networks Using a Public Model of Cooperation. Paper for the IAMCR.

Hjarvard, S. (1995a) *Internationale tv-nyheder. En historisk analyze af det europeiske system for udveksling af internationale tv-nyheder*. Copenhagen: Akademisk Forlag.

Hjarvard, S. (1995b) Eurovision news in a competitive marketplace. *EBU Diffusion*, Autumn.

Hjarvard, S. (1995c) TV news flow studies revisited. *Electronic Journal of Communication*, 5(2, 3), 24–38.

Hjarvard, S. (2001) News media and the globalization of the public sphere. In Hjarvard, S. (Ed.) *News in a Globalized Society*. Goteborg: Nordicom.

Hodgson, J. (2000) Western media accused over African coverage. *Guardian*, November 17. Retrieved from: http://www.guardian.co.uk/media/2000/nov/17/broadcasting1.

Horton, P. (Ed.) (1978) *The Third World and press freedom*. New York: Praeger.

Housel, T. J. (1984) Understanding and recall of TV news. *Journalism Quarterly*, 61(3), 505–508.

Hudson, T. (1992) Consonance in depiction of violent material in television news. *Journal of Broadcasting and Electronic Media*, Fall, 411–425.

Hujanen, T. (1992) The textuality of the Gulf War in TV news compared. *Nordicom Review 2*.

Husseini, S. (1994) Felons on the air: does GE's ownership of NBC violate the law? *Extra!* November/December.

Hutchins Commission. (1947) *A free and responsible press*. Chicago: University of Chicago Press.

Image of Africa (1988) Introduction to synthesis of the European national reports. In *Report of the International Exchange on Communication and Development Between Africa and Europe*. Rome, Italy.

International Exchange on Communication and Development Between Africa and Europe (1988). In *Report of the International Exchange on Communication and Development Between Africa and Europe*. Rome, Italy.

International Federation of Journalists (2005) *Journalists and media staff killed in Iraq involving US forces*. Retrieved from: http://www.ifj.org/pdfs/IraqMar03Aug05.pdf.

International Telecommunication Union. (2010) *World Telecommunication/ICT development report: Target 8—ensure that all of the world's population have access to television and radio services.* Retrieved from: http://www.itu.int/ITU-D/ict/publications/wtdr_10/material/WTDR2010_Target8_e.pdf.

ITV (1984) The British desk: South Africa's intelligence operations in Britain. ITV, May 8, courtesy Bodleian Library, Oxford University.

Jameson F. (2000) Globalization and strategy. *New Left Review* 4 (July/August), 49–68.

Johnston, C. B. (1995) *Winning the global TV news game.* Boston: Focal Press.

Jones, A. (1984) UPI's continuing struggle. *The New York Times*, August 16, via Lexis/Nexis.

Juluri, V. (2003) *Becoming a global audience: longing and belonging in Indian music television.* New York: Peter Lang.

Jurkowitz, M. (2003) Media protest treatment in Iraq: letter to Pentagon accuses US troops of intimidation. *Boston Globe*, 13 November.

Katz, J. (1991) Collateral damage to network news. *Colombia Journalism Review*, March/April, 29.

Kavoori, A. P. (2009) *The logics of globalization: studies in international communication.* Lanham, MD: Rowman and Littlefield.

Kellner, D. (1992) *The Persian Gulf TV war.* Boulder, CO: Westview Press.

Kelly, T. (1995) APTV to set up new talks on pooling for safety in Sarajevo. *UK Press Gazette*, June 19, 10.

Kenneth, L. (2007) *UPDATE 2-CNN to stop using Reuters news service.* Reuters, August 31. Retrieved from: http://uk.reuters.com/article/idUKN3043986420070831?feedType=RSS&feedName=technology-media-telco-SP.

Keune, R. (1991) Television news exchange: is the future over before it began? *Intermedia*, 19(2), 37.

Kirby, M. D., and Jackson, L. J. (1986) International humanitarian law and the protection of media personnel. *University of New South Wales Law Journal*, 9, 1.

Kline, L., Greene, T., and Noice, H. (1990) The influence of violent video material on cognitive task performance. *Psychology in the Schools*, July.

Knightley, P. (2003) History or bunkum? *British Journalism Review*, 14(2).

Kozol, W. (1989) Representations of race in network news coverage of South Africa. In Burns, G., and Thompson, R. J. (Eds.) *Television studies: textual analysis.* New York: Praeger.

Kull, S., Clay, R., and Lewis, E. (2002) Misperceptions, the media, and the Iraq War. *Political Science Quarterly*, 118(4), 569–598.

Lamerton, J. (1995) Reuters gets primetime on NBC super channel. *Broadcast*, July 21.

Lansipuro, Y. (1987) Asiavision News Exchange. *Intermedia* 15(1), 22–27.

Larson, J. (1984) *Television's window on the world: international affairs coverage on the US networks.* Norwood, NJ: Ablex.

Larson, J. (1988) Global television and foreign policy. Paper for the Foreign Policy

Association.

Layne, B. (1994) ABC, Japan's NHK tighten ties. *Hollywood Reporter*, April 27, via Lexis/Nexis.

Lee, J. (2001) Why TVnewsweb failed. *The Guardian*. Retrieved from: http://www.guardian.co.uk/technology/2001/jul/09/internetnews.mondaymedia-section.

Lewis, J. (2010) Democratic or disposable? 24-hour news, consumer culture and built-in obsolescence. In Cushion, S., and Lewis, J. (Eds.) *The rise of 24-hour news television: global perspectives*. New York: Peter Lang.

Lewis, J., Williams, A., and Franklin, B. (2008) Compromised fourth estate? UK news journalism, public relations and news sources. *Journalism Studies*, February.

Lewis, N. (1986) Charges filed in plan to buy *Washington Star* for Pretoria. *Washington Post*, November 1, A2, via Lexis/Nexis.

Li, K. (2007) CNN to stop using Reuters news service. *Reuters*, Aug 31, Retrieved from: http://in.reuters.com/article/idINIndia-29248520070831.

Life, R. (1993) ITN puts question mark on WTN deal. *Broadcasting*, April 2, 10.

Lipscomb, G. (2002) APTN ups showbiz news. *Broadcast*, January 11. Retrieved from: http://www.broadcastnow.co.uk/news/multi-platform/news/aptn-ups-showbiz-news/1134645.article.

Loyn, D. (2005) *Frontline: The true story of the British mavericks who changed the face of war reporting*. London: Michael Joseph.

Maass, P. 2001. Deadly competition. Crimes of War Project, February 2001. Retrieved from: http://www.crimesofwar.org/archive/archive-deadlycomp.html.

MacBride, S. (1980) *Many voices, one world*. Paris: UNESCO.

Macdonald, A. (2006) *US offer Iraq journalists new safeguards*. Reuters, March 20.

MacGregor, B. (1997) *Live, direct, and biased?: Making television news in the satellite age*. London: Arnold.

Mahoney, J. (1975) The news exchange: the agency dimension. *EBU Review*, 26(3), 32–34.

Malik, R. (1992) The global news agenda. *Intermedia*, 20(1).

Masmoudi, M. (1979) The new world information order. *Journal of Communication*, 29(2), 172–198.

Mater, G. (1989) Conus: a satellite success story. *Washington Journalism Review*, 11(4), 54.

McCarthy, J., and Morrell, J. (1994) *Some other rainbow*. London: Corgi.

McClellan, B. (1993) The growing focus on global news. *Broadcasting & Cable*, May 31, 40–41.

McClellan, B. (1994) Reuters eyes growing TV presence. *Broadcasting & Cable*, August 1, 28.

McKernan, L. (Ed.) (2002) *Yesterday's news: the British cinema newsreel reader*. London: British Universities Film and Video Council.

McLuhan, M. (1962) *The Guttenberg galaxy: the making of typographic man.* Toronto: University of Toronto Press.

McManus, J. (1994) *Market-driven journalism.* Thousand Oaks, CA: Sage.

McNelly, J., and Izcaray, F. (1986) International news exposure and images of nations. *Journalism Quarterly,* 63(3), 546–553.

McPhail, T. (1987) *Electronic colonialism.* London: Sage.

McQuail, D. (1987) *Mass Communications Theory: An Introduction.* 2nd ed. London: Sage.

Meade, A. (2010) ABC cuts claim Middle East correspondent Anne Barker. *The Australian.* Retrieved from: http://www.theaustralian.com.au/business/media/abc-cuts-claim-middle-east-correspondent-anne-barker/story-e6frg996-1225947 749030.

Melnik, S. (1981) *Eurovision news and the international flow of information: history, problems and perspectives 1960–1980.* Bochum: Studienverlag Dr. N. Brockmeyer.

Melody, W. (1993) On the political economy of communication in the information society. In Wasko, J., Mosco, V., and Pendakur, M. (Eds.) *Illuminating the blind spots: essays honoring Dallas W. Smythe.* Norwood, NJ: Ablex, 63–81.

Mickelson, S. (1998) *The decade that shaped television news, CBS in the 1950s.* London: Praeger.

Mirabella, A. (1994) News explosion of '95. *Columbia Journalism Review ,* 33(4).

Mitra, S. (2010) *Transcultural productions: photojournalists of the Third World in Western news agencies.* Unpublished master's dissertation, Swansea University.

Molina, G. G. (1990) *The production of Mexican television news: the supremacy of corporate rationale.* Unpublished doctoral dissertation, University of Leicester.

Moncrieff, C. (2001) *Living on a deadline: a history of the Press Association* London: Virgin Books.

Mooney, B., and Simpson, B. (2003) *Breaking news: how the wheels came off at Reuters.* London: Capstone.

Morales, W. Q. (1984) Latin America on network TV. *Journalism Quarterly,* 61(1), 157–160.

Murphy, C. (1980) Rhoodie's fraud conviction reversed in S. Africa scandal. *Washington Post,* September 30, A17, via Lexis/Nexis.

Musa, M. (1990) News agencies, transnationalization and the new order. *Media, Culture & Society,* 12, 325–342.

Musburger, R. B. (1991) *Electronic news gathering.* Boston: Focal Press.

Naets, T. (1987) The EBU offices in the United States. *EBU Review,* May, 8–15.

Nash, C., and Van der Gaag, N. (1988) Summary of the United Kingdom report. In *Report of the International Exchange on Communication and Development Between Africa and Europe.* Rome, Italy.

Negrine, R., and Papathanassopoulos, S. (1991) The internationalization of television. *European Journal of Communication,* 6, 9–32.

Newsday (1988) NBC may buy part of Visnews *Newsday*, August 2, II, 11, via Lexis/Nexis.

Nimmo, D., and Combs, J. (1985) *Nightly horrors: crisis coverage by television network news*. Knoxville: University of Tennessee Press.

Nordenstreng, K. (1984) *The mass media declaration of UNESCO*. Norwood, NJ: Ablex.

Nordenstreng, K., and Varis, T. (1974) Television traffic—a one-way street? a survey and analysis of the international flow of television programme material. Paris: UNESCO.

Ogundimu, F. (1992) Media coverage, issue salience, and knowledge of Africa in a Midwestern university. Paper presented to the *African Studies Association* meeting, Seattle.

Ottaway, D. B. (1987) Reporting the Third World: how governments silence foreign correspondents. *Index on Censorship*, April, 25–27.

Owen, J., and Purdey, H. (Eds.) (2009) *International news reporting: frontlines and deadlines*. Chichester: Wiley-Blackwell.

Palmer, M. (2011) *Homo informans: news now*. Paris: Editions de l'amandier.

Pan, Z. (2008) Framing of the news. In Donsbach, W. (Ed) *The international encyclopedia of communication*. Malden, MA: Blackwell Publishing.

Parenti, C. (2004) Al Jazeera goes to jail *Nation* March 11, . Retrieved from: http://www.thenation.com/doc.mhtml?i=20040329&c=1&s=parenti.

Park, C. I. (1994) *A comparative analysis of the selection process and content of television international news in the United States and Korea: a case study of the US CNN Primenews, Korean KBS 9 o'clock news and SBS 8 o'clock news programs*. Unpublished doctoral dissertation, Ohio University.

Parker, R. (1994) *The future of global television news, research paper r-13*. Joan Shorenstein Barone Center, JFK School of Government, Harvard University.

Paterson, C. (1990) *Western television news and the frontline states: a case study of Third World news coverage*. Unpublished master's thesis, Boston University.

Paterson, C. (1992) Television news from the frontline states. In Hawk, B. (Ed.) *Africa's media image*. New York: Praeger.

Paterson, C. (1998) Global battlefields. In Boyd-Barrett, O., and Rantanen, T. (Eds.) *The globalization of news*, 79–103. London: Sage.

Paterson, C. (1999) Agency source influence on television foreign reporting: the case of Mururoa and Tahiti. *Asia Pacific Media Educator*, 7, July–December, 16–36.

Paterson, C. (2001) The transference of frames in global television. In Reese, S., Gandy, O., and Grant, A. (Eds.) *Framing public life: perspectives on media and our understanding of the social world*. Mahwah, NJ: Lawrence Erlbaum Associates.

Paterson, C. (2004) News—local and regional. In Newcomb, H. (Ed.) *Encyclopedia of television*. New York: Routledge.

Paterson, C. (2007) International news on the Internet: why more is less. *Ethical Space: The International Journal of Communication Ethics*, 4(1), 57–66.

Paterson, C. (2010) The hidden role of television news agencies: "going live" on 24 hour news channels. In Cushion, S., and Lewis, J. (Eds.) *The rise of 24-hour news television: global perspectives.* New York: Peter Lang.

Paterson C., Andresen, K., and Hoxha, A. (forthcoming) The manufacture of an international news event: the day Kosovo was born. *Journalism: Theory Practice Critique,* 13(1).

Paterson, C., and Sreberny, A. (Eds.) (2004) *International news in the twenty-first century.* Eastleigh, U.K.: University of Luton/John Libbey.

Paterson, C., and Zoellner, A. (2010) The efficacy of professional experience in the ethnographic investigation of production. *Journal of Media Practice,* 11(2), 97–109.

Payette W.C. (1952) Just like radio, news develops as tv staple; '52 key year. *Billboard,* September 20. Retrieved from: http://books.google.com/books?id=Rho EAAAAMBAJ&pg=PA11&dq=%22United+Press%22+Fox+Movietone&lr.

Perlmutter, D. D., and Hamilton, J. M. (Eds.) (2007) *From pigeons to news portals.* Baton Rouge: Louisiana State University Press.

Philo, G. (2004) The mass production of ignorance: news content and audience. In Paterson, C., and Sreberny, A. (Eds) *International news in the twenty-first century.* Eastleigh, U.K.: University of Luton/John Libbey, 199–224.

Pinder, R. (2001) Interview. *Transnational Broadcasting Studies,* 7, Fall/Winter. Retrieved from: http://www.tbsjournal.com/Archives/Fall01/pinder.html.

Plante, J. (1986) Reporting by satellite, a challenge for the networks. *Intermedia,* 14(3), 34–35.

Prato, L. (1994) Expect more TV news from abroad. *American Journalism Review,* 16 (10), 48.

Press Gazette (2007) Reuters accused of betraying principles. May 25. Retrieved from: http://www.pressgazette.co.uk/story.asp?sectioncode=1&storycode=37635

Preston, A. (1999) The development of the UK television news industry 1982–1998. Ph.D. thesis, University of Stirling. Retrieved from: https://dspace.stir.ac.uk/dspace/bitstream/1893/1425/1/Preston%201999–07072009.pdf.

Pronay, N. (1972) British newsreels in the 1930s: their policies and impact. *History,* 57(189), February.

Putnis, P. (1994) *Displaced, re-cut and recycled: file-tape in television news.* Gold Coast, Queensland, Centre for Journalism Research and Education, Bond University.

Putnis, P. (1996) Producing overseas news for Australian television. *Australian Journal of Communication,* 23(3), 1–22.

Rai, M., and Cottle, S. (2008) Global 24/7 news providers: emissaries of global dominance or global public sphere? *Global Media and Communication,* 4(2), 157–181.

Rai, M., and Cottle, S. (2010) Global news revisited: mapping the contemporary landscape of satellite television news. In Cushion, S., and Lewis, J. (Eds.) *The rise of 24-hour news television: global perspectives.* New York: Peter Lang.

Ramaprasad, J. (1993) Content, geography, concentration, and consonance in foreign news coverage of ABC, NBC, and CBS. *International Communications Bulletin,* Spring.

Rathbun, E. (1994) Associated Press tackles international video. *Broadcasting and Cable,* July 18, 44.

Read, D. (1992) *The power of news: the history of Reuters 1849–1989.* Oxford: Oxford University Press.

Reese, S. (1990) The news paradigm and the ideology of objectivity: a socialist at *The Wall Street Journal. Critical Studies in Mass Communication,* December.

Reese, S., Ballinger, J., and Shoemaker, P. (1993) The roots of media sociology: Mr. Gates and social control in the newsroom. Paper prepared for the *Association for Education in Journalism and Mass Communication Conference,* Kansas City.

Regan T. (2005) Rumsfeld says he will look into detention, shootings of journalists. *Christian Science Monitor,* 3 October.

Reuters (2006) Reporting the world. *Broadcast,* 27 April.

Reyes Matta, F. (1979) The Latin American concept of news. In Martin, L. J., and Hiebert, R. E. (Eds.) *Current issues in international communication,* 251–257. New York: Longman.

Robinson, J. P., and Levy, M. R. (1986) *The main source: learning from television news.* Beverly Hills, CA: Sage.

Robinson , P. (2002) *The CNN effect: the myth of news, foreign policy, and intervention.* New York: Routledge.

Rodriguez, A. (1996) Made in the USA: the production of the Noticiero Univision. *Critical Studies in Mass Communication,* 13(1), 59–82.

Romano, A., and Kerschbaumer, K. (2005) The accidental journalist; The London bombings turned ordinary citizens into reporters. *Broadcasting & Cable,* July 11, 17.

Rosenblum, M. (1993) *Who stole the news?* New York: John Wiley.

Sabreen, R. (1985) News is no longer enough. *Broadcasting,* 109(9), August 26, 24.

Sanit, T. (1992) The new unreality: when TV reporters don't report. *Columbia Journalism Review,* May/June, 17.

Schiff, F. (1996) The Associated Press: its worldwide bureaus and American interests. *International Communication Bulletin,* 31, 7–13.

Schiller, H. I. (1989) *Culture, inc.* New York: Oxford University Press.

Schlesinger, P. (1987; originally 1978) *Putting 'reality' together: BBC News.* 2nd ed. London: Routledge.

Schlesinger, P. (1980) Between sociology and journalism. In Christian, H. (Ed.) *Sociology of the press and journalism.* Keele, England: University of Keele.

Schonfeld R. (2001) *Me and Ted against the world: the unauthorized story of the founding of CNN.* New York: HarperCollins.

Seidman, S. (Ed.) (1989) *Jürgen Habermas. On society and politics: a reader.* Boston: Beacon Press.

Semati, M. (2001) Reflections on the politics of the global rolling-news television genre. *Transnational Broadcasting Studies*, 6. Retrieved from: http://www.tbsjournal.com/Archives/Spring01/Semati.html.

Semati M. (2010) Islamophobia, culture and race in the age of empire. *Cultural Studies*, 24(2), 256–275.

Semetko, H., Brzinski, J., Weaver, D., and Willnat, L. (1992) TV news and US public opinion about foreign countries: the impact of exposure and attention. *International Journal of Public Opinion Research* 4(1).

Shaw, D. (1987) Paper tainted by ties to right wing Moon church. *Los Angeles Times*, April 26, pt. 1, 1, c1, via Lexis/Nexis.

Shoemaker, P., and Reese, S. (1991) *Mediating the message: theories of influence on mass media content*. New York: Longman.

Shoemaker, P., Danielian, L., and Brendlinger, N. (1991) Deviant acts, risky business and US interests: the newsworthiness of world events. *Journalism Quarterly*, Winter, 781–795.

Shuster, S. (1988) Foreign competition hits the news. *Columbia Journalism Review*, (27)1.

Silcock, B. W. (1994) Television news coverage of the Maastricht summit: testing theories of the global newsroom. Paper presented at the *Association for Education in Journalism and Mass Communication Conference*, Atlanta, Georgia.

Simpson, J. (1994) Royal Television Society lecture.

Simpson, J. (1995) A joke, a shot, a pool of blood. *Independent* (London), August 15, 2, 15.

Smith, A. (1980) *The geopolitics of information: how Western culture dominates the world*. New York: Oxford University Press.

Sonwalkar, P. (2001) India: makings of little cultural/media imperialism? *Gazette*, 63(6), 505–519.

Sonwalkar, P. (2004) News Imperialism: Contra View from the South. In Paterson, C., and Sreberny, A. (Eds.) *International news in the twenty-first century*, 111-126. Eastleigh, U.K.: University of Luton/John Libbey.

Sparks, C. (2004) The global, the local and the public sphere. In Allen, R. C., and Hill, A. (Eds.) *The Television Studies Reader*, 139–150. London: Routledge.

Sreberny-Mohammadi, A. (1996) the global and local in international communication. In Curran, J., and Gurevitch, M. (Eds.) *Mass Media and Society*, 177–203. 2nd ed. London: Edward Arnold.

Sreberny-Mohammadi, A., Stevenson, R., and Nordensteng, K. (1984) The world of the news study. *Journal of Communication*, 34(1), 120–142.

Stenvall, M. (2003) An actor or an undefined threat? the role of terrorist in the discourse of international news agencies. *Journal of Language and Politics*, 2(2), 361–404.

Stenvall, M. (2008) Unnamed sources as rhetorical constructs in news agency reports. *Journalism Studies*, 9(2), 229–243.

Stephens, M. (1993) *Broadcast news*. 3rd ed. Fort Worth, TX: Harcourt Brace Jovanovich.

Stevenson, R. (1988) *Communication, development, and the Third World: the global politics of information.* New York: Longman.

Stevenson, R. (1991) The world of US network television news: eighteen years of foreign news coverage. Paper presented to the *Association for Education on Journalism and Mass Communications* meeting, Boston.

Stone, P. (2007) There's a lot more to that story about CNN dumping Reuters. *followthemedia.com*, September 7. Retrieved from: http://followthemedia.com/bigbusiness /reuterscnn07092007.htm

Straubhaar, J. D. (1991) Beyond media imperialism: asymmetrical interdependence and cultural proximity. *Critical Studies in Mass Communication*, (8)1, 39.

Straubhaar, J. D. (2007) *World television: from global to local.* Thousand Oaks, CA: Sage.

Sultan, D. (1948) Video newsreel producers looking for sponsors. *Boxoffice*, National Executive Edition, June 19, 16. Retrieved from: http://issuu.com/boxoffice/ docs/boxoffice_061948/16.

Taylor, J. (1991) Reuters holdings plc. In Hast, A. (Ed.) *International directory of company histories,* vol. iv. Chicago: St. James Press.

Taylor, P. (1992) *War and the media: propaganda and persuasion in the Gulf War.* Manchester: Manchester University Press.

TeleCinco Television (2004) *Hotel Palestine: killing the witness.* Video documentary.

Tetley, B. (1988) *The story of Mohamed Amin: front-line cameraman.* London: Moonstone Books.

Thompson, M. (1994) *Forging war: the media in Serbia, Croatia and Bosnia-Herzegovina.* Luton, U.K.: Universty of Luton Press.

Thussu, D. K. (2000) Legitimizing "Humanitarian Intervention"? CNN, NATO and the Kosovo crisis. *European Journal of Communication*, 15(3), 345–361. Retrieved from: http://ics.leeds.ac.uk/papers/pmt/exhibits/1863/Thussu.pdf.

Thussu, D. (2004) Media plenty and the poverty of the news. In Paterson, C., and Sreberny, A. (Eds.) *International news in the twenty-first century.* Eastleigh, U.K.: University of Luton/John Libbey.

Thussu, D. (2007) *News as entertainment: the rise of global infotainment.* London: Sage.

Transnational Broadcasting Studies (2001) Interview: Khalid Kazziha. *Transnational Broadcasting Studies* No. 6, Spring/Summer. Retrieved from: http://www.tbsjournal.com/Archives/Spring01/tech.html.

Trigoboff, D. (2002) Journalists' survival schools: before reporters head out for war zones, networks teach them how to stay alive. *Broadcasting & Cable*, May 6, 2002.

Tuchman, G. (1972) Objectivity as strategic ritual: an examination of newsmen's notions of objectivity. *American Journal of Sociology*, 77, 660–679.

Tuchman, G. (1978) *Making news: a study in the construction of reality.* New York: Free Press.

Tumber, H., and Webster, F. (2004) *Journalists under fire.* London: Sage.

Tunstall, J. (Ed.) (1970) *Media sociology.* London: Constable.

Tunstall, J. (1977) *The media are American*. New York: Columbia University Press.

Tunstall, J. (1992) Europe as world news leader. *Journal of Communication*, 42(3), 84–99.

Tunstall, J., and Palmer, M. (1991) *Media moguls*. London: Routledge.

UK Press Gazette (1995) APTV signs up four new clients. October 16, 13.

Utley, G. (1997) The shrinking of foreign news: from broadcast to narrowcast. *Foreign Affairs*, 76(2), 2–10.

Van Dijk, T. A. (1991) *Racism and the press*. London: Routledge.

Van Ginneken, J. (1998) *Understanding global news*. London: Sage.

vanden Heuvel, J. (1993) For the media, a brave (and scary) new world. *Media Studies Journal*, 7(4), Fall, 11–19.

Venter, E. (2005) *The safety of journalists: An assessment of perceptions of the origins and implementation of policy at the two international television news agencies*. Unpublished master's thesis, Rhodes University.

Venturelli, S. (1993) Democracy as fiction in the transnational public sphere. *Media Development*, 4, 21–24.

Vidal-Beneyto, J., and Dahlgren, P. (Eds.) (1987) *The focussed screen*. Strasbourg: Amela.

Visnews (1979) *Visnews: Newsroom operating handbook*. Internal document.

Volkmer, I. (1999) *CNN news in the global sphere: a study of CNN and its impact on global communication*. Bedfordshire: University of Luton Press.

Waite, T. L. (1992) As networks stay home, two agencies roam the world. *The New York Times*, March 8, 5.

Wallis, R., and Baran, S. (1990) *The known world of broadcast news*. London: Routledge.

Walpole, A. (1995) Killing fields. *Broadcast*, November 10, 21.

Weaver, J., and Porter, E. (1984) Patterns of foreign coverage in US network TV: a ten year analysis. *Journalism Quarterly*, 61(2), 356–363.

Weiner, R. (1992) *Live from Baghdad: gathering news at ground zero*. New York: Doubleday.

Weisman, J. (1983) Ignorants abroad. *TV Guide*, May 28, 8.

Westcott, T. (1995a) Getting mighty crowded. *Television Business International*, November.

Westcott, T. (1995b) War stories: the agencies. *Television Business International*, November.

White, D. M. (1950) The gatekeeper: a case study in the selection of news. *Journalism Quarterly*, 27, 383–390.

Wilson, J. (2003) US troops "crazy" in killing of cameraman. *Guardian*, August 19.

Winseck, D. (1992) Gulf war in the global village. CNN, democracy and the information age. In Wasko, J., and Mosco, V. (Eds.) *Democratic communication in the information age*, 60–75. Toronto: Garamond.

Winseck, D. (1997) Contradictions in the democratization of international communication. *Media, Culture & Society*, 19(2), 219–246.

Wolper, A. (2004) Reuters still seeking answers on alleged abuse of three staffers.

Editor and Publisher, December 5.

Wu, H. D. (2003) Homogeneity around the world? Comparing the systemic determinants of international news flow between developed and developing countries. *Gazette,* 65(1), 9–24.

Wyand, P. (1959) *Useless if delayed.* London: George G. Harrap.

Zabkova, Z. (2009) *The rise of television news agencies.* Unpublished master's dissertation, Birkbeck College, University of London.

Zelizer, B. (1992) CNN, the Gulf War and journalistic practice. *Journal of Communication,* 42(1), 66–81.

Zier, J. A. (1994) Profitable WTN invests in itself. *Broadcasting & Cable,* July 18, 42–43.

Interviews Cited (where consent to be quoted by name has been granted)

Ailes, Andrew (Visnews, Reuters Television)

Amin, Mohammed (Visnews, Reuters Television)

Baker, Nigel (Associated Press)

Boccardi, Lou (Associated Press)

Braun, Eric (Associated Press)

Connor, John (Reuters Television)

Donovan, Tony (Reuters Television, APTV)

Henderson, Peter (TVNewsweb)

Heron, Ken (TVNewsweb)

Kogan, David (Visnews)

Lipscomb, Lowndes (WTN)

MacIntyre, Sandy (Associated Press)

Mahoney, John (WTN)

Schonfeld, Reese (UPITN, CNN)

Wald, Richard (WTN, ABC)

Watson, Lloyd (Reuters Television)

Index